The Art of the Restaurateur

The Art
of the
Restaurateur

Nicholas
Lander

INTRODUCTION

The title, *The Art of the Restaurateur*, sprang into my consciousness as soon as I started thinking about writing this book. Several emotions lay behind this reaction. The first was personal: I was a successful restaurateur myself from 1980 until 1988 at L'Escargot, a bar and restaurant in London's Soho. Happily, these exciting years formed the basis for my career as a journalist, and since 1989 I have had the good fortune to write the restaurant column for the *Financial Times* and many magazines as well – a most unusual role reversal. During this period I have also acted as a consultant to a string of arts organizations on how best to manage their bars, restaurants and cafés. I could not have done any of this without my own formative years as a restaurateur.

However, the main purpose of this book is to correct a misconception that exists, I believe, in many restaurant-goers' minds as to who is mainly responsible for a successful restaurant. Since the emergence of the new wave of French chefs, including Paul Bocuse, Michel Guérard and Roger Vergé, who transformed French cooking with *nouvelle cuisine* in the 1970s, chefs, in my opinion, have been elevated to an overly lofty position. They have been the main focus of the restaurant media, to the detriment of the restaurateur's profession.

Many chefs are extraordinarily talented individuals whose food I have had great pleasure in eating, a pleasure I hope will continue for many years. But great chefs do not necessarily make great restaurants. The partnership of a visionary restaurateur alongside a talented chef can create restaurants of even more outstanding character than those created by a chef alone. They generate enormous pleasure and sustain inordinate levels of interest. These – with their sense of warmth, of being looked after by a team led by an inspirational individual – are the restaurants that I, and many others, choose to return to time and time again, and they form the basis of this book. *The Art of the Restaurateur* starts with my own experiences as a restaurateur and restaurant correspondent. This is followed by the stories of twenty of the leading and most inspirational restaurateurs, each of which is concluded with an analysis of an area of the business that each restaurateur highlights.

Among the great restaurateurs in these pages are Juli Soler, who alongside the far better known Ferran Adrià, took elBulli to such worldwide renown; Maguy Le Coze, who while running Le Bernardin in Paris in the early 1980s, dreamed of opening in New York, and then did so; Gilbert Pilgram, whose initial career in the law did not stand in the way of his subsequent restaurant career alongside Alice Waters at Chez Panisse, California and then with Judy Rodgers at Zuni Café, San Francisco; and Trevor Gulliver, whose first career was as a manufacturer of T-shirts for pop concerts, before he moved into restaurants and spotted a young chef called Fergus Henderson, then cooking above a pub. Together, this like-minded and highly opinionated pair opened St. John, and transformed not just British cooking, but also how British cooking is now viewed around the world.

The twenty restaurateurs profiled may have very different restaurants and come from very different backgrounds, but they share one common characteristic, a distinctive quality at the professional and the personal level: they each possess an extraordinary vision for what they want their restaurant to be. A vision that includes in many cases the ability, which is almost a sixth sense, to divine what their customers will want to eat, as well as providing the most exhilarating surroundings. Along with this – and what I believe distinguishes the most successful restaurateurs from the rest – is their innate ability to locate and bring the best out in the necessary specialists and management team to turn this vision into reality. Then, crucially, they manage to run it profitably, day in and day out.

Hence my choice of the word 'art' to describe what these restaurateurs do. While chefs may use plates for their art, restaurateurs' imaginations work on much bigger canvases. They look at empty spaces – modern, old, on one floor or on several, in bustling parts of town or in down-at-heel areas – and begin to paint pictures in their heads of what these spaces will look like when they are full and bustling with customers and staff. I know from having done this with the five-storey, eighteenth-century London townhouse that became L'Escargot that this exhilarating experience is, per-haps more than any other, the most exciting aspect of this noble profession.

All the restaurateurs in the book possess this talent. Danny Meyer originally demonstrated it when he wandered round what had once been a lacklustre vegetarian restaurant, which in his hands was to become the Union Square Café in New York. Mark Sainsbury worked the same magic when he transformed what had been a supermarket in Exmouth Market, London, into Moro restaurant. Across town, Nigel Platts-Martin saw the potential of a pub on the corner of Ledbury Road, Notting Hill, renovated it, and then installed a young Australian chef called Brett Graham. Together, they opened The Ledbury, a restaurant that has been winning awards ever since.

While researching this book, one fact of restaurant life has become abundantly clear: that even the most successful restaurateurs have had to close one of their restaurants at some time or other, because they got it wrong. Only those who have stuck to one restaurant or a very specific location, such as Juli Soler, Hazel Allen at Ballymaloe in Ireland or Marie-Pierre Troisgros in Roanne, France, have not undergone this painful experience. The only exceptions to this rule are Nigel Platts-Martin, whose five restaurants continue to thrive (a tribute to his ability to spot talented chefs as well as to all he learned during his two previous careers as a lawyer and merchant banker), Russell Norman, and Sam and Eddie Hart's three restaurants in close proximity to one another in central London.

This book seeks, first and foremost, to show the importance of the restaurateur's profession by telling the stories of those professionals I most respect and admire, based on my longstanding relationships with them, as well as interviews especially for the book, and many enjoyable visits. Many of them are revealing their experiences for the first time. Although I hope it will be of great interest and usefulness to those considering a career in restaurants, this is not a manual for opening a restaurant. There are already plenty of those, and anyone who is excited at the prospect of doing it, and possesses the requisite appetite, courage and resources, should consult them and make as many acquaintances as they can in this very friendly business in which it is very difficult to keep anything secret for long. Contained within these pages, though, is much sage advice, many sources of inspiration, and several cautionary lessons for all those who dream of becoming restaurateurs – or, indeed, entrepreneurs in any area.

The other aim of this book is to reconnect the restaurateur's profession with its noble roots. Over the past thirty years I believe I have had the good fortune to live through what can, without hyperbole, be described as a golden era for restaurants. During this period restaurants have emerged in the most unlikely of locations, serving the most extraordinary food and attracting the most exceptional following, all aspects that were unthinkable when I first opened for business on 2 June 1981. There have been many reasons for this. One is the extra disposable income many people enjoy, which has been a great stimulus to demand. Restaurants have also become the focus of so much media attention that they have become increasingly attractive investments for the wealthy. Also, rising rents, along with with so many TV cookery shows, have contributed to a big social change witnessed by all the major cities over the past decade:

a new market of restaurant goers aged twenty-five to thirty-five, who increasingly use informal restaurants as public spaces to meet in the early evening rather than going home.

The vital social role that restaurants play in the lives of many was concisely explained to me in 1993 on my first professional visit to New York, by Bryan Miller, then the restaurant critic of the *New York Times*. At that time there were far more restaurants in New York than there were in London and I asked him why. 'It's simple,' he explained, 'unless you earn above a certain amount of money in this city you can't afford an apartment with a dining room, somewhere to sit down, to eat in and to entertain your friends in. And if you don't have one, you have to meet your friends elsewhere.' This is precisely what, beyond food, wine and hospitality, the best restaurateurs provide today, as our cities become increasingly crowded and our personal spaces smaller and more expensive.

In fulfilling this very basic human need, today's restaurateurs are providing a service very similar to that of the original restaurateurs when they first appeared in Paris during the 1760s and 1770s. At that time a new class of independent professional emerged whose principal skill lay in preparing a *restaurant*, or restorative, a clear consommé that had the property of restoring lost strength to a sickly or tired individual. In her fascinating book *The Invention of The Restaurant*, Rebecca L. Spang charts how restaurants first emerged, announcing to those who walked past 'I shall restore you', at a time when the French elite was increasingly preoccupied with the pursuit of good health, as well as a burgeoning fascination with cuisine. Restaurateurs derive their professional name from the French verb *restaurer* (to restore): only the noun, the restorative soup that was to give its name to the restaurant in which it was served, has the 'n'. It is a fascinating footnote that, 260 years on, how well any restaurant makes soup, particularly the now rarely seen consommé, remains a critical test for any restaurant reviewer to assess.

Over the next sixty years restaurateurs would benefit from the social upheavals of the French Revolution and the immediate consequences of having so many British troops stationed in Paris in 1815 after the Battle of Waterloo. These soldiers became their biggest-spending customers. By then, the menus had grown substantially but what they introduced to Paris, and what began to feature in the writings of many journalists, novelists and travellers, was the excitement these restaurants generated, and how they could accommodate, and gratify, private pleasure in a public space.

This was the discreet charm of the restaurant, which from the 1840s onwards was to radiate from Paris around the rest of France, then across Europe and finally across the rest of the world. It was initially a French monopoly, although in the case of the partnership of French chef Auguste Escoffier and Swiss hotelier, César Ritz, who initiated such significant changes in the kitchen and the restaurant, a Franco-Swiss co-production. From the first half of the twentieth century it was a profession principally populated by Europeans, whether in London, New York or Rio de Janeiro.

The most significant change in restaurateurs over the past thirty years, and the one I believe that has been more responsible than any other for the profession's current golden age, has been the recognition that it is no longer solely the prerogative of the French, German or Swiss, however talented they may have been. It is a legitimate, highly satisfying and equally risky future for anyone, regardless of their nationality, training or background. I was inadvertently a small part of this transformation, as I was one of the first young Englishmen to enter this profession in 1980, at a time when my fellow restaurateurs in London were predominantly professionally trained Austrian, German, Swiss, French or Italian. Many others were to follow, and to bring with them their own distinctive national characteristics to add to the French and Italian cooking styles that were then the norm around the world. It is this combination that created such excitement, as restaurateurs in New York and London, who had always deferred to Paris as the centre of excellence, began to open restaurants that were to rival them, and in some cases to surpass them.

The ostensible rivalry between the cities, though, much discussed in the press at the time, was more imagined than real. However successful or admired restaurateurs in London or New York might have felt, they all recognized that the ultimate restaurateur's restaurateur, Jean-Claude Vrinat, was still based in Paris and still working lunch and dinner in Taillevent, the restaurant he had inherited from his father. Vrinat was the last French professional restaurateur (as opposed to chef) to hold the coveted three Michelin stars. Taillevent was demoted to two stars in 2007 the year before his death, an event that for many marked a significant shift in the balance of power from restaurateurs to chefs. As well as having the great good fortune to watch Vrinat in action while a customer at Taillevent, I also interviewed him at length in 1999 for the *Financial Times*. He was not only adamant about the one essential factor in any successful restaurant – 'restaurants must come from the heart' – I can still hear him saying that the profession demanded three qualities of any restaurateur: a love of food, a love of wine and a love of one's fellow human beings. These three are intricately and inexorably linked because of the bonds of trust that have to exist between a customer and the restaurateur. While we can rely on specialists for advice as to how we can best lead our lives, only the restaurateur is charged on a daily basis outside the home with guaranteeing the safety of the food and drink we put into our mouths to keep our bodies going. It is a great and exciting responsibility.

It is one that the next generation of restaurateurs, those entering the business in their mid twenties will, I believe, meet with growing confidence. I am delighted that today so many young people are going into the restaurant business, or are planning to do so, attracted by the excitement of dealing with seasonal produce, the daily interaction with their fellow human beings, and the opportunity not to have to spend their working day staring at a computer screen. If these stories make their restaurants more successful, this book will have achieved its goal. I will be happy from a purely selfish perspective, as it will mean that there are even more exciting restaurants for me to take my family and friends to in the future.

THE ACCIDENTAL RESTAURATEUR

I woke up to the life of a restaurateur on the morning of 2 June 1981, when my restaurant L'Escargot in Soho, London, finally opened for business. Aged twenty-nine, I had absolutely no professional experience for the job. I had never worked in a restaurant. I had no training as a cook, let alone as a chef (and I came to learn that there are significant differences between the two roles). None of my friends were in the business. It was certainly not a profession I had ever envisaged for myself, although it has since taken me around the world, given me a good living for over thirty years, and provided far more fun and friends – not to mention good meals and wonderful wine – than I had imagined possible. I was very much an accidental restaurateur.

The accidents that led directly to the opening of L'Escargot began when my late father suffered the first of a series of strokes that were to lead to his premature death. As the eldest son of a close-knit family, I promptly took a leave of absence from my job as a metal trader in London and went home to Bowdon, just south of Manchester, to assist my mother with his recovery. As he got stronger I faced a predicament: should I go back to my old job or, at twenty-eight and relatively footloose and fancy-free, do something on my own? An advertisement from a Californian winery looking for a UK agent caught my eye, and I decided to pursue it. Along with an old friend (with whom I soon parted company) I secured the agency, believing that the wine was better than it was, and that all the talk of the British pound constantly strengthening against the US dollar would make our wine unbeatable value. We were also in love with the California dream, and wondered how anyone could turn down our enthusiastic sales pitch.

It quickly transpired that nearly everyone could. Sales were extremely difficult: with a limited range of wines to sell, I found it almost impossible to get in to see any of the powerful supermarket buyers, and while customers were beginning to be intrigued by New World wines, they were not prepared to part with their money for them. In addition, I soon began to appreciate that wine bottles are highly fragile, that they can easily be stolen and that wine storage costs mount rapidly. What I needed, I told myself, was a wine bar through which I could sell the wines at a decent margin.

The reason I ended up with a twenty-five-year lease on one of London's oldest restaurants was primarily due to the charms of the building itself, plus a superabundance of naivety. L'Escargot Bienvenu at 48 Greek Street had opened in the 1920s as the first restaurant in London to specialize in French bourgeois cooking – a more homely, less expensive style of food compared to the more expensive haute cuisine then found in many

restaurants and hotels. The owner also farmed snails in the basement kitchen, making it the first restaurant in Great Britain to produce its own. I had asked my old friend, the designer Tom Brent, to help me find a suitable site for the wine bar I had convinced myself I needed. Tom was to play a large part in the launch of L'Escargot because he was later responsible for dealing with the builders, the design and the interior, as well as the unforgettable carpet complete with snail trails. But I don't think he ever believed, when we first walked round what was to become my professional home for the next eight years, that I would emerge with the keys to its front door.

From the moment I walked into the building I fell under its spell. 48 Greek Street had been built as a townhouse for William Cavendish-Bentinck, the third Duke of Portland and twice the Prime Minister of Great Britain, and it exuded history, charm and character. The rooms were dignified, they had a great sense of proportion and each one was unique. It was a building, I believed, that would make all my customers feel welcome. Its conversion to a restaurant in the 1920s had not affected its character too much. The ground floor housed the main restaurant, complete with lampshades held at each corner by plastic snail shells. There was a stunning private dining room on the first floor with all its original features intact and windows overlooking Greek Street, which was to play host to numerous wedding lunches, including my own. There was a most unusual room on the top floor with a glass barrel-vaulted roof that was perfect for wine tastings. And there was a fully equipped kitchen in the basement, although it had been condemned on forty-four counts by Westminster Council and would have to be completely renovated.

First, there was the question of how to finance the purchase of the building, let alone the renovation. My goal at this stage was fairly modest: to convert the ground floor into the wine bar I thought would be the answer to my surplus wine stock, and then, once the business started to generate some profits, to do up the two rooms at the back of the building, including the one with a barrel-vaulted roof, which I realized had enormous potential. I managed to secure the lease with the help of Archie Preston, a friend of my father's, whom he had helped to establish his first business in Manchester in the late 1940s. Now the director of a significant property company, his son-in-law Stephen Lindemann very generously bought the freehold for around £150,000 ($235,000) for 438 square metres (5,200 square feet) of central London property. He granted

16

me the twenty-five-year lease and an option to buy the freehold at a fixed price, which happily I never exercised. Had I done so, I would have tied up too much cash and when my health deteriorated in the late 1980s I would not have been able to sell so quickly. Restaurateurs are principally traders, I quicky learned.

Between the time that the purchase was completed in September 1980 and the opening of L'Escargot in June 1981, many momentous things happened and many have been forgotten, partly due to the first of a series of grand-mal epileptic fits that the stress of opening the restaurant caused me to experience, and which first made their presence felt in the month before we were due to open. I do remember, though, a great party we held in the restaurant on a Saturday night before the builders moved in. And I recall going for lunch that day to Bianchi's, then a renowned Italian restaurant one block away, and telling its highly respected manager Elena Salvoni about my plans and the party that night. She came over to join us, and, excited by so many young faces in the building, promptly decided that she would come to work with me. This was to prove a great blessing, since she brought all her loyal customers with her, but in the short term I had a problem. I had just hired London's best maitre d', but I hadn't really planned to open a restaurant. Well, I told myself, at least I had the two empty rooms at the back of the building.

Two other women were to play a significant role in my restaurant. The late Sue Miles was once a hippy, then a midwife, before turning to cooking. She was redoubtable. Long before it became the norm, she had an unwavering belief in good, simple ingredients and the charms of Italian cooking, combined with a will of iron. I remember the flavours of the bollito misto she cooked for me one night in her house in Kentish Town as though I had eaten it only yesterday. Sue was to be my consultant on all kitchen-related matters: its redesign, the purchase of the new equipment, the hiring of a full-time chef, and, together with that chef and me, the menus. I wanted the food to be as good in my restaurant as the best I had eaten in others'. Sue had another great quality. As far as she was concerned, the more customers the restaurant attracted, the better it would be. Some people in the business believe that quality is synonymous with a restricted number of customers. Sue, however, believed that the menu should be written in a way that allowed an efficient service for as many people as possible.

The two L'Escargot menus – one for the restaurant and a separate one for the ground-floor brasserie – were groundbreaking for 1981.

Firstly, they were written in English, whereas most menus of that era, particularly in expensive restaurants, were entirely in French. Secondly, they were both relatively brief, with about eight starters and eight main courses, because we wanted even then to be seasonal, and to serve the best possible food despite the constraints of a basement kitchen. Perhaps most unusually, on the restaurant menu we never listed more than one fish main course. Instead, the two or three fish dishes of the day were written on a small specials card that was printed before each service and attached to the main menu. Typical dishes from the restaurant menu at that time included a ramekin of snails, garlic and parsley topped with puff pastry; pasta and seafood salad with Dover sole, squid, shrimps and cockles and an olive oil and lemon dressing; suprême of brill and smoked haddock mousse with cucumber and dill sauce; rack of English lamb with a hot onion tartlet; and saddle of venison with pears and cranberries.

I would have achieved only a fraction of what I have been able to do during the past thirty years had it not been for a chance encounter with the wine writer Jancis Robinson, whom a year later I was fortunate enough to marry. When I met Jancis in autumn 1980, she had already written her first wine book, *The Wine Book,* and was the wine correspondent of *The Sunday Times.* Wine brought us together at a tasting, and then in early 1981 we travelled together along the west coast of the US, buying wines for the restaurant's list, which was initially to feature only American wines. When she finally realized quite how inexperienced I was, it was too late – she was already married to an accidental restaurateur. There were compensations: most notably on the night of 22 October 1981, when we were married, as our wedding lunch took place in the private dining room at the front and that night's party took over the whole restaurant. We drank our entire stock of Bruno Paillard 1973 Champagne, and for some time afterwards it seemed worth opening the restaurant just for that party.

My negotiations to buy the restaurant had taught me a few valuable lessons. The first was how not to treat customers. Although the restaurant had already been closed when I acquired the lease, its bars were still stocked because the vendors were keen to sell it as a going concern. It still rankles that after long negotiations and an eventual agreement to pay very close to the asking price, the previous owner never offered a celebratory drink, something to mark the occasion. I was determined from then on to err on the side of generosity, as most restaurateurs do. Then there was the issue of the kitchen, which was located in the basement, as so many of them are

in London's tall and narrow buildings. It was connected to the floors above with two electric lifts. These lifts were to prove extremely temperamental and were liable to get stuck, usually just before lunch or dinner when we were fully booked, and were expensive to maintain on service contracts. But I did not realize at the time quite how fortunate I was to take over a restaurant with a kitchen already in place. From a cost perspective, it is much better to take over a restaurant in which the kitchen is an already integral part. And it is not just a question of the cost of fitting out a kitchen. When you build from scratch there is often the inclination to keep adding more elements to make the customer's experience more comfortable and the kitchen even more exciting for the chefs. This can adversely affect the restaurant's income. At the St. John Hotel in Leicester Square, for example, a discrepancy between the final computer drawings and the actual physical space meant that it was not possible to fit in four of the tables that had been outlined on the architect's drawings. Over the course of a busy year this could mean an annual loss of income of £50,000 ($80,000).

In June 1981, however, I had more than enough to worry about. The builders had gone into receivership only a month before we were due to open, thereby locking me out of my own restaurant. Hiring good staff was difficult, and the number of shifts in which we had planned to do dry runs in the restaurant was growing smaller and smaller as the building delays mounted. I remember one trial dinner in the barrel-vaulted room on the top floor, when we were using the table furthest away from the kitchen to test whether the dishes could travel that far without losing their heat. Our first set of waiting staff included a number of 'resting' actors. One of them, Clive Merrison, who went on to have a distinguished acting career, performed the role of a dumb waiter in front of the dumb waiter, the manually operated lift that brought the food from the kitchen. It was all I had to laugh about at the time.

As so often happens, we had gone significantly over budget before we opened and I had been turned down in my application for a wine-only licence on the ground floor, which was the principal reason I had decided to become a restaurateur. I thought I had prepared everything correctly, as did the expensive licensing solicitor I had hired to represent me. But what no one told me was that we were to attend the final sitting of this particular licensing authority, so all thirteen magistrates turned up instead of the usual three. They were put out by the fact we had only provided three sets of the expensive drawings that have to accompany any such application, and they turned me down imperiously. Overnight, my wine bar had to become a brasserie, where no alcohol could be served without food. Eventually, though, I looked back on this as a very lucky break, because it meant not only that the average spend on the ground floor was higher than I had initially budgeted, but also that L'Escargot remained distinctively different from the nearby pubs and clubs of Soho.

It certainly looked different, thanks to Tom Brent. He had chosen bespoke-furniture-makers to produce lamps that curved inside the barrel-vaulted room. He had come up with a green-and-blue colour palette for the (then innovative) rag-rolled walls, and he had designed the large letters for the sign that still hangs outside the building, which allows it to be recognized by customers approaching from either end of Greek Street. At the same time he had restored the cast of the original owner riding a snail, which also still hangs outside. Then he decided we should have a snail carpet, a feature that is still remembered by customers who ate at L'Escargot in the 1980s, because seeing it as they walked in immediately brought a smile to their faces. The carpet had a dark-blue background on which the outlines of green snail trails linked up to a border of a similar blue, detailed with snails. When Tom first had this apparently impossible idea my father spoke to a former colleague of his in a Yorkshire carpet mill. Thanks to the recession, their looms were quiet at the time, so they produced the carpet within six weeks at a very friendly price.

At least the carpet gave the customers something to smile about in the first few weeks, when the food and service were pretty poor. Later in my career, when I was one of several advisors working with British Airways on their food, I heard the phrase 'DOB' being bandied about by the man in charge of choosing what would appear on their club and first-class menus. 'DOB' stands for 'Doable on Board' and means taking into consideration all the limiting factors of cooking at 10,000 metres (33,000 feet) from a tiny kitchen before putting it on the menu. Similar restrictions apply to certain dishes sent out of a basement kitchen to dining rooms four floors away. Sue and Elena were both keen to serve pasta, but it lasted only a week on the menu because no solution could be found to the fact that the glistening dish that left the kitchen was irrevocably transformed into a coagulated mess by the time it arrived in front of my customers. Knowing your building, I learned quickly, is as important as knowing your guests.

Right from the beginning, we were never short of customers. The combination of Elena's welcome, the original interior, the fact that restaurant openings were much rarer then than they are today, plus a generous review by Fay Maschler in the *London Evening Standard* made sure of that. The problem was how to look after them. Gradually, an experienced team gathered around me. Nick Smallwood, who had worked at the Hard Rock Café and Zanzibar, a members club in Covent Garden, strengthened the management and introduced me to an indispensable bookkeeper. Sue Miles found us a chef, a young man called Alastair Little, one of the first of the home-grown British chefs who were to become so well known in the 1980s (among his friends and contemporaries were Simon Hopkinson and Rowley Leigh). Alastair valiantly saw us through the first six months, but was clearly better suited to smaller establishments such as the eponymous restaurant he was to open one street away from L'Escargot in Frith Street. He now runs his own delicatessen, Tavola in Notting Hill, which is devoted to the food of Italy, a country he loves with a passion. As we got busier, Martin Lam (now at Ransome's Dock in Battersea) came to work in the kitchen, initially just in the evenings, and then as head chef on a permanent basis. His culinary principles, based firmly on seasonality – now the byword for most chefs, but pretty revolutionary twenty-five years ago – were to guide L'Escargot. Here again I was very fortunate, particularly as he and Elena got on so very well. Martin had, and still retains, a love of preparing the best seasonal ingredients and cooking them for as many customers as possible, an essential quality to look for in a chef if you want to make money. Equally importantly, he had the organizational ability to see how we could best do this to ensure every customer left happy and on time. He also had an easy-going approach: Martin wanted to get on with everybody, and this proved important when Elena wanted to accommodate all her customers' foibles. Martin and I often used to laugh at the number of times Elena marked her order VIP, which seemed to be in the majority of cases.

Since Martin pursued our policy of constantly changing menus, we developed some very strong friendships with our suppliers: Michael Hyams for fruit and vegetables; Ian Woodhouse for meat and game; Julian Birch and William Black for fish, the latter delivering every week from Boulogne in northern France; Jack Morris in Bury for his black puddings and the late Bob Baxter in Morecambe Bay for his potted shrimps. This experience reinforced a business lesson my late father had drummed into me at an early age, one that has become increasingly important, I believe, for restaurateurs and chefs. 'Any fool can sell,' he used to say, 'but there is far more skill required in buying.' Looking after your suppliers, above all paying them on time, is an increasingly important aspect of the restaurateur's role, and one that pays significant dividends. Not only do the suppliers give you the best and most timely advice (crucial when planning menu changes), but they also become customers, using your restaurant as the location for a business lunch or a place to celebrate. It is an approach that makes for very good business and long-lasting friendships.

The black pudding and potted shrimps were constant and incredibly popular features of the brasserie menu. We devoted equal attention to both menus, the main difference between them being that the restaurant menu featured more expensive cuts of meat, fish and game, such as rack of lamb, duck breast, fillet of turbot, sea bass and monkfish. By contrast, in the brasserie the biggest-selling dishes were salads, fish pie, sausages of any description and calves' liver. The increasing popularity of the brasserie had a hugely beneficial effect on the kitchen's profitability, as the combination of the two menus ensured that there was little wastage. The benefit of this synergy is one reason why so many top chefs have over the past twenty years opened restaurants serving less expensive dishes, and is also why ingredients such as pork belly, lamb shoulder and salt beef have shot up in price. Being able to use both sets of ingredients in one kitchen was, I came to appreciate, not only a commercial benefit, but also an extra attraction for our customers.

With his penchant for art and cabaret, as well as his connections in the fashion world, salonist Stephen Chamberlain joined us as brasserie manager some time after Martin Lam and brought an inspirational new identity to the ground floor in the evenings. It had been busy at lunchtime from the beginning, but because we could not sell alcohol alone, the early-evening business was very poor. Two innovations changed that. Firstly, he introduced a rota of art exhibitions on the walls that changed every month. This was great for business because the artist held an opening party on the Monday evening (invariably the quietest night of the week; how to fill Monday evenings remains a perennial challenge for restaurateurs everywhere), and many stayed on to eat afterwards. Secondly, he introduced cabaret evenings on Thursday, Friday and Saturday nights, which filled the place up and brought in a younger audience keen to have a good time in a distinguished setting. I always liked to think that the Duke of Portland would have approved. Suddenly, I had not just a restaurant, but a business of different but distinct parts that complemented one another. The inexpensive ground floor was a place people visited several times a week; the more expensive restaurant upstairs also attracted its own set of regular customers, who naturally wanted 'their' table whenever they came; and there were two rooms of different sizes that could be used for private parties, a side of the business that began to pick up quickly as the economy improved.

Opening in a recession was tough, but I didn't fully appreciate at the time that, tough as it was, my timing had not been that bad. Fortuitously, Channel 4 television had recently opened offices nearby and because it did not have its own production facilities, it immediately gave a new lease of life to all the service industries that had long had their homes in Soho. Casting agencies, editing suites and post-production facilities all enjoyed an immediate boost to their business, and a new wave of independent production companies suddenly emerged. All of them needed somewhere to meet, discuss, pitch for business, eat, drink and, from time to time, celebrate. Their existence promptly justified L'Escargot's. Restaurants have to serve a purpose for their customers – plying them with good food, drink and service is never enough – and fortunately we stumbled upon ours very quickly. We provided a business service, one that was noticed by several regular customers who went on to open the Groucho Club two streets away in 1985 as a club for those in the media. Although I recall feeling threatened at the time, I soon began to appreciate one of life's great maxims, particularly pertinent to the restaurant business: that imitation is the sincerest form of flattery. Tony Mackintosh, the Groucho's first MD, invited me round soon after they opened to tell me he was making Jancis and me life members because L'Escargot had inspired so much of what they had done (including the original eau-de-nil paintwork). I didn't relish the rivalry at the time, but there proved to be enough customers for us both.

Because of our proximity to theatreland, and the fact that we established a reputation as a meeting place for the media, and also because there were fewer restaurants then, L'Escargot quickly attracted a fascinating clientèle. Princess Diana, Ella Fitzgerald and Mick Jagger (whose cup the waitress assured me she would always keep because it had had his lips on it) all came, along with numerous eminent politicians whom journalists interviewed across the more discreet corner tables in what became known as Elena's room; so did Michael Palin, numerous literary agents including Caradoc King, and many visiting chefs, restaurateurs and winemakers. A visit from someone well known always sent a frisson of excitement through the waiting staff, and it obviously delighted Elena too.

The fact that she had already spent forty years looking after her customers – and was to carry on until 2010 at Elena's L'Etoile in Charlotte Street – gave her unique insight into the pleasure of working in a restaurant and the reason for her extraordinary rapport with customers. Customers' surnames or claims to fame meant nothing to her, she said. When she looked through the list of the thirty-three tables we had booked for a busy lunch, she did her best to make sure that they each got their favourite table and, most crucially, that no one was sitting next to, or even close to, anyone else in the same profession. Then, time permitting, a little bit of reminiscing would begin, and she would explain that watching people come in to eat during the various stages of their lives gave her the utmost pleasure. To see them together initially as 'courting couples', as Elena always referred to them, then married, then bringing in their children for their first meal in a restaurant, then watching their children grow up, then finally welcoming the children in as adults at the beginning of their professional and family life: nothing and nobody, however famous, gave her as much pleasure as this sequence of happy events.

Early one evening she let slip her own view on why she had been so successful at making her customers feel at home, which was perhaps the first and only time I ever heard her talk about herself. 'It's all to do with my lack of height,' she said. I was too stunned to say anything, so I waited for an explanation. 'I'm only five feet [1.52 metres], which gives me a great advantage when I approach customers sitting around the table because there is no height difference between us. We look each other straight in the eye. I don't look down on them and they never have to look up to me. It's as simple as that.' Elena then went off to check on a pre-theatre table and I knew I had just been privy to one of the most insightful, but certainly not one of the most easily reproducible, secrets of restaurant management.

I was soon to learn what my contribution would be to the running of a restaurant that, once established, employed ninety to 100 staff, served over 400 customers a day and had weekly sales of over £55,000 ($85,000), with customers in four different rooms and the kitchen staff in the fifth down below. Effectively, I was in charge of staff morale. Successful restaurants are, above all, team efforts and it was my job to go from floor to floor, area to area, to make sure that everyone responsible for my customers' having a good time were themselves in the right frame of mind to do their best. Monday mornings were always difficult because we were closed on Sundays, so this meant the kitchen had to get into gear from a standing start, and there was always the most sickness and absenteeism (the bane of any restaurateur's life) immediately after the weekend. As the week got busier, the restaurant settled into a rhythm of its own, but Wednesdays were always tricky for no other reason, it seemed to me, than that the previous weekend seemed a distant memory and the next one still some way off. I always used to come into the restaurant on Saturday afternoons, often with our eldest children Julia and William, who got great pleasure from helping the waiting staff arrange the chocolate snails we used to serve with the coffee, helping themselves to several at the same time. Saturday nights always started slowly, but got busy quickly as people flocked into the West End.

My first job working in a rapidly expanding textile business in Manchester stood me in good stead. There too we were always up against deadlines, not quite the two per day every restaurant faces, but the need to get orders processed through the factory so they could be dispatched on time was a huge challenge, albeit one I enjoyed. In the factory, as at the restaurant, meeting deadlines depended on everyone co-operating towards a common, determined goal. Nobody can run a successful restaurant on their own, so learning to inspire your staff is essential. In fact, motivating your staff is the key to being a successful restaurateur. Whatever happened last night, however good the service was, however happy everyone left, each restaurant starts the day from scratch. There is, hopefully, a pretty busy reservations list, but at 8.00 a.m. every morning, or much earlier if the restaurant is open for breakfast, the kitchen and the waiting staff have got a lot of work to do. And inevitably the first couple of phone calls are from staff who don't feel well enough to come in to work.

In fact, most of my day, from 8.30 a.m. until 7.00 p.m., was spent encouraging my staff. The two things I did first upon walking through the heavy front door were to check the reservations book to make sure that nothing had gone wrong the night before, and to switch on the coffee machine on the ground floor so that everyone could make themselves a coffee when they came in. The latter was critical to staff morale. The next couple of hours were spent in the office, checking the takings, going to the bank and ensuring that we had plenty of cash, not just for the floats that each cashier needed (and we had one in each in the brasserie and restaurant at lunch and dinner), but also to ensure we had enough cash to meet the demand for 'subs' that arose from many members of the team during the week. Although credit cards were common in the 1980s, cash machines were not and internet banking did not exist. Cash was still king and this was how most of my staff were paid every Friday. By the beginning of the following week, quite a few, particularly the younger ones, had little left, and at around 5.00 p.m., at the end or beginning of their shift, would climb the stairs to my office in search of a £10 or £20 ($15 or $30) 'sub', that would be taken out of their following week's wages. Offering this interest-free service was an important and constant role in keeping my staff happy.

By 11.00 a.m. the pace started quickening. The specials were ready and on the menu; the waiting staff had arrived and were anxious for their staff lunch at 11.15 a.m., which took place around table 18, the large round table at the back of the brasserie; the front of the restaurant and the front steps had to be mopped down (something I could check on by sticking my head out of the office window above); the delivery hatch was firmly closed; and the bookings lists were distributed to the restaurant and the reception desk.

Although we all knew we had thirty-three tables to fill across the three dining rooms (we didn't take bookings in the brasserie), the number of unreserved tables that we calculated were left to fill, and what the front-of-house team decided were left available, was often very different. It was crucial to tell the receptionist as soon as possible exactly how many tables we wanted her to fill once the phone was switched down from the office to the front desk at midday. Once customers started to arrive, I would hand over responsibility for this to those who, I quickly came to realize, could look after my customers far more skilfully than I could. Around 1.00 p.m. I would take off my jacket and tie, slip on a chef's apron and take my place in the kitchen by the manual lift that took food up to the brasserie to ensure that the service was as efficient as possible. This was a role I loved: being in the heat of the kitchen, using my authority and my hands to ensure that we served our customers as well and as swiftly as possible. Lunches were very busy, with 180 to 200 customers in ninety minutes, and when they went well (which, I am delighted to say, they mostly did), brought me a great deal of personal and professional satisfaction. I would be back in my jacket and tie by 2.30 p.m. in time to walk around the restaurant and talk to the customers I knew, or who wanted to see me. Then at around 3.00 p.m. I had lunch with Martin, usually at a table in the front window of the brasserie, watching the world go by on Greek Street and hearing how things had gone from Elena, before she went home for a break, returning at 7.15 p.m.

The late afternoon schedule included doing the banking from that day's lunch and preparing everything for that night's service:

The Accidental Restaurateur

the reservations list, the specials and any special menus for parties that may be taking place anywhere in the restaurant or the brasserie. The hour between 4.00 p.m. and 5.00 p.m. was always quite hectic in the kitchen because that was when the evening brigade arrived to take over from their colleagues who had worked during the day (each would work different shifts on alternate weeks). It was always quite an anxious time too, because if someone failed to turn up for work, either a kitchen porter or a chef, we would have to find a replacement. The St Mungo's hostel for the homeless close by often provided immediate and all-too-keen substitutes for the former, but if the fish chef failed to appear, this could result in delicate and costly negotiations to persuade someone who had already worked an eight-hour shift to stay on and work another.

I rarely worked in the evenings. This was when Elena and Stephen took over, and although we could be even busier in the evenings than for lunch, the immediate pressure was less because the dinner service is spread over a longer period than lunch. I wanted to put my then two small children to bed, a pleasure which I sometimes even managed. I remember that as I closed the curtains in our bedroom before collapsing into bed, my thoughts were often of the restaurant, wondering quite how busy we had been that night.

My time as a restaurateur did change me in one significant and enduring way. When I opened L'Escargot I had a secret ambition: to have one of London's most successful restaurants while being the world's worst cook. I loved eating, not cooking. All that changed after I spent time in the kitchen calling orders for the brasserie; as I watched the chefs at work I became fascinated by all they did and by the beauty and dexterity with which they did it. Excellent hand-eye coordination is as essential in a chef as a good palate. This coincided with the arrival of our children, Julia in 1982 and William in 1984, at a time when Jancis was filming a series of wine programmes for Channel 4. I have been the cook at home ever since.

Eventually, my years as a restaurateur took their toll, and I was forced to sell the restaurant in 1988. I now know that I have been suffering from ulcerative colitis all these years. I was hospitalized twice and while lying in hospital the second time, it became obvious to me that I had a rather one-sided choice: to carry on as a restaurateur at a significant cost to my young family, or to sell up and try to find a less stressful profession. For me, there wasn't really any choice.

Selling a single restaurant is not an easy proposition. We had never pursued profitability as an end in itself and I had always planned to expand; towards the end I even dreamed of buying the small restaurant next door and opening an Italian restaurant serving more authentic Italian food than existed in London at the time. Sadly, it was not to be. However, any restaurant's most valuable asset – its lease – was in good condition. There were still seventeen years left on it and the first rent review in 1986 had not been too onerous. Interested buyers soon appeared; the difficulty lay in negotiating with them while the restaurant remained busy, as I did not want to lose key staff or customers in the interim. I had told Elena and Martin (both of whom I had now made shareholders) of my decision, and because they were both very keen to stay at L'Escargot I had also made them a promise: in the event of two buyers offering me the asking price, I would defer to them as to which one they would prefer to work with in the future. Ultimately, this promise was to prove costly because when the situation indeed arose, the buyer they had declined immediately increased his offer by five per cent, but by this stage we had shaken hands on the deal. An anxious month followed, as the transfer of the funds was far slower than anyone had anticipated, but finally it came through. By May 1988 L'Escargot was no longer mine.

I remember walking out of the front door, having said goodbye to all the staff just before they got busy for lunch and turning left towards the tube station. At the first corner I came to it finally hit me that I was no longer a restaurateur, and that, most importantly, I would no longer be working with such a fascinating team, nor having my life enriched twice a day by interesting customers walking in through my front door to be fed and entertained. I felt very empty. I also believed that I had reached the end of my restaurant career. In that I was to be proved quite wrong, and much more quickly than I could have imagined – it was really just the end of the first course.

RESTAURATEUR TO CRITIC

There is one tell-tale sign that I have been a restaurant critic for the last twenty-two years, although it is not obvious. The clue to my profession lies in my shirts, and it is something that comes to my attention whenever I put one on in the morning. On virtually every shirt there is at least one black pen mark, often several, which are the consequences of the tools of my trade: a black pen and a small Moleskine notebook that will fit into my jacket pocket.

Although I have done my utmost to preserve my anonymity over the years – for a very long time the only photo of me that ever appeared was of my red socks – I do go through almost the same ritual whenever I walk into a restaurant. My jacket comes off; my tie, if I am wearing one, gets tucked into my shirt; and my napkin is draped as widely as possible to minimize any spills. Never, as Jeffrey Steingarten once wrote in his excellent book *The Man Who Ate Everything*, allow the waiter to indulge in that most pretentious habit of unfurling the napkin and placing it on your lap. I then pull out my notebook, take the top off my pen and set to. And this is the combination that does the damage to my shirts. For the next hour and a half, the pen is facing towards me and as I combine eating, drinking, letting my eyes roam the room and making notes, the pen inevitably comes into contact with some part of my shirt, resulting in the ink spots that give me away.

Every restaurateur has a different opinion about the critics who review them (and, of course, about the increasingly influential restaurant bloggers), which is inevitably a result of how well they have been treated in the review. But two views, in particular, are widely held. The first is that although almost every new restaurant will be subjected to many articles, the reviewers rarely return. Most other art forms, such as exhibitions, films, books or DVDs, are complete when they are reviewed and don't change afterwards, but restaurants do. Chefs come and go; sommeliers bring in new approaches to wines; and, above all, the restaurateur and the waiting team will be creating something that just gets better with the patina of age. Despite this, restaurants are rarely re-reviewed, and it is difficult for restaurateurs to lure the reviewers back in. The offer of a free meal may be misconstrued as a bribe (and restaurant expenses are a considerable cost for the newspapers, although most other arts correspondents do get free tickets), while press releases are rarely as effective today as they once were.

The second complaint is that while a good working knowledge of the world of music, opera, cinema or theatre are required before anyone becomes a critic in these highly disciplined fields, the role of restaurant critic is often handed to those with no professional experience whatsoever. There are notable exceptions, of course, such as François Simon of *Le Figaro* and Fay Maschler at the *London Evening Standard*, but by and large restaurant critics do not have the same level of intimate, professional knowledge of their subjects as other critics. While a good appetite is a prerequisite, many restaurateurs are disappointed that so few restaurant writers have a working knowledge of areas such as the wine list, into which considerable time and effort is invested, and which is a major source of revenue and customer satisfaction. This second complaint, at least, is one I am fortunate enough to have been able to address during my second career in the industry.

It is not surprising, perhaps, that the most significant steps in my career as a professional restaurant critic should have taken place around the dinner table. My initial break into journalism was over dinner at our house in north London in 1990 with J.D.F. Jones and his partner. JDF, as he was known worldwide, a Welshman who loved his food, wine and gossip, was then the editor of the *Financial Times'* Weekend section. Over a bibulous dinner, talk turned to the topic of why it was one of the few newspapers not to have a regular restaurant column. I can still recall his response: 'We get a lot of articles sent in, but they all tend to be along the same theme: "We went here, I had the lamb, my partner had the salmon, and the bill came to such-and-such amount." I am looking for something different.' Like all the best editors, as I was to appreciate, JDF knew what he didn't want, even if he didn't know what he did want.

His words stayed with me a few days later when we went out for dinner to Bibendum restaurant in South Kensington, which had been opened by a forceful trio of designer Sir Terence Conran, publisher Paul Hamlyn and chef Simon Hopkinson. Bibendum had garnered considerable praise for its elegant design in the former Michelin building, and for Simon's precise and delicious renditions of classic French and British dishes. During our meal something kept nagging at me, a thought that all was not as it should be. I remember being struck by a sense of obvious friction between the waiting staff and the kitchen. One of the most constant challenges for any restaurateur is to manage the very different goals of the kitchen brigade on the one hand and the front-of-house team on the other. In fact, I would go so far as to say that it is the quintessential challenge for any restaurateur. Although the waiting staff have to face their customers at every turn and be as accommodating towards them as possible (above all to maximize their tips), chefs operate in isolation, cut off from their customers and more preoccupied with the perfection of the finished dish than any customer's foibles. This may sound like an irreconcilable situation, but in reality the circle is squared most of the time by the best restaurateurs' ability to encourage both teams to work to everyone's mutual benefit, particularly that of the customer. If not, the restaurant goes out of business.

During the next few days I wrote a review of what we had experienced – painfully slowly, as I seem to remember – then printed it out and posted it to JDF with a note saying that if I were still a restaurateur then this is the kind of review I would like to read. He promptly responded by saying he was going to print it a week on Saturday, and that I would then write a fortnightly column. He had, he added, only one question and one word of advice. The first was how I would like to be known professionally. Hitherto I had always been known as Nick, but the tone of his voice implied that a column by Nicholas Lander would carry more gravitas. I concurred and professionally I have been Nicholas ever since. The second was a good piece of advice for anyone about to embark on a journalistic career: 'Obviously, I want you to write the very best you can. But don't forget that however good it is, some time the following week Saturday's paper will be wrapping up someone's fish and chips somewhere.' This was a salutary and invaluable reminder never to take myself, or my subject, too seriously. As I started to write I became increasingly confident in my approach and grew more aware, as the *Financial Times'* international circulation grew, of just what a fortunate position I was in to be able to write about restaurants all over the world.

My career underwent another turning point – and an even more pleasurable one – while I was waiting to be seated at restaurant L'Ami Louis in Paris in late 2004 at a dinner for Johnny Apple, a leading *New York Times* journalist and renowned gourmand. Among the many friends from the worlds of politics, the arts, food and wine, there were also several notable journalists present, including Charles Eisendrath, who runs a fellowship programme for journalists at the University of Michigan. He and I got trapped in a corner and started talking about newspapers. At that time the internet was viewed as a major threat to the future of many newspapers, as it has indeed proved to be, and there was much speculation about what the future would hold for many journalists. As someone not blessed with much self-confidence, I repeated my professional concerns to Eisendrath.

He dismissed them. He said that in his opinion the world would come to appreciate more professional expertise rather than less, and in this he has proved to be correct. The specialist, certainly in the fields of food and wine, has come to be much more appreciated. It was what he went on to say about the *Financial Times* in particular, though, that has stayed with me ever since, and that I remember whenever I sit down in front of a blank screen to write my next article. 'Every time FT readers give up ten minutes of their weekend to read your column they are paying you a huge compliment. You are duty bound to repay that compliment by making what you write as interesting, as pertinent and as much fun as possible.' And that is what I have always subsequently tried to do.

A little later, Lorna Dolan, one of my editors, astutely picked up on the unique perspective from which I was writing and suggested adding the subtitle 'The Restaurant Insider' to my column, an addition I have been very happy with. Although I have long since sold my restaurant, I have, I hope, managed to keep one foot in the restaurateurs' camp, with the other one firmly in that of the consumers. I can see things from a restaurateur's perspective, which allows me to explain a business that can be fascinating, all-consuming and emotionally draining by turns and occasionally simultaneously. I also spend a lot of time and money in restaurants as a customer, and I hope that what I write helps customers appreciate what restaurateurs are trying to do, and vice versa. The fortuitous combination of being a former restaurateur, along with writing for a newspaper with an international platform and a well-off readership, and being married to one of the world's top wine writers, has also been instrumental in introducing me both professionally and socially to most of the world's top chefs. Certainly, restaurants are fun, but there is a more serious side to them, too. They employ many people around the world. Since they can require limited capital and very low technology, restaurants are often the business many new immigrants turn to first when they arrive in a new country with little by way of possessions other than recipes and the desire to recreate the flavours and aromas of the cooking of the homeland they have left behind. At the other end of the scale, restaurants can also be extremely expensive, not only for those who find the experience disappointing for whatever reason, but also for those who, often without doing due diligence, choose to invest in them. In the UK, restaurants are consistently second in the league table for the highest number of bankruptcies, second only to those in the building industry. A number of my early columns were specifically aimed at pointing out quite how risky investing in restaurants can be.

I realize now that during this period my approach to writing about restaurants changed significantly. At first my reviews were either too forgiving towards the profession I had reluctantly left behind, or weighted too much in favour of the consumer. Since that happy rendezvous in L'Ami Louis, there has been a shift in my focus towards writing about restaurants in a way that not only reveals their secrets, but also tells a story that can be appreciated wherever it is read. How and what I write has to be enjoyed by someone picking up the paper or online whether in Tokyo, London, Paris, New York or San Francisco. Food and wine can only be a part, albeit a significant part, of what I write, the rest has to be the sense of fun, coupled with a good story, that most restaurants represent. My role is to describe this magic to the best of my ability. It is a wonderful job, but the credit for creating the magic, and ensuring it is performed to the highest level of critical acclaim, day in and day out, lies with the world's great restaurateurs.

HAZEL ALLEN

THE BALLYMALOE WELCOME

Hazel Allen was the first restaurateur I thought of when I began to compile the *dramatis personae* for the book. As I did so, I began to realize quite how significantly some of the world's best restaurateurs have been under appreciated. Hazel, along with her sister-in-law Darina and mother-in-law Myrtle – the first two always referred to by their Christian names, the last always most respectfully as Mrs Allen – make up a triumvirate of remarkable women who have established Ballymaloe House, a forty-minute drive outside Cork, south-west Ireland, as one of the very finest restaurants, country-house hotels and cookery schools in the world since it first opened for business in May 1964. Hazel is married to Myrtle's son Rory, Darina to his older brother Timmy.

The house, the surrounding buildings and its staff seem capable of adapting to any visitor's demands and requests, which is almost certainly a result of the establishment's rather unambitious origins. Myrtle Allen and her late husband Ivan bought the house because it came with the surrounding farm. Overwhelmed by its produce, and revealing the skills and determination that have been her hallmark ever since, Mrs Allen put an advertisement in the *Cork Examiner* headed 'Dine in a Country House'. Since then neither Ballymaloe nor the Allen family (which now numbers over sixty), nor, it has to be said, the quality of cooking in Ireland, have ever looked back.

While both Darina and Mrs Allen have received justifiably extensive coverage for all they have achieved at Ballymaloe, it is always Hazel's presence that I have felt pulling the strings behind the scenes. It is her curly red hair, her smile, her peripheral vision (a crucial quality for any restaurateur), and her quiet approach to a table just to check that everything is going smoothly that I have noticed. Yet she has always seemed to slip back into the shadows between the reception area and one of the restaurant's seven dining rooms before I get a chance to ask her too many direct questions. I sensed a tentativeness, too, when arranging a time to meet at Ballymaloe, although her apprehension turned out to be down to the fact that she has never given an interview before. For the last forty years Hazel's priorities have been talking and listening to her guests, rather than talking about herself.

My last visit to Ballymaloe began with the ritual I always go through when arriving, although it was a particularly wild and windy autumn night. No sooner had I driven through the gates than I stopped the car, lowered both front windows and let the air sweep across my face and arms. I knew I was in a very calm haven and that, until the moment I drove out again,

I would be wonderfully looked after. This feeling persisted as I opened the glass-panelled front door and was instantly greeted by the warm voice of the receptionist, who sits at a desk directly in front of the door, in full view of anybody coming in or going out. I could not have been made to feel more warmly welcome. Even the ivy-covered exterior of the hotel seemed to exude a warm welcome, a theme continued inside by large open fires, comfortable chairs and sofas in the lounge off to the left and the fascinating art that covers every wall, the collection of which has been the Allens' passion since they first bought the house. Everything inside seems to have been built, or bought, for comfort. As we walked out of the hotel the following afternoon, I mentioned this experience to Hazel. She explained that she had introduced the transparent front door and the positioning of the desk twenty years ago: 'Those first few seconds are absolutely crucial in putting the guest at ease, making sure that they feel welcome. It always surprises me how many hoteliers and restaurateurs get this wrong. It is absolutely vital to get it right.'

Dinner that evening was in the best Ballymaloe tradition. Comfort came with a potato and herb soup; simplicity with a plate of peeled prawns from Ballycotton harbour five kilometres (three miles) away, with herb mayonnaise; culinary dexterity via half a local lobster, diced and returned to its shell with a butter sauce; and generosity with the trolleys of cheese and desserts that are explained and served by young waitresses in simple blue dresses that evoke a bygone era. Hovering in the background, whichever way one looked, was sommelier Colm McCan, who has spent sixteen years with the Allens and is still engagingly enthusiastic and solicitous. The cooks at Ballymaloe have the advantage of access to countless excellent local ingredients, but the menu is written with great simplicity, clarity and style. On the night I was there it included a carrot and savory soup; a bruschetta of courgettes, Knockalara ewes' milk cheese and pine nuts; and a frittata of roast peppers and garden greens. The vegetarian dishes are highlighted rather than neglected. Jason Fahey, the head chef, is given a clear and definitive name check. The menu states firmly but politely that mobile phones are not permitted. And the back page contains testimony from Mrs Allen, giving due credit to all her kitchen's suppliers.

'Ballymaloe is not run by fashion but by quality, by the confidence we have in what we're doing and the determination to go the extra mile for our guests,' Hazel explained, leaning back in a green high-backed armchair in a small, extremely comfortable drawing room just off the conservatory. I had just poured us both a cup of Barry's tea, the famous Cork blend, and

Hazel Allen

there were a couple of peacocks strolling past the window. The quality Hazel exudes, other than an overriding consideration for others, is of extraordinary proficiency, the ability to manage any situation. She would have made an exceptional occupational therapist, the career she had initially planned, but when the Dublin college she had applied to said they could not accept her for a year, her mother steered her towards a course in hotel management, which she could start immediately. 'In those days you didn't argue with your mother.'

Her memories of her time at the college in Cathal Brugha Street (where Darina was a fellow student a couple of years ahead of her) include many happy ones: of being taught how to cook French classics such as *sole bonne femme* and *gâteau Pithiviers*; of a stint one summer in Switzerland working in a family-owned hotel where the concept of days off was simply unheard of; and, finally, and most significantly, of a job working in a hotel in Montreal, Canada in 1970. This was to prove life changing, not for what she did, but for what she read. 'I wasn't looking forward to coming home because most hotels in Ireland at that time were pretty dreary. I was on a train and I just happened to read an article in a magazine about Ballymaloe and there was a photo of Myrtle with all her children. I decided that's where I wanted to work.'

She applied to Ballymaloe on her return to Ireland in October 1970 and, rather to her surprise, was taken on to start on 26 December. Five days later came an experience she would never forget. The New Year's Eve parties in those days were very big, very formal affairs. The house was full and all the carpets had been rolled up so that everyone could dance and a lot of the furniture had been moved into the outhouses. The menu was the very best local produce: lots of hams, pork and platters of oysters and shellfish. Hazel recalled: 'Suddenly, the door opened and in walked an extraordinarily smartly dressed group of guests whom we quickly recognized as Cork's entire Jewish community and who, for religious reasons, could not eat anything on the buffet.' It quickly transpired that there had been a mix-up in the bookings and they were expected the following evening, but it was obviously too late to do anything about it, so Mrs Allen went off into the kitchen and started preparing a whole range of dishes they could eat. Hazel had experienced immediately what most excites her and so many other restaurateurs: they love a crisis, and finding the solution to it.

Hazel stayed on and brought much-needed discipline to the reservations process. She recalled that when she arrived the system was chaotic: there was only one phone in the hotel, and it was at the opposite end of the hall from the office where all the bookings were written down on a single sheet of paper.

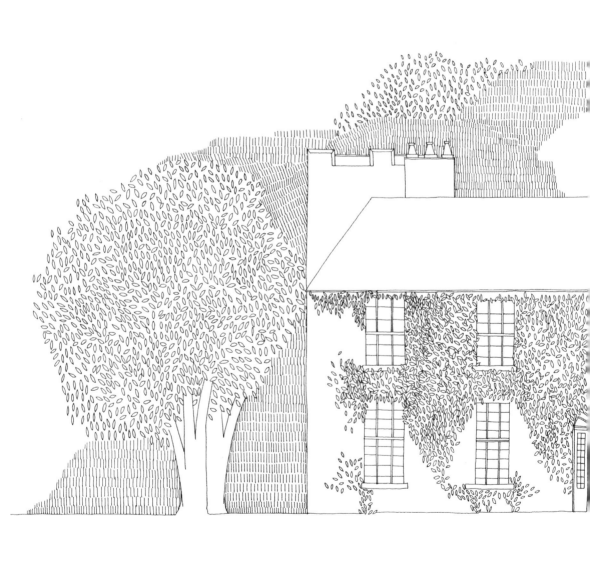

Then, love intervened and she married Myrtle's son Rory. And, having travelled to Australia and New Zealand, they both returned to Ballymaloe. Their five children provide the continuity into the next generation, particularly Roisin, whom I watched working in reception alongside her mother (one child runs the Ballymaloe relish business, another the successful Cully & Sully food business, another the farm next to the hotel). Hazel's quiet accession took place over the next few years; at first alongside Darina and Mrs Allen in the kitchen in the early 1980s, while they also ran La Ferme Irlandaise in Paris, a restaurant that was an outpost for the best Irish produce. (Hazel described Mrs Allen setting off on the night ferry with a suitcase full of Irish porridge oats, flour, potatoes and lobsters!) Then, in the winter of 1982, something took place at Ballymaloe which no firm of management consultants could ever have conceived of, but which has had the most extraordinary impact on the hotel and restaurant ever since.

In an attempt to fill the quiet winter period, the Allens decided to run their first 12-week cookery course, turning over the bedrooms in the hotel to the students. It was slightly chaotic, but it was extremely well received. So much so, in fact, that the following year Darina and her husband Tim decided to establish the school on separate premises at Shanagarry, three kilometres (nearly two miles) away. It is now one of the most highly regarded cookery schools in the world and receives students four times a year from, on average, thirteen different countries.

The school has had many unforeseen and highly beneficial consequences for the restaurant and all those who work there. It has allowed Hazel to blossom in her role as restaurateur and hotelier, since it gave her and Darina separate spheres of influence and businesses to grow into. It has launched Darina on her career as teacher and champion of Irish producers and farmers (she is a great supporter of the Irish Slow Food Movement), and has generated extra synergy between the two of them. The school has also brought in new and very different influences from all over the world to this hotel and restaurant at the end of a road deep in the Irish countryside. Producers, wine-makers, farmers and writers continually make their way down to Ballymaloe, knowing that they will be talking to a highly appreciative audience comprising chefs, farmers and other potential clients, as well as extremely well-connected communicators for their cause. On the night I arrived, an example of such synergy had just taken place. Dermot Carey and David Langford had been giving a talk at the school about the largest private collection of potato varieties in Ireland (at the Victorian kitchen garden on the Lissadell Estate, Co. Sligo), and were then having dinner in the restaurant. Regular visits from people such as this are an inspiration to those working in the kitchen only a few steps away.

Hazel explained that she came to recognize the informal manner in which a country house hotel should be run during her childhood in the Irish countryside. The countryside is simply more relaxing, and that is what Ballymaloe is all about. 'I know what to expect, even if it is very difficult for me to lay down precisely what the principles are behind what I do, as many who come to work here wish I would. It is more a way of life.' Her role today in communicating this way of life to her guests begins with the bedrooms, and ensuring that the level of comfort is maintained and certain distinctive features remain. These include the absence of a television and tea- or coffee-making facilities, although the latter will always be brought to the room. Nor do the rooms have safes, and until guests began to bring their laptops a few years ago, none of the bedrooms had locks on them either. The bedrooms are filled with old wooden furniture and thick swagged curtains; the bathrooms are warm and practical, but certainly not of an ultra-modern design.

This idiosyncratic approach is also reflected by the fact that Ballymaloe is still registered professionally as a guest house rather than a hotel, something that Hazel does not want to change. The reasons behind the apparent lack of facilities would not be appreciated by a hotel guide, she feels, so they would always be poorly rated as a result. They may also expect the staff to dress more uniformly, which is something she would not want.

A change in Ballymaloe's staff has also brought a change in Hazel's role. While there are still several members of the team who have been with the Allens for over forty years, the strength of the Irish economy in the early twenty-first century led to an acute shortage of staff, a situation that was solved when Ireland's Restaurant Association brought in waiters from as far afield as Tunisia, and introduced a stricter form of record keeping and legal management, which Hazel now supervises.

It is at 2.00 p.m. every afternoon that Hazel's professional heart begins to beat a little faster, with the start of a process that will not finish until after breakfast the following morning. 'Two p.m. is when Jason hears what the boats have landed at Ballycotton, then the rest of the suppliers start arriving and we can plan that evening's menu, which is printed at about 5.30 p.m.,' Hazel explained, before rattling off the names of their regular suppliers. 'There's Brenda O'Riordan who runs a local fish supply company and brings the fish from the boats; Mrs Ahearn, a farmer's wife, who brings the ducks

Hazel Allen

and guinea fowl; hams come from Gubbeen, also the source of one of Ireland's best cheeses; pork from the land our son farms; Angus and Hereford beef from two other farmers; and chickens from Annie Fitzsimmons. Bill Casey and Frank Hedermann bring the smoked fish and the eggs come from our own chickens, of course. And then there's the mackerel my husband Rory catches.'

The communal goal, until the guests set off after breakfast the following morning, is converting all these ingredients to meet their guests' expectations. The Ballymaloe breakfast is the most satisfying I have ever experienced, renowned partly because it is a combination of a buffet with cooked items (the eggs, bacon, black pudding and fish are cooked to order), and partly because the basics of it are so wonderful. A large pot of porridge gently bubbles away and there is an array of breads, both made earlier that morning, as well as the pots of jams and marmalades to dip into, and, of course, the famous Barry's Tea from nearby Cork. Meeting customers' expectations is the aspect of her role that Hazel, rather like a chess master facing a difficult board, finds the most challenging and the most engaging. 'Accommodating your guests is what is most exciting,' she added. 'Those who only want Tanqueray gin before dinner or soya milk with their breakfast, those who come to eat here at the time when they know we will be harvesting fresh peas.' She cited with pride the time when a receptionist had realized that a guest was a particularly enthusiastic rugby fan, and had used her own credit card to subscribe to a satellite channel so that he could watch the games.

Hazel was particularly emphatic about the different skills required in running an hotel and a restaurant. 'I don't believe that there are many skills on the hotel side that require training, it is more a matter of aptitude. But the principles of restaurant service, of how you look after and serve your guests in the dining room certainly do. Those skills have to be ingrained.' It is therefore in the dining room where Hazel feels she is most essential to Ballymaloe's continuing success, even if, as she confessed, she is not quite as quick to spot any minor omissions as she once was. She does know, however, precisely when her presence around the dining rooms is most crucial. Things tend to go wrong late at night, and she is there to ensure that they don't. She always puts the younger staff in charge of the cheese and dessert trolleys because it encourages them to be enthusiastic and charming and it is a great boost to their confidence. 'But both they, and the food that is on these trolleys, do tend to wilt a bit and it is absolutely essential that I watch this, to ensure that the last table in the restaurant receives the same quality of food and service as the first.' This role means that Hazel usually leaves the restaurant after midnight when, as she described it, she has 'put the place to bed'.

One predicament resulting from Hazel's long reign at Ballymaloe is that she has never been able to find a restaurant manager who she believes can match her demanding standards. But in reality she never will, because although Ballymaloe employs over 150 people, there is still only one restaurant and one family that guests want to be greeted by. One major reason that restaurateurs have no choice but to expand is to create higher ranking positions for their best managers to develop into, but this cannot be the case here until she decides to retire.

Another general challenge for Hazel (and increasingly restaurateurs worldwide) is how to address the question of dress code: what and how to tell guests what they should wear and how to monitor any such policy. 'Smart-casual is a phrase that drives me mad,' she explained, 'but I haven't been able to come up with anything better. On some nights there can be any number of guests who have chosen to dress smartly and there will be others in trainers. I am not sure how we can ever resolve this satisfactorily.' But this is one minor irritation in the professional life of a woman who enjoys spending long hours doing what comes naturally to her: pleasing people, chatting to them and taking care of their quirks and demands before sending them on their way to enjoy her beloved country. Aside from this, she relishes catching up on what other people are doing. When we met she had just returned from London with a young sous chef, during which time they visited five different restaurants and the Algerian Coffee Stores in Soho, her favourite coffee shop.

Another of her favourite aspects of the job is Ballymaloe's renowned Sunday-night buffet, when the distinction between the Allens and their guests becomes less obvious as both sit down to enjoy the large platters of roast meats, salads, fish and shellfish. This ritual began many years ago as a way of ensuring the kitchen brigade could get a relatively early night at least once a week, but it has become a distinctive gathering in its own right, at which those who dispense the hospitality sit down with those who have travelled to Ballymaloe to experience it.

It would be facile to conclude that Ballymaloe is simply the achievement of three remarkable women: Mrs Allen, Darina and Hazel. When I mentioned this to Tom Doorley, the perceptive Irish writer on food and restaurants, he completely disagreed with me. 'Perhaps,' he pointed out, 'the credit should go to the Allen men who seem to have the knack of marrying such extraordinary women.'

The art on the walls

At some stage during the planning of their first restaurant every inexperienced restaurateur will wake up to the fact that as well as satisfying their future customers' appetites, there is also the challenge of doing the same for their eyes. What will they look at while they hand in their coats at the front desk, wait for their companion to arrive, or head off down the corridor that leads to the lavatory?

Novices will start with a number of particular disadvantages. They will probably be preoccupied with more immediate issues, such as dealing with the builders or the bank; they will start with little in the way of knowledge as to what will work artistically; they are unlikely to own anything suitable; and, perhaps most critically, they may not have the right connections to obtain it. However, as the remarkable collection at Ballymaloe demonstrates, the connections between restaurateurs and artists have been strong for decades, with the former often – and farsightedly – acting as patrons of the latter. Certainly, it is the art on the walls of the Kronenhalle restaurant in Zürich, Switzerland, or at La Colombe d'Or in Saint-Paul de Vence in the south of France, with their extraordinary collections of works created at the restaurants by visiting artists such as Picasso, Matisse, Chagall and Braque, that provide an extra reason for eating in either place.

The chances of this being repeated today, though, are very slim. The only original art I received at L'Escargot came one afternoon from an artist who so enjoyed his dish of a civet of hare that he took a paper napkin, drew a hare eating from a dish while sitting on a tree trunk by a forest with the words 'The civet of hare is delicious'. I had it framed and it subsequently hung proudly in the first floor restaurant.

There are several ways to approach the problem. For example, I hired the first floor of L'Escargot to a gallery owner who lent me works in return for meals he would subsequently enjoy. Then, at Stephen Chamberlain's instigation, we loaned the wall space on the ground floor to artists, who put up an exhibition of their work for a month at a time. This policy worked for everyone: my customers saw a regularly changing art show, the artists sold their works, and I benefited because the walls of my restaurant looked interesting. I even ended up buying a few myself, which now hang at home to remind me of my previous life. We also rescued large portraits of my wife's Victorian ancestors from her family's attic, and they hung, smiling and welcoming, in the restaurant lobby, looking as though they had been there for decades.

Today, much larger and often more dramatic pieces created by contemporary artists can provide an even more stunning backdrop to a restaurant, as shown by the association between chef Mark Hix and his artist friends Tim Noble, Sue Webster and Tracey Emin at his various London restaurants, and all that surrounds the Bar Room and The Modern at MoMA, New York.

At Ballymaloe, the combination of continuous ownership over so many years with conspicuous good taste makes the walls of the restaurant as attractive as what is on the plate. One dining room was often erroneously referred to as the 'Eats Room', an abbreviation of the name of Jack Yeats

(younger brother of the poet W.B. Yeats), whose paintings were among the first to hang on the walls here. Hazel explained that it had all started with her father-in-law, who used to go to the agricultural shows in Dublin, where the London gallery Waddingtons would set up a stand to waylay the cash-rich farmers. Over the years he bought about ten paintings by Jack Yeats, several of which used to be together in the breakfast room, but most have now gone because they became too valuable. 'We still have a couple, though,' she added with great pleasure. Over the ensuing decades, Mrs Allen, Darina and Hazel have bought works by a succession of younger Irish artists, many of them based in nearby Cork. There are works by Patrick Scott, Jane O'Malley, Michael Farrell, Norah McGuinness, Paul Moss and Mainie Jellett that continue to delight her.

'It's great to have the walls to play with,' she explained, 'and it is lovely, and a particular challenge to change the pictures from time to time, to move them around. But the best thing about having what is effectively our own gallery space is that it has provided the opportunity to get to know these artists, so many of whom have become our friends over the years. That's a particular, and most unexpected, aspect of being in this business.'

Far more people today buy the work of promising young artists than when the Allens started collecting, so prices have increased substantially. It is important, though, to start thinking about how the walls will be decorated from the moment the prospective restaurant becomes yours.

JOE BASTIANICH

ITALY IN THE USA

Joe Bastianich has opened more than a dozen restaurants across New York with Mario Batali, his business partner, chef and fellow media star. They also run outposts in Las Vegas and Singapore, and they have several more planned for Hong Kong. Surprisingly, though, our latest meeting was not scheduled to take place in one of his restaurants – which would make it the first time, I began to realize, that I had seen Bastianich outside what has been his natural habitat ever since he grew up in his parents' Italian restaurant. A true restaurateur's restaurateur, Bastianich has been immersed in the world of restaurants from the day he was born. However, at the very last minute I received an instruction from Kim Reed, his extremely patient personal assistant, to meet him at Esca, his seafood restaurant on West 43rd Street.

When I was shown to the table I realized that not only had I never seen Bastianich looking so dapper, but also that this was the first time I had seen his legs. In the past, I had watched Bastianich working, or talked to him from in front of the bar or service counter at Babbo (illustrated page 57) or Eataly, or across the table at Otto or Del Posto. But here he was in a sleek blue suit with white piping around the collar, a white shirt with a flap hiding the buttons and an elegant pair of black brogue shoes with white crepe soles. Sunglasses, a baseball cap and a smartphone were his only other accoutrements. He accepted my sartorial compliments nonchalantly. 'I picked them up in Milan recently when I was filming *Masterchef Italia*,' he replied (he also fronts *Masterchef* in the US). The suntan, he added, came from competing in a recent Ironman event in Hawaii.

There was still a definite buzz in the air as the restaurant began to calm down after a busy lunch service before gradually gearing up for an even busier evening. The receptionist, overshadowed by a large floral display, was scanning the list of bookings; a single diner at the bar was shaking hands with the barman and complimenting him on the meal he had just enjoyed; and the busboys were streaming back and forth from the kitchen to lay the tables. On arrival I had been taken past the bar to the table any experienced restaurateur would occupy, at which Bastianich was polishing off a plate of *bomboloni* (plum fritters with zabaglione). From this corner he had an uninterrupted view of the main route every waiter has to take in and out of the kitchen. Nothing, from this vantage point, could escape his eagle eyes.

While many fall into the profession at an impressionable age during their late teens or early twenties, Bastianich grew up in a restaurant.

His parents, Felice and Lidia (with whom he has subsequently collaborated on several restaurants, cooking shows and cookbooks), ran their own Italian restaurant in Queens for many years. The first was Buonavia on Queens Boulevard in 1970, followed by a second, Villa Seconda, in Fresh Meadows. They sold them both in 1980 to open Felidia on 58th Street. His childhood revolved around the restaurant: family meals were taken with the staff before they opened for dinner; he was put to work at an early age preparing the salads or helping the grill man; and he did his homework at a corner table to keep out of the staff's way. There was, however, often the bonus of finding lost change by stretching his slim arm down the back of the banquettes.

His parents had opened their own restaurant because at that time it was one of the few career paths open to immigrants. As is so often the case, they willingly undertook the extremely long hours of hard, physical work with one main goal in mind: that their children would never have to do the same. In fact, Joe Bastianich initially did what his parents dreamed of. He graduated from college and set off to do something considered important in their eyes by joining an MBA programme with Merrill Lynch and working on Wall Street. Corporate life was not for him though and by 1990 he had earned enough to spend two years in Italy, which convinced him that his future lay in food, wine and restaurants. It is the juxtaposition of the two very different experiences – as the son of a chef and a restaurateur, and then as a highly successful restaurateur in his own right – that combine to make Bastianich such a fascinating character.

Deep within him is the sense, which was prevalent in the UK and the US a generation ago, that a restaurant is a battleground in which the customer or supplier is always trying to get the better of the restaurateur. Today, any restaurateur is in a much stronger position, thanks to a market of far more interested customers and much more sophisticated systems to protect the business against petty theft, whether by the staff or suppliers. But this sense of vulnerability never seems to have left Bastianich. He is quite right, of course, to stress how important such considerations are for any would-be restaurateur. He lays down hard and fast the rule that any restaurateur's prime enemy is waste. It is impossible to eliminate it completely, but minimizing it at every opportunity has to be a continuous, if decidedly unglamorous, priority. This is a mentality, a business approach that was inculcated into him by his parents.

Another impression I always take away from any time spent with Bastianich is one that reminds me of something my wife once said when she walked into the office of my restaurant in the days before mobile phones. 'Now I understand,' she remarked, looking around at what I can only describe as the prevailing organized chaos, 'there's no such thing in a restaurateur's life as an in-tray.' Any restaurateur's day and night is a series of immediate and constant, but often minute, calls to action. Since Bastianich grew up in this world, this is his day-to-day modus operandi whichever restaurant he is in.

I had just sat down when he asked me whether I would like to share a pot of Earl Grey tea. He called over a waiter by name and prefaced the tea order by asking after the waiter's wife and children. Then, excusing himself, he walked past the bar, but not without stopping to congratulate the pastry chef on her dessert, and then getting the latest update on bookings from his receptionist. Television appearances, the best reviews and all the awards from the industry mean nothing without this constant support every restaurateur has to give to their staff, an approach that comes naturally to Bastianich. I can run these restaurants, his words and body language imply to his staff, because I can do every job as well as you can.

The immediate beneficiaries of this life in restaurants are his teenage children, all of whom view restaurants with a very different perspective from the one he had at their age. 'They've all got prospective restaurateur DNA inside them,' he added with a proud smile. 'They get it, they ask all the right questions and, of course, they've eaten at a lot of good restaurants around the world, and not just mine. It will be exciting to see quite what they make of it.' It will certainly be fascinating to see whether his children's restaurant careers get off to the same flying start as their father's. Back in 1993, he borrowed $80,000 (£50,000) to put down a deposit on a brownstone building in the theatre district of New York, an area he reckoned would generate the highest volume of customers and therefore stand the biggest chance of success. He recalled the time fondly and proudly, as every restaurateur does of their first baby. Bastianich's was Becco, where the rent was $3,000 (£2,000) per month, and he worked there morning, noon and night. Twenty years on, its turnover is $12 million (£8 million) and it is still the most profitable restaurant in the group. Becco's longevity is down to a great location and keen pricing – all-you-can-eat pasta dishes at $23 (£15) and wines at $25 (£16) – which generate a high volume of customers.

While he was coordinating the wines for a James Beard Awards dinner, an event that celebrates the highest achievers in food, wine and restaurants across the US, Bastianich met Mario Batali, who was to cook the dinner.

First their friendship 'snowballed', as Bastianich puts it, and subsequently their business partnership, which now includes twenty-five restaurants, three wineries in Italy and a staff of over 2,500. Bastianich is convinced that, having grown up in the rigid business hierarchy of his parents' restaurant, he is particularly well equipped to appreciate and accommodate a chef as talented as Batali as his partner. 'A chef's life is one of the last few bastions of true apprenticeship and I have a great deal of time for that and all it represents. But chefs do see things in terms of black and white while restaurateurs see the world in various shades of grey.' The struggle between chefs and restaurateurs, between the back and the front of the business, is a great and timeless one. 'But if you can reconcile these two views of the world, and bring about a sense of equilibrium, it's wonderful. This is what makes great restaurants great.' Having spent time with Batali and Bastianich both together and separately, I can testify that they have a genuine fondness for one another and a sense of bonhomie towards the world that they feel fortunate they can express through food and wine. Their working relationship works well because their spheres are very separate: Mario is the chef and Joe the restaurateur, who looks after the wine and the business. Both also have an extremely useful media presence. 'We pick our fights,' Bastianich explained, 'and at times we undoubtedly test the limits of each other as friends and partners. But after twenty years we're in this to the finish.'

It was as friends walking around the West Village that they found their first site together, the boarded-up, long-established and once-loved Coach House restaurant, which then had a large 'For Rent' sign outside. Today it is Babbo, open only in the evenings but capable of generating so much raw energy from those waiting by the door, eating at the bar or along the banquettes down either side of the restaurant, from the waiters running up and down the central staircase and from the sommeliers somewhat more sedately pouring wine from the large service table in the centre, that I am never sure whether I want to eat and drink, or just inhale. It has certainly achieved Bastianich's goal at the outset of emanating the spirit of Italian food that is 'local, brash, visceral and authentic'. While the synergy between Batali and Bastianich has obviously been a major factor in their success, so too has Bastianich's ability to synthesize a restaurant's appeal before they have even decided to embark on it. You need to be able to explain your restaurant in one short sentence. Like a proud parent, he rattled off a list of their restaurants. 'Esca, where we are, is crudo, raw

shellfish and regional seafood. Lupa, on Thompson Street, is a Roman trattoria. Otto, in Greenwich Village, is an enoteca and pizzeria. That's all that a consumer can take in and remember. And I've never been able to understand why restaurateurs describe their restaurants as Mediterranean. That's a sea, not a type of cooking.'

The serendipity of Batali as a partner; their decision to focus later restaurant openings south of 23rd Street, where Bastianich believes 'the world is your oyster'; the fact that so many people choose to eat out in New York, which he thinks of as the restaurant capital of the world (like London, he says, but with a fifty per cent discount); and the fact that many in New York treat restaurants as their living rooms, have all given Bastianich the opportunity to use every restaurant opening to experiment, to break moulds. These innovations, once the public has finally accepted them, have particularly delighted him because they show the influence a restaurateur can have in shaping human behaviour. But the first two experiments, at Babbo and Otto, involved struggles he had to overcome. At Babbo it was his decision not to serve wine by the glass, but by the *quartino* (a quarter of a litre, or a third of a bottle), which initially shocked consumers but has since been widely copied, in London most notably by Will Smith at Arbutus, Wild Honey and Les Deux Salons. There is no doubt that it brings benefits to the consumer, allowing a table of two, for example, the opportunity to share a quartino of white wine with the first course, followed by a quartino or a bottle of red with the main course. It brings benefits to the restaurateur too: a slightly higher spend and, because of how it is served, the potential to minimize waste.

At Otto it was the introduction of the stand-up tables, at which customers could enjoy a glass of Prosecco and a plate of prosciutto in the front part of the building, which was authentically designed in the image of the waiting room in an Italian railway station, that caused the consternation because of its novelty. Again, the tables were eventually accepted by the public and copied by other restaurateurs. Within the pizzeria itself these tables have also succeeded in creating the necessary distinction between the front and back room, which has ordinary table service, and ensuring that both are equally popular.

In 2005 Bastianich embarked on Del Posto, reclaiming a vast former Nabisco bakery building in Chelsea with one specific aim: to construct a glamorous Italian restaurant that would be on a par with the city's top French restaurants and win a coveted four-star rating from the

New York Times. It involved a radically different approach from before; rather than concentrating on one particular region of their beloved Italy, Bastianich and Batali sought to deliver the best from the entire country: the most authentic *bollito misto* from Turin, the freshest mozzarella from Naples; and the most delicate *agnolotti* from the Piedmont region all combined with their distinctive brand of showmanship. The term *primo assaggio* was even created to replace the French *amuse bouche,* as Bastianich joked that he would rather cut off his right hand off than use a French word in this unequivocally Italian restaurant.

As Bastianich talked about Del Posto, which took two years to create and has continually improved until today he believes it is now very close to what they both dreamed of at the outset, there was a definite sense of exhaustion in his voice. 'I know now that there is only one restaurant as ambitious as this in the life of any restaurateur and I am delighted that we seem to have created a new customer, those who want the very finest Italian food and wine in this city. Del Posto is how Mario and I could express ourselves artistically as restaurateurs. But never again – it's one four-star restaurant per person per life. In many ways it is a restaurateur's restaurant.'

Eataly, which Bastianich and Batali opened on Madison Square in autumn 2010 in partnership with its creator Oscar Farinetti (who has other branches of Eataly across Italy and Japan), is far, far bigger and its appeal is far more popular. It is a very successful rendition of all that Italy produces in food and wine inside one vast building, with the added bonus of great visual and sensual pleasure, too. It comprises a café, *gelateria* and wine shop on the outside; long aisles devoted to pasta, cheese, meat, fish and vegetables as well as ready prepared food; and in the centre, a series of counters where New Yorkers in a hurry can eat well and swiftly, as well as a more formal steak restaurant. The figures behind its bustling cafés, food shops, restaurants, ice cream, beer and wine shops are staggering: an investment of $26 million (£17 million); 20,000 customers on a busy Saturday; a staff of 700; and sales in its first year of $70 million (£45 million).

While relieved at its immediate success, Bastianich was not completely surprised. 'Everything about Eataly makes you hungry and that, coupled with the location, meant that New Yorkers took to it.' What he is most delighted by is that Eataly has in effect become 'the piazza of New York, a great gathering place where people can eat, drink, have fun and be seen, just like the traditional centre of an Italian town. That's the magic, what everyone goes there for, whether it's for an espresso, an ice cream, or to spend $100(£65) on dinner for two in Manzo, the steak restaurant.' For that, Bastianich continued, is Italy's big advantage over France. French food just doesn't have that instantaneous, impulsive appeal: there's no equivalent of the pit stop, however brief, for an espresso, an ice cream or a slice of pizza. French food is the food of kings, Bastianich proclaimed, Italian the food of peasants – and there is no doubt as to which one he is delighted to have championed.

He did in fact once open a French bistro, Bistro du Vent, close to Esca and with its talented chef, David Pasternack, but he closed it after fifteen months for reasons that an outsider might imagine a professional like Bastianich would have taken into consideration well in advance. 'The location was bad; my heart wasn't in it; and if you invent a restaurant to fill a space, as we did here, then it's sure to fail,' he explained. This is a common cause of failure: the idea that the building comes first, which is followed by an attempt to shoehorn whatever the restaurateur thinks will work into it. The Hart brothers have faced a similar problem with Quo Vadis in London.

Recalling this episode, though, allowed Bastianich to philosophize on the business in which, even though he is only in his mid forties, he has spent more successful years than many others. The two big challenges for any restaurateur in New York are labour – 'that's what we sell' – and the rising cost of property. For the past three years a series of class actions concerning the alleged unfair distribution of service charge, brought on behalf of groups of waiting staff against all the major restaurant groups, has been bubbling quietly under the surface across the city. When these are finally resolved they may prove to be financially extremely painful, but the very fact that they are happening has left Bastianich (and other leading restaurateurs) with the sense that the commercial future of his company may very well lie outside New York. He spoke of possible openings in Orange County, California, and branches of Luppa, Otto and a more expensive Italian restaurant in Hong Kong, with a view, perhaps one day, to opening in China.

As for the rent, he repeated the rule drummed into him by his father: that the monthly rent must never be greater than the gross daily takings on your quietest day of the week, but commented that with rising land prices and conversion costs, this is now much harder to achieve. These figures, he explained, are forcing restaurateurs to be far more ambitious – his analogy was that every new opening has to be the equivalent of a grand slam in baseball. 'And that's very tough to pull off,' he sighed.

It was time for Bastianich to head off to his next meeting, downtown at Del Posto, but such is his love of everything that restaurants represent, he could not end on anything but a positive note. 'For me, being in any of our restaurants when they are firing on all cylinders is the greatest buzz,' he said with an utterly emphatic smile. 'The power of a restaurant is like a lightning rod, it knows no social stratifications. You can be running a room that contains hipsters, captains of industry and families from Wisconsin. And it is more than just the satisfaction of feeding and nurturing so many from all walks of life. The routine of doing this twice a day, of saying hello, seating them, feeding them and then saying good-bye is mentally and spiritually fulfilling. And when I'm away from my restaurants, I miss that routine.' He acknowledged that not every day goes to plan, however. 'When it is good, it is all good, but when a service goes wrong, being at the helm of a sinking restaurant is an awful feeling. I've had my fill of those, too.' As we headed for the door, Bastianich turned to me and said, 'And I don't subscribe to the view that the restaurateur's biggest enemy is the critic, either. The restaurateur's biggest enemy is his ego. Once you believe that you are more important than the customer, you've lost the plot.'

The ageless profession

In his autobiography *Restaurant Man*, Joe Bastianich explains that during his forty-six years, the only time he wasn't happy was the period he spent away from the restaurant business, when he followed his brain rather than his heart and worked on Wall Street. Before and after that, his life has been completely absorbed by restaurants. The profession can do this to anyone, regardless of age, race or background. I fell into it at the age of twenty-eight and I can vouch for the fact that it proved to be a completely compelling way of life. Although being a restaurateur can be physically, emotionally and financially demanding, the profession also brings with it certain distinct advantages.

Most importantly, age is no barrier to entry (or exit). One of the most exciting aspects of the restaurant business today is that an increasing number of emerging restaurateurs are in their late twenties or early thirties, younger than ever before, and they are creating an engrossing career path for themselves that can last for decades. A chef's career, on the other hand, tends to mirror that of a talented sportsman. They exhibit great talent in their late teens; they travel, learn and begin to display their individuality in their early twenties; show off their skills and develop their style of cooking, often in their own restaurants in their early thirties; but by the time they reach their mid thirties they have often endured a work and social life that has exhausted them physically and mentally. Their next move tends to be out of the arena that has made them well known and into an executive chef position, a role in the media or, on occasion, a jump across the great divide into the role of the restaurateur.

Restaurateurs may start later, having worked their way up to a senior position in someone else's restaurant before establishing their own business, but only they can determine when they want to retire. Every major city can boast restaurateurs who have continued successfully for many years, for example Warner Le Roy and George Lang in New York, Peter Langan in London, Jean-Claude Vrinat in Paris and Arrigo Cipriani, who has masterminded the expansion of the Cipriani group of restaurants from his base in Venice. The best restaurateurs all believe they are involved in something that will make the world a better place, if best practice continues to be observed and passed on in the best possible way. They do not just lead by example, but ensure they transmit their knowledge, experience and concern for their fellow human beings to the staff they believe will best maintain the standards they have striven to maintain for decades.

The restaurateur's profession is also one in which the family business can still play an important role. Many restaurateurs in this book have created restaurants that can and will travel the world, such as Nobu, Remi, Shake Shack, wagamama and The Ivy. However, there are almost as many that remain firmly in family hands, managed by second, third or even fourth generations, for example the Harts, who have travelled from Hambleton to London; the Bertaiola family in Italy; the fourth generation of Troisgros behind the stoves in Roanne, France; and the numerous members of the Allen family

in Ballymaloe, Ireland. The opportunity to establish a business where human contact is so strong, coupled with the ability to hand it over to the next generation, only makes the appeal of life as a restaurateur more attractive.

It is certainly a profession that runs in the blood, as I can see from watching my son begin to formulate his plans to open his own restaurant after two years in the hospitality industry working for others. Although he is the same age as I was when I opened my own restaurant, he seems far better qualified and a better judge of food and wine than I was at twenty-eight. More importantly, he has friends who are already cooking, working in restaurants or hotels, or travelling the world to taste food and wine that they have never experienced before. Has all this come about because when he was four years old I used to take him into my restaurant with his sister on a Saturday afternoon, where they would help the waiting staff get the sugar bowls and plates of chocolate snails ready for that night's busy service? I will never know. What I do know is that he is unlikely to find such a rewarding profession elsewhere, or one that is as likely to be in demand in our rapidly changing world. In this respect I agree with Gilbert Pilgram of Zuni Café in California: that the profession of restaurateur is like that of a craftsman, a set of skills that can be distilled from one generation to another that will only improve with age.

Joe Bastianich

ENRICO BERNARDO
II VINO:

A PARISIAN MECCA FOR WINE LOVERS

In 1990, when he was only fourteen years old, Enrico Bernardo travelled from his small home town of Limbiate in Lombardy, northern Italy, to train as a cook at the Scuola Alberghiera Carlo Porta, the hotel school in Milan. He was driven by a single ambition: by the time he was thirty, he promised himself, he would have opened his own restaurant. He missed by a year. In September 2007, Bernardo opened Il Vino on an attractive corner site at 13, boulevard de la Tour Maubourg in Paris's chic 7th *arrondissement*, opposite Petrossian Caviar and with two even more venerable neighbours, Les Invalides and the Eiffel Tower, on either side. The preceding seventeen years had seen Bernardo travel the world as the culinary career he had embarked upon eventually gave way to a fascination with wine. In Athens in 2004, aged twenty-seven and at his very first attempt, he beat off impressive competition from around the globe to become the 'Best Sommelier in the World', awarded by ASI (Association de la Sommellerie Internationale). He knew he had to accomplish this arduous feat that year because the competition takes place only once every three years, and had he failed his restaurant ambitions would have been delayed by even more than a year.

Il Vino is neither a restaurant nor a wine bar in Bernardo's mind, but rather something new and different: somewhere he can take his customers on a journey, disarm any preconceptions, and introduce them to pairings of food and wine that most other menus or wine lists would not lead them to. Il Vino is, in his firm opinion, a wine restaurant. It has also fundamentally changed the fundamental profit calculations that lie at the heart of every restaurant, for the benefit of both the customer and the restaurateur.

Before I could ask a single question, though, Bernardo wanted to introduce me to someone he described as equally important to his own success and that of Il Vino. He came back with his arms around a woman: 'This is my sister Mary, and since 2002 she has been responsible for all that I have achieved. She is my muse.' Mary supplies the advice, the vision and the strategy, and she is the person to whom Bernardo always turns. 'Although she doesn't work alongside me in the restaurant' he explained, 'Il Vino is the two of us, nobody else. I am only too aware that I wouldn't have achieved anywhere near what I have done without her.'

The Bernardo family would also be proud of the smart interior of Il Vino that Enrico and Mary have created, despite the fact that when they took it over in 2007 they could not afford an architect and their total budget was only €200,000 (£170,000 or $260,000). Their first course of action, to take over an already established restaurant, is the most sensible and most cost-effective for new restaurateurs because the most expensive items (the kitchen and all the necessary ductwork and extraction) are already in place. While half their capital was sunk into improving the kitchens and upgrading the lavatories, the rest went into making the two halves of the restaurant more comfortable, introducing leather chairs, tables at different heights to create one relaxed and another more formal eating and drinking area, and the comfortable banquettes that are synonymous with the best Parisian restaurants. Immediately visible on the bar opposite the front door are a couple of colourful flower displays, contrasting with the black-and-white photos of vineyards on the walls. On the far wall is a glass display of wine bottles, perched horizontally (and correctly) so that the wine stays in contact with the cork and prevents it from drying out. There is a general feeling of professionalism in the air. So far, it would appear, so normal.

Il Vino begins to show its very different ambitions, however, just outside its front door, where there is a conspicuous sign proclaiming that it is home to the Best Sommelier in the World. Also on the outside are the menus that highlight the restaurant's unique approach. While the lunch menu comprises three or four choices for each course, there is nothing so ordinary at dinner. Instead, there is just a series of wine flights (tasting sequences of wines by the glass) at different prices. The customer chooses their wine flight first, which is based on those on offer that week and will always include a series of wines served 'blind', without the customer knowing what he or she is about to enjoy, or a couple of bottles from the wine list. Then, on the back of this, and a discussion about any food allergies or dislikes, Bernardo, his team of five waiters, who are all sommeliers, and his highly talented chef, Michele Biassoni, create a four- or five-course menu. Dinner at Il Vino can therefore be a real adventure, and quite how negatively customers can react to this approach – and just how skilled Bernardo has become at converting even the most curmudgeonly customer to his way of thinking about food and wine – was brought home to me while I was sitting at a corner table for two with my wife one Saturday evening.

We had just ordered when a table of four, consisting of two very well-dressed middle-aged Parisian couples, came to sit at the next table. One was clearly the host, and Bernardo immediately introduced himself and explained the principles on which Il Vino works. The expression on the face of the host's male guest grew increasingly angry. First of all, he was not going to be allowed to choose from a menu. On top of that, there was no wine list. Finally, he was going to have to leave the crucial choice of what he

Enrico Bernardo

was going to eat and drink to this young whippersnapper who also happened to be Italian, to boot. I nudged my wife under the table and what we then witnessed from Bernardo was a lesson in how to deal with a recalcitrant customer and convert them to your cause. Without being defensive or oleaginous, or giving them anything out of the ordinary, Bernardo completely charmed them. He was pleasant, attentive, smiling and seemed genuinely concerned to correct the misconceptions they obviously harboured. He remained extremely patient throughout as he explained the unusual principles on which Il Vino is based. The first well-chosen glass of wine broke down their anger and from the first plate of well-cooked food this man's good humour, and therefore that of the whole table, returned. By the end of the meal he was Bernardo's – and Il Vino's – biggest fan, and I would not be surprised if, back in his office on Monday morning, he was proudly telling his colleagues of the wonderful, novel restaurant he had recently discovered.

Bernardo's culinary progress had seen him win the Best Young Chef in Europe competition in 1993 in the kitchens of the Grand Hotel in Stockholm, Sweden. Then, aged nineteen, he became the youngest *chef de partie* (the person in charge of one particular section of the kitchen, in this case the busy fish and shellfish section), at Maison Troisgros, the acclaimed three-Michelin-starred restaurant in Roanne, eastern France. 'This was very tough,' Bernardo admitted with a smile, 'a period I've always described as the equivalent of my military service because the restaurant was so busy and the organization so hierarchical.' Bernardo also became interested in wine, partly because his working axis in France and Italy was very close to the vineyards of both countries, which he used to visit at the weekends and on his days off. He began to appreciate that the overall taste of a dish was more important than its constituent parts and that finding the right balance in a dish, and the right balance between a plate of food and the most appropriate glass of wine, was much more exciting than anything else. His fascination with wine grew as he began to visit the vineyards, and he remembers precisely where he was and what he tasted that changed his career. 'We were tasting with Marcel Deiss, a winemaker in Alsace, and we did not know what the wines were. I recall recognizing one as a Gewurztraminer Vendange Tardive, and that was it.'

Having switched to the life of a sommelier in 1999 at Le Clos de la Violette restaurant, Aix-en-Provence, Bernardo then joined restaurant director Eric Beaumard and chef Philippe Legendre as head sommelier at Le Cinq restaurant, the plush Hotel George V in Paris in 2000, where he was in charge of the 50,000-bottle cellar. The five years at Le Cinq, from which he could tour

the world's vineyards and was tasting up to thirty-five wines a day in the
run-up to the competition in Athens in 2004 was, he recalled, 'the most
exciting period of my life'. It was also to prove crucial in the evolution of his
plans and principles for Il Vino. Firstly, working at the George V made him
aware of a maxim he describes as 'service, service, service'. 'It was drilled into
me that the guest is king,' he continued, 'and that every day is a competition
to do better.' Contact with so many wealthy guests made him realize quite
how personalized the service has to be in order to please them. With this
approach came an awareness of the attention to detail, and ultimately a love
of detail, that are necessary to achieve it. 'Finally, alongside this knowledge
of the process came my own personal maturity. Thanks to my years at the
George V, I now know how to handle most critical situations that arise in
my own restaurant. And, above all, I know not to panic.'

At the same time, Bernardo grew increasingly frustrated by the fact
that in so many restaurants the sommelier always seems to have the smallest
walk-on part, and it is one that often intimidates rather than delights the
guest. The usual sequence is that once the table is seated they will be asked
whether they want an apéritif; then water; then they are introduced to the
maître d' and then the menu; and only when they have chosen their food
will the sommelier come along with an intimidating-looking book that
the host may not even bother to look at. So often, in Bernardo's experience,
the sommelier will be asked to find a white wine for a table where the order
for the first courses ranges from oysters to foie gras to soup and a salad.
Increasingly, Bernardo came to believe, the ultimate consumer satisfaction
lay in serving a series of wines by the glass. This also began to coincide with
his growing obsession for directing his guests towards a pairing of food
and wine that was as close to ideal as possible. Hence Il Vino, where all
the waiters are sommeliers. It's the wine selection that comes first, then
a discussion as the sommelier explains what will follow, taking into account
allergies and personal dislikes, and then a very different kind of meal gets
under way, in which the final dishes are a surprise until they are explained
by the waiter who serves them. A meal in which, Bernardo smiles with some
satisfaction, his guests are both delightfully surprised by the range of wines
they are served – much wider in terms of geography and style than that
offered by most restaurants in France – and by the food, as they discover,
and enjoy, ingredients they would never ordinarily have ordered.

The first of two combinations of wine and food when we ate there was
called 'On The Wine Routes of France' and took in wines from Corsica,

Burgundy, Fronton in the south west and the Rhône. The accompanying meal began with stuffed squid, moved on to fillets of red mullet with an olive tapenade, then milk-fed pork with Swiss chard, and finished with a chocolate tart and orange ice cream. The second, where all the wines were served 'blind' in opaque glasses, began with a German Riesling and a tartare of beef; then paired Brittany lobster with sorrel and a Savennières; an Italian Nebbiolo with a rack of lamb; cheeses from Madame Quatrehomme, one of Paris's top *affineurs* (cheese-maturing specialists), with a red burgundy; and ended with a confit of figs, vanilla ice cream and a glass of Rivesaltes.

In the very beginning, though, Bernardo was certainly not smiling, as Il Vino was not easily understood. 'It could not be pigeon-holed either as an Italian restaurant,' he sighed, 'or as a wine bar.' But the journalists in Paris were very supportive and after two months Il Vino had become the place to be. 'It felt like travelling from hell to paradise.' Il Vino's financial performance has only got better too, with turnover in 2011 even better than it had been in 2010, previously its best year to date. The restaurant is serving forty-five to fifty customers every evening, sixty-five to seventy on a Saturday night, and around twenty for a weekday lunch. Bernardo believes it is considerably more profitable, and more efficient, than any other restaurant with a Michelin star – which Il Vino gained in 2008. This is because, he explained, such restaurants have to offer a far more comprehensive menu: five first courses; three fish and three meat main courses, then five desserts, plus a cheese selection which, because there is so much waste, is never very profitable. At Il Vino the range of dishes is far more limited and when one fish or meat dish runs out it is just replaced with another. 'We throw away very, very little,' he concluded with pride.

This concentration of choice means a more efficient organization. 'To serve the same number of customers from a normal à la carte menu,' Bernardo explained, 'I would need at least one more cook and one more waiter. But here we are only twelve in total, five in the kitchen and five sommeliers plus one kitchen porter and my invaluable PA, Aline, whom I first met working at the George V.' These two factors mean that for the guest, dinner at Il Vino can be €20–30 (£17–25 or $25–40) less expensive than dinner at a restaurant of a similar quality. The food, wine and service, as well as the novelty, have been packaged more cleverly and effectively. By changing his menus every four weeks, rather than every three months as is the norm, Bernardo also believes he can not only innovate, but also avoid being at the mercy of rising prices. 'Wild sea bass can go up from €20 to €35

Enrico Bernardo

(£17 to £30 or $25 to $45) per kilo between September and November and if it is there, fixed on your menu, a steep rise like this can be financially very painful,' Bernardo added.

The consequences of this approach for the restaurant's overall profitability are significant, Bernardo has discovered. Most restaurants with a single Michelin star will be delighted with a ten per cent net profit at the end of the busier months. At Il Vino he has managed to achieve twelve per cent regularly and fourteen per cent during the busier months. This appreciation of the harsh economic facts of life that underpin every restaurant is particularly important here, where there are few economies of scale. Il Vino is a small, independent restaurant – the kind that so many dream of – which prospers on the number of guests it can attract every day. 'If we have forty-five booked, it will be a good night. Thirty-five to forty-five will be OK, and if it is less than thirty-five I begin to get worried,' Bernardo explained, sipping his espresso. These numbers are important because a trading year for a formal restaurant like Il Vino consists of only 200 days when they can possibly be full, another 100 when at best they can only be half full – those days, say, before and after the numerous French public holidays – and the rest of the time they are closed. 'We must maximize these trading opportunities.'

The relaxed nature of his team's approach to wine and the fun that they create for the customer has attracted some specific groups of restaurant-goers. Women in particular, Bernardo continued, have been drawn to it, not just with other women, but also bringing their partners and husbands. Children have brought their parents; parents their fellow wine lovers. Il Vino has appealed above all to the growing number of people who know about wine and the even greater number who want to learn more about it. Bernardo laughed when I asked him whether being an Italian in Paris had been a factor in Il Vino's success. 'There's a bit of a contradiction here. The French seem to love the Italians but they still cannot be shaken from the belief that to be the best food and wine has, first and foremost, to be French.' Although he has been schooled in the best French culinary and wine practices, Bernardo believes that not having come from a completely French background has been an advantage in his role as 'maverick', someone who has turned the restaurant's normal style of presentation on its head.

He has had involvements with others in restaurants in Cassis in the south of France and in the ski resort of Courchevel, but these have proved less successful as their operating seasons are so short. Since the continued success of Il Vino in Paris, Bernardo has been approached by hoteliers and potential partners all keen to open outposts in Monaco, Dubai, London and Shanghai but, so far, without any deal being struck. The reason, I suspect, is that none of them could replicate the Bernardo effect. 'If you want to be a successful restaurateur you have to be sensitive to what is going on every second of the day and night, to the guests, to your staff, to every new dish that comes out of the kitchen. You have to be supremely generous, to give yourself twice a day when the guests arrive and to imbue your staff with your motivation, philosophy and sense of personality. And when you do that you go to bed at the end of the night really tired.' In a voice that sounded almost pleading, he added: 'Nobody should go into this unless they've had the training, an insight into the background, and stress, of trying to please eighty different people, all of whom have different expectations from the moment they walk through my front door. I have learned over the years that it is much easier to give bad service than to surprise a guest. One needs to be really open, smiling and positive. A restaurateur has to be so elastic,' Bernardo concluded, holding his hands wide apart.

This turned out not quite to be the end: 'But I do love it,' he continued. 'There's so much passion and involvement in running a restaurant like this and the fact that I need to have such trust in my team. There are so many different lives and histories around you and that is even before you have started talking to the guests. I am really proud to be a restaurateur, to be able to be so reactive every day. You can never be bored.'

Bernardo's success as a restaurateur, combined with his wine knowledge, has taken him into other areas, most notably designing wine glasses, writing books and consulting at wine dinners. But the most recent, and most fascinating for him, has taken him into the very opposite of his working day and seen him advise wealthy Parisians on building, and filling, their own wine cellars at home. All of this is a long way from the original dream he had at the Milan hotel school, but he is convinced that his different lives as cook, sommelier and now successful restaurateur have empowered him to have a far better and clearer vision of the dining room than he would have had if he had stayed in the kitchens. Chefs are preoccupied with themselves, their dishes and their ideas, Bernardo maintains, and cannot see their guests objectively. Only life as a restaurateur can expose you to this, he believes. It's *la verité*, the ability to see the restaurant as it is, that makes his life as a restaurateur so exciting, so challenging, and so exhausting.

The stranger's advantage

Enrico Bernardo is not the only restaurateur to have found fame outside his native city. Sam Hart travelled from the north of England to Mexico City before settling in London; Michelle Garnaut ended up in Hong Kong and China after leaving her native Australia; Maguy Le Coze is still very French, despite spending the last twenty-five years in New York, 3,000 miles away from her beloved Paris; Alan Yau came to London via Hong Kong and Norwich. Danny Meyer hails from St Louis, Missouri (he hasn't lost his passion for the Cardinals, their baseball team), and is absolutely convinced that his mid-Western sense of hospitality was among the most important factors in the success of the Union Square Café, the first of his many New York restaurants. I opened L'Escargot in London's West End only five years after moving down from my native Manchester. Why have so many restaurateurs succeeded outside their native habitat?

The first part of the answer to this question is the most obvious. The world's major cities have long had the biggest concentration of restaurants, so over the years numerous waiters, managers and chefs have gravitated towards them and progressed professionally through the kitchen or the restaurant, before succumbing to the desire, and finding the necessary backing, to open their own restaurants. After all, the major cities bring not only the highest concentration of future customers, but also access to potential backers and suppliers. The competition may be fiercer, but that too can be an advantage: a cluster of good restaurants will benefit both customers and restaurateurs.

However, perhaps a more subtle explanation can be found in other qualities that lie at the heart of any successful restaurateur. The first is that since this profession tends to a universal human need – to be welcomed, to be looked after, to be fed and watered – it is one of the very few professions that truly crosses national boundaries. Master the skills and travel or, alternatively, master the skills as you travel. This free market in international talent is a particular attraction of the restaurateur's profession and will quickly be keenly appreciated by anyone who chooses to embark upon it.

On top of this, being an outsider brings with it certain advantages. Hart, Garnaut, Le Coze, Yau and Bernardo, amongst many others, have successfully provided something that was previously lacking in their adopted city, and they have done so not just with the conviction of youth and their own beliefs, but also because they have a hunch. They believed, based on even a brief stay, that their new home was missing something, a style of restaurant that they alone could provide. The range of what has ensued is as varied as the restaurateurs behind them. An authentic, fun Spanish restaurant; a modern American bistro; menus in Shanghai and Beijing that resound with dishes from Greece and the Middle East; and, in my own case, a bistro and restaurant with modern British and French dishes where the wine list was entirely American. At the outset, all these restaurants may have sounded unlikely to succeed, but they have

certainly changed the face of the cities in which they have opened.

These opportunities may only have been visible to outsiders, who probably chose, as I know I did, not to listen to those better acquainted with the local restaurant scene and gave their ideas little chance of success. It is fascinating to speculate what would have happened had the still-naive Alan Yau not dismissed his builder's advice – that the English would not take to his plans for communal seating – when the first wagamama was under construction in 1992. Arriving as an outsider, with a strong conviction and a clear vision, can be a great advantage for a restaurateur, particularly as this phenomenon relates to another factor that is also part of every restaurateur's challenge: the fear of failure.

Restaurants are very public ventures, increasingly so now that every opening is followed in such detail by so many. When they close, they are conspicuous failures. But, as Enrico Bernardo admits, this failure, if and when it should happen, is less embarrassing if it does not take place in your home city. London, Paris and New York witness so many restaurant closures that failure, however painful, may feel less personal, and in turn their size may quickly provide another opportunity for a restaurateur to prove themselves. There are many reasons why restaurants fail, but it is rarely down to a lack of conviction on the part of the restaurateur. And that is the one attribute that so many nascent restaurateurs bring to the big cities they choose to open in – and one major reason why they seem to succeed.

Enrico Bernardo

GABRIELE BERTAIOLA

A TRADITIONAL ITALIAN LOCANDA

After my first meal at Antica Locanda Mincio, set in the countryside outside the small town of Borghetto di Valeggio between Verona and Mantua in north-west Italy, I wondered whether I would ever again come across such an atmospheric restaurant in such a magnificent setting, run by such a charismatic individual. This is one of those restaurants I enjoy the most when I am in Italy – a place where the owners take the food and wine and the care of their customers seriously, but certainly not themselves. Several tables of families with small children help create a relaxed atmosphere, and there is a sense as you walk through the front door or onto the terrace that you are participating in a performance that has been taking place for a long time, and will continue for many years. The regular customers come for the performance, and the extensive menu and wine list play useful supporting roles. And all of this comes enveloped in a thousand years of history.

On my return two years later, I saw immediately the toll that running the restaurant for the past thirty-five years has taken on its owner, Gabriele Bertaiola. What I also saw was the potential therapeutic value his involvement with a place that has been in his family since 1919 could have. The surrounding natural beauty had remained virtually unchanged. The area is part of the broad, verdant Po Valley that runs in a wide corridor across Italy. Around here it is particularly green because it encompasses the River Mincio, which flows down from Lake Garda to join the River Po. To reach the restaurant one must cross the fourteenth-century Ponte Visconteo, while another wooden pedestrian bridge links the restaurant to a windmill, still turning but no longer to any purpose. Today, the beauty of the countryside is a magnet for hikers, cyclists and families. Over the preceding millennium, however, it has provided the backdrop for the activities of the Knights Templar, Napoleon's army and many combatants in Italy's struggle for independence. There is a real sense of history in the air.

An outline of this history can be found on the back of the twenty-four-page booklet that Bertaiola has considerately collated as a combined menu and wine list, interspersed with paintings by the Veronese artist Federico Bellomi. The design reflects not only Bertaiola's pride in the place he was born, and where he has lived and worked all his life, but is also an unusually democratic approach to the showing of the wine list. Although it is customary for every guest to receive a menu when they sit down, the standard practice is to hand a copy of the wine list to only one person at each table, and usually to the man. This is not only highly divisive, and fails to recognize the increasingly important role of the woman as host, but is also often plain wrong: I don't believe I am the only husband in the world whose wife knows far more than he does about wine. I have lost count of the number of times, especially in France, when the wine list has been given to me and I have promptly handed it to my wife. Nevertheless, I am then shown the bottle even though I have not ordered it, and all too often I am also asked to taste the wine my wife has ordered only minutes before – usually in better French than mine. The other great disadvantage of offering only one wine list is that it limits any discussion about the wine that may take place around the table and puts the eventual choice in the hands of one person, who may or may not be feeling magnanimous. Commercially speaking, anything that can be done to open up the discussion about the wine choice often leads, in my experience, to the purchase of a more expensive wine or more than one bottle, which clearly is good for the restaurant.

The most simple, elegant and effective solution to this problem has long been the large four-page menu at Taillevent in Paris. Here the first and main courses appear on the first page and the cheeses and desserts on the final page, and the whole thing opens up to reveal *la cave de Taillevent*: the contents of the restaurant's renowned wine cellars. Bertaiola goes one further, since on his menu the food gives way to the wine list, listing (unusually for Italy) wines from all over the world, including Israel and New Zealand, as well as dessert wines and digestifs. Equally unusually, there is a list at the end of forty whiskies from Scotland, Canada and the US, which Bertaiola was persuaded to buy a decade ago by a waiter who was passionate about them.

Both menus acknowledge their restaurant's respective historical roots. Taillevent is named after the chef to France's royal court in the fourteenth century (also the man credited with writing the first cookbook in French). The final page of Bertaiola's menu is a list of key dates, including the site's origins in the eighth century and its church in the ninth, with various battles in between; the first appearance of a tavern in its current location in the fifteenth century; and finally, its integration into the new state of Italy in 1866. It then became a *locanda* (inn) with rooms as well as a restaurant, until legislation twenty-five years ago stipulated a minimum of seven bedrooms for all inns. When that came into force the Bertaiola family moved in above the shop and have continued to live there with great pleasure. 'One of the great attractions of being a restaurateur here,' Bertaiola explained, barely concealing an almost boyish pleasure,

Gabriele Bertaiola

'is being able to wake up, draw back the curtains, listen to the birds and the river flowing by and watch the first rays of the sun shining on the hills opposite.' I got the impression that it more than made up for waiting for the last customer to leave, and the noise of their cars as they drove off into the early morning.

When Bertaiola wakes up he looks out onto another of his restaurant's assets, one that makes it a pleasure to visit, but also presents one of the most difficult operational challenges for restaurateurs anywhere. Outside the Locanda's main building, which houses the kitchens, lavatories and the two exquisite dining rooms that seat 140, is a short zebra crossing that leads to a shaded terrace by the banks of the river. This has capacity for 150 people, and it is difficult to imagine a more delightful place to sit. It is ringed by tall linden trees, which Bertaiola himself planted in the 1970s, so it is cool in the hot midday sun, and has lovely views of the river. The trees and the noise of the water provide the perfect backdrop for conversation, as they seem to create a vacuum within which everyone can talk, laugh, eat and drink with unbounded pleasure. It is such a wonderful spot that some customers were sitting down at their tables long before the restaurant was due to open. The combination of the sunlight streaming in through the tree tops and the waiters in their formal black uniforms reminded me of a background in a Toulouse-Lautrec painting of something similarly hedonistic from the nineteenth century. Only the sight of men in shorts, and the ubiquitous mobile phones, brought me back to the present.

There isn't a restaurateur in the world who would not envy Bertaiola this terrace. Outdoor seating has become de rigeur in recent years and a huge boon for restaurateurs everywhere. This is partly simply because sitting outside makes the customer feel more relaxed, conveying the impression that although the office is only a ten-minute walk away, it feels far longer. It is also down to the almost universal ban on smoking inside restaurants that has finally, and justifiably, come into force. An outdoor heater and a few tables squeezed precariously onto an uneven pavement (which, with smokers seemingly impervious to the cold, can be very useful, even during the winter) may not constitute everyone's idea of a romantic outdoor terrace, but it does provide a lucrative source of income. However, the most memorable meals on sunny Mediterranean or Sydney harbour terraces, for me at least, cannot easily be repeated on the terrace of a restaurant in London, Paris or New York. They can never be the same experience.

Terraces do provide management challenges. The first is that the terrace, or any outdoor seating, is almost by definition the furthest section of the restaurant from the kitchen, so it may be necessary to adapt the menu to fit the location. On the tried-and-tested principle that food does not travel, the combination of distance, plus the fact that a terrace will often be shaded, means that any dish can lose its heat quickly. The Bertaiolas overcome this by serving the food rapidly, and they have the advantage that they only use the terrace in the warm weather, which allows the food to stay hot for longer. Terraces also have one inherent fault that no one, even the most experienced restaurateur in the world, can control. The weather, so wonderful at 10.00 or 11.00 a.m. when a customer calls requesting a table on the terrace, or even at 12.30 p.m. when the first few customers have been seated outdoors, may suddenly turn windy, cool, wet or any combination of these, and the customers will want to move indoors. The restaurateur will then face an extremely stressful few minutes.

How this is handled is a sign of how well the restaurant is managed and, in particular, of how well the receptionists have been trained, especially in the most basic rule of taking a booking: never promise a customer a particular table, no matter how important they may be, or how often they come to the restaurant. Any request for an outdoor table should be greeted with either 'I will make a note of that for you' or 'We will do our best to oblige.' If this rule is not followed, the resulting chaos is not a pleasant sight for those who believe in the fundamental good nature of humankind.

The other basic rule of terraces is not to fill them up. Since they are sometimes larger than the seating area indoors, it can be tempting to take as many bookings as will fit outside. Come a shift in the direction of the wind or a sudden squall, though, this can be another recipe for disaster, because once the customers move inside there will not be enough seats for everyone. Although Bertaiola can seat 150 people outside he knows never to take more bookings than for 140 because that is the maximum he can seat indoors.

Paolo, twenty-seven, and Elena, twenty-five, Bertaiola's two children, have experienced just how swiftly this can all go horribly wrong from the most exposed vantage point: the reception desk by the Locanda's front door. While Paolo has worked by his father's side for the past six years, Elena has been away at university but any time at home is usually spent handling the reservations or acting as cashier. Elena's description of the scene when the weather turns nasty, and a sudden queue of customers appears by the front door, was suitably graphic. 'It's war. We no longer know which section they were in when they were sitting outside, so there is a very good chance that some of the chits for what they have ordered will have gone missing.' And the customers will want very different things: some want to come in and carry on as before, some want their bill immediately so that they can leave straight away, and some want to hedge their bets in the hope that they can go back outside, but the chairs and tables are usually too wet for them to do so. 'I do prefer it here in the winter when the big fires are burning and everyone is inside.'

Bertaiola then pulled out a piece of paper to show me how he plans for every service on the terrace, his 'battle plan' as he called it. An A4 sheet has been divided into seven sections, each of which is the responsibility of one waiter who is named on the sheet. Within each section are the names of the bookings and the number of covers, which ranged on the day I was there from tables of two to tables of sixteen (the latter a table of women who held their hands up like schoolchildren for the waiter to take their order, but seemed to amend slightly everything they wanted to eat from the menu). Finally there was each waiter's number for the computer to recognize. That way, he assured me, there was a good chance of minimizing the risk of anything going too wrong should the weather suddenly change.

The Gabriele Bertaiola who explained this to me looked almost the same as the man I had encountered on my first visit: tall, impeccably dressed and very concerned with his customers' well-being, but in the intervening eighteen months he had suffered a severe setback to his health, directly attributable, his doctors believe, to the stress of running this restaurant to such demanding standards. At the age of sixty-three he had suffered a stroke so severe that he had had to spend five months in hospital and was told he may never walk or speak again. To confound such pessimism he was now walking again, albeit with a limp, doing what he enjoys most: *vivere con le gente*, or living with his customers.

In 1977 he had taken over the restaurant from his father, who had died young and suddenly, and running the restaurant rather than the kitchen had been the natural choice. 'I live alongside my customers,' he explained. 'I enjoy seeing them happy and delighted with the food and wine we serve. A lot of people come from afar and it's my job to see that everything is all right for them.' His sudden departure to hospital put a considerable strain on Paolo, even though they had been working together for six years. His return has obviously presented challenges of the opposite kind, as suddenly there are two Signor Bertaiolas in the restaurant used to running the show, although Gabriele is quite aware of how dependent he, and the restaurant, are on Paolo's slender shoulders. Sitting next to his father, Paolo, perhaps not surprisingly, said that it was the fun of being with the customers he has inherited that he enjoys most about the life of a restaurateur. Far less enjoyable was the challenge of reconciling the two days the restaurant is closed, Wednesday and Thursday, with a social life, the desire to be with his girlfriend and the need to sleep. As soon as he finished, his father said (in far better English than he had led me to believe he could speak): 'But I think the hardest thing for him is working with his father!'

A pause in the conversation allowed us all to check on the time. It was now 12.30 p.m. and time for another daily ritual in the life of a busy rest-aurateur: a quick bite to eat. While the waiting staff were coming out to seat their customers and take their apéritif orders, Paolo led his father off for what I guessed from his hand gestures would be a very swift bowl of pasta. Before I went for my own lunch, I asked Elena for a tour of the kitchens.

While the Bertaiolas encapsulate the role of restaurateurs in their concern for their customers, they are also custodians of a building and a way of cooking that goes back even further. Walking into their kitchens is definitely a form of culinary time travel. They occupy two large rooms barely touched by technology. In the first is a large wooden table on which various plates of antipasti are placed for the waiters to pick up and serve. On the first occasion I ate there, a young boy, less than ten years old and wearing an Italian football shirt, was conscientiously coating a large fruit tart with icing sugar. The far wall, which once contained a fireplace, is now home to shelves of soup bowls and tureens that are used to serve their pilgrim's soup, a recipe that dates back to 1700 and contains meat stock, chicken livers, black truffles, morel mushrooms and cinnamon, which was then a luxury ingredient. Most of the cooks are women, the eldest and smallest of whom, I could not help but notice, was sporting a pair of pink plastic clogs.

It is in the second room where the action is, although it comes in two different varieties. In the right-hand corner is a large range where one chef is in charge of the pasta and soup section, fourteen different dishes in all. To the left is a large open grill that is used for all the meat and fish main courses, from the simple but succulent fillets of eel that today, Bertaiola explained to me, come from Venice rather than Lake Garda as they once did (as these are now considered toxic), and the fillets of horse meat, which is a local speciality. Standing beside the young chef in front of the grill, and closing my eyes briefly, I felt as though I could have been watching the preparation for a dinner any time over the last couple of centuries.

This impression coincided forcibly with what we ate: pumpkin ravioli, which are a speciality of Mantua; ravioli stuffed with cheese and topped with cubes of pear; grilled trout and baked kid with polenta; and finally strawberries in lemon and sugar, served in a Royal Wessex blue-and-white bowl depicting a horse and carriage drawing up at a tavern – the very English equivalent of Antica Locanda Mincio. When we were finishing dessert, Bertaiola came to say goodbye, as it was time for his siesta. Although his voice sounded weak, his spirit was unquestionably strong. 'I am here,' he said, 'so I must be optimistic about my future.' As he walked off I could not help but notice Paolo standing over a table in the centre of the restaurant listening attentively to a table of customers, exactly as his father has done for the past thirty years. I left Antica Locanda Mincio with the feeling that it was in very good hands for at least the next generation.

Gabriele Bertaiola

A sense of history

Many restaurateurs would envy the strong historical links of the area around Antica Locanda Mincio. Since it is an area through which many people have travelled across the centuries on their way to Rome, the hospitality providers along its roads have established a tradition of welcoming their tired and hungry guests that few other countries can rival. That is why walking into a well-run *trattoria* or *ristorante* in Italy generates such instant pleasure: it is the immediate realization that you are in the hands of experienced professionals. I first began to recognize the value of such a history when I walked into the deserted L'Escargot in 1980 and moved beyond the fact that it was originally an eighteenth-century townhouse. As I walked around its five floors, I also started to see that, more importantly, it had traded successfully for the past fifty-five years as a restaurant specializing in the French provincial dishes that are now very much back in fashion. This sense of continuity, of being part of a chain of ownership of a building that dates back to the time when restaurants first began to emerge in our cities in the early nineteenth century, grew over time until it became one of the distinct pleasures of being able to call myself a restaurateur.

The restaurant whose history is most acutely felt by the customer is perhaps Le Grand Véfour in Paris, just north of the Palais Royal, where the rather cramped tables and chairs are an immediate physical reminder that the customers who first sat there when it opened its doors in 1785 were considerably smaller than we are today. London can boast nothing quite so old, although

Scott's in Mayfair began life as an oyster warehouse in 1851 before subsequently becoming a restaurant. The lure of gently restoring an old restaurant back to life is very strong. I remember sitting with Sam and Eddie Hart shortly after they had opened Quo Vadis in London, when they mentioned that one of the things that had impelled them to undertake this project had been the realization that by doing so they were preserving a restaurant and a building for future generations.

Restaurants themselves are part of our history, but they are also sometimes responsible for maintaining historic buildings that were never built for that purpose, but nevertheless have the interior, character and charm to become restaurants. One of the most striking examples of this has been the transformation of what was originally a girls' school built in the late nineteenth century close to London's Liverpool Street station. Chris and Jeff Galvin (brothers and chefs who cooked at different times at L'Escargot), along with their backer, Malaysian-born Ken Sanker, won the competition to transform this neglected site, and today, as Galvin La Chapelle, it is packed with customers enjoying the more expensive restaurant and more informal bar and café. The elegance of the historic building adds a vital sense of excitement.

Restaurants have also made a significant difference to the composition of many British high streets by taking over, as I believe no other business could have done, the former banks that once dominated these streets. As the major banking groups consolidated, many branches, often occupying rather grand corner sites, had their roles usurped by the internet and were converted into restaurants of all kinds, with the Pizza Express chain among the first to exploit them. When I first investigated this phenomenon I was told that although the transformation of the ground floor and offices (formerly the scene of many a difficult meeting with the bank manager) into the kitchen and dining area was relatively inexpensive, the most costly element was removing the safe at ground level, which had once received the nightly bags of cash and cheques. These were built to last and frequently needed dynamite to remove them. When Drew Nieporent opened the first Nobu in New York on a corner site that had once been a bank, the safe was too big to remove, so they promptly turned it into a walk-in wine safe.

At the Antica Locanda Mincio, every part of the surroundings contributes to the sense of history, and the Bertaiola family realize that their role as restaurateurs belongs to them only for as long as they want to follow in the footsteps of those who have gone before them. Surely no other profession can combine such immediate gratification with an equally strong sense of history, twice a day, seven days a week.

Gabriele Bertaiola

MICHELLE GARNAUT

Eclectic Western
Food In The Far East

5

Michelle Garnaut is the most peripatetic of restaurateurs. Born in Melbourne, Australia, the eldest of nine children, she came to London in the late 1970s to train as a cook before travelling back east. Hong Kong became her resting post in the mid 1980s, and it was there in 1989 that she opened M at the Fringe in the centrally located Fringe arts club. This was the first in a trio of memorable restaurants that reverberate with her style and bear the trademark capital M, which has become the symbol of her inimitable presence. After a stint as a guest chef in the Peace Hotel in Shanghai in 1996 – and against everyone's advice – Garnaut was the first Western restaurateur to open on the Bund, Shanghai's waterfront area, in January 1999, five years before the competition. She chose to open in China because it was the logical next step after her success in Hong Kong, and she could see that the opportunities, as well as the challenges, were huge. In 2006 she added M the Glamour Bar on the floor above the restaurant. Having played a significant role in the renaissance of Shanghai, Garnaut then decided to open in Beijing: proof, as if any were needed, that all successful restaurateurs have a very strong masochistic streak. Negotiations began in 2002 on a site on the corner of historic Qianmen Street, which overlooks Tiananmen Square, with an opening in time for the Beijing Olympics in 2008 as the ultimate goal. Planning and building delays, and then politics, intervened, so that in the end Capital M finally opened its doors in 2009.

My encounters with Garnaut over the years have always been exciting, and have left strong impressions of a restaurateur and entrepreneur with a highly developed social conscience. The first time we met was in Shanghai during the not-for-profit International Literary Festival, which Garnaut, as a result of her strong interest in the arts, founded in 2002, and which has brought in writers from all over the world ever since. She later expanded to create a sister event in Beijing. Watching Garnaut in action during this hectic period revealed a woman of great charm and iron determination. 'You know I am very pig-headed, don't you?' she once commented, and my response was that, as well as deep admiration for all she had achieved, this was her one characteristic on which all my sources had agreed. Garnaut's pursuit of potential restaurants in China certainly demonstrates her unique approach. 'In the mid 1990s, most people were running scared of China, many leaving for residency rights elsewhere in Canada or the UK. But it seemed to me that being a part of China was the future for Hong Kong, whether we liked it or not, and so I decided to pursue it. It seemed mad at the time, and everyone said I was mad.'

We shared a cup of tea one February afternoon at Capital M (illustrated page 97) on the day before Chinese New Year. Snow was falling outside in Tiananmen Square as dusk was descending, and the restaurant had a film set-like quality, with warm colours that made everything seem peaceful. Garnaut had just given the waitress a tough grilling on all the ingredients on the tray she had delivered when Espen Harbitz, her longstanding general manager, came to tell her that Party officials were asking for her. 'This should be fun,' she laughed. What followed was testimony to the impact she has made in a city and a market so many Westerners find difficult to penetrate. This impact has largely been in making her restaurants focal points for locals and tourists alike; in training so many young Chinese in the hospitality business; and in paving the way for so many other restaurateurs to follow her example, some of whom have seemed to enjoy far more resources, but have fared less well.

We were led into a room full of Party and Town Hall dignitaries drinking tea and eating snacks, and I was introduced as the man from the *Financial Times*. A lot of bowing ensued. Next, a sliding door opened and we were led onto a balcony, accompanied by children in colourful costumes, and into the full glare of state television cameras. Down below us, Tiananmen Square was packed and all eyes were on us. A countdown began. We had been instructed to place our hands on the panels by the balcony at the final moment, which, as we did so, lit up the entire square. Everyone applauded and cheered, not many of them realizing, I suspect, that one of the few women on the balcony was an Australian restaurateur with a very limited working knowledge of Cantonese and Mandarin.

Garnaut has a true passion for restaurants, coupled with a clarity of vision for what she wants them to be, that I have rarely encountered before. Quite how besotted with restaurants she is became immediately obvious when we met at The Groucho Club in Soho, London, en route to lunch at Hix on Brewer Street. The night before, she explained, she had spent with her former flatmates from the 1970s at a production of *The Kitchen*, the National Theatre's revival of the Arnold Wesker play about life in a professional kitchen. Then, before our lunch, she wanted me to take her on a mini restaurant crawl, so we called in at the new next-door establishments Duck Soup and Cây Tre on Dean Street. As we passed Randall & Aubin on Brewer Street she stopped abruptly and walked straight in. The interior of this restaurant, built in 1911 as a butcher's shop and still replete with hooks, marble tops and mirrors, had charmed her,

Michelle Garnaut

and she took a card and promised to be back. Then as we were being shown to our table at Hix, she walked off again. I had chosen this restaurant because Mark Hix, its chef-proprietor, has a strong friendship with talented artists such as Tracey Emin, Mat Collishaw and Damien Hirst, whose works litter the restaurant and the bar downstairs and which I knew she would find interesting. Minutes later, having checked out the artworks, Garnaut came back to join me. The waitress brought the menus and asked us whether we would like to see a tray with the fresh cuts of meat. While we declined I noted Garnaut's striking outfit, which seemed so illustrative of her style as a restaurateur. Her red hair was complemented by orange lipstick, tights and a large ring and a matching orange lining on a three-quarter length black coat (an old favourite, she disclosed, from the Finnish designer Marimekko).

Seeing Randall & Aubin had caused Garnaut to reflect on the integrity of the space that any restaurant occupies. 'There are very few properties left in Asia that have any sense of history,' she said with real sadness in her voice, 'When I was looking for a site in Beijing I was shown a few fascinating temples, but we were immediately told that a gas supply couldn't be fitted in them, so that ruled them out. In Hong Kong the price of property and the fact that the property companies want an almost immediate return on their investment is strangling the development of any independent restaurateurs.' This is particularly ironic for Garnaut who, having established the role of independent restaurateur with M at the Fringe in Hong Kong in 1989 at a time when few people ate Western food outside hotels, was forced to close it in 2009 because her lease had expired. At the time of writing she is still looking for the right location for its reincarnation. She had just spent several hours that morning talking to her designer in Hong Kong about two possible sites, one over three floors that had, many decades before, produced *char siu* pork, and another, less poetically, in a shopping mall. Her spirit is willing but the commercial and bureaucratic elements may be against the project: the three-floor building would be expensive to manage because of labour costs, and to incorporate all the new legislation for disabled access would remove so much of the floor print (the amount of floor space that can be used to accommodate paying customers) that it is not commercially viable.

As Garnaut looked down the menu, the expression on her face changed. At the bottom of the list of robustly priced main courses was a section headed 'Sides, vegetables and potato dishes' that would add another £3.50–£4.75 ($5.50–$7.50) per item to the bill, plus, of course, twelve-and-a-half per cent

94

service. 'This is something I refuse to do,' she expostulated. 'Dishes should complement each other and all the main ingredients should be served on the same plate.' In fact, the question of what the menu should be in order for a restaurant to succeed is key to the integrity of Garnaut's success. Having started to cook in different kitchens in Hong Kong, and having done quite a lot of cooking for events and parties, she began to realize that there was a gap in the market for the kind of food she and those she had come to know would like to eat. While it would be based on recipes she had gleaned from her travels across Europe, North Africa, Turkey and the Middle East, it would have to adhere to three principles: the menus must be smart, carefully thought out and executed, and receptive to what is currently available in the market. Certain rules would also apply to the choice of dish: 'Firstly, we can never put anything on the menu unless we really know and understand what it is. I cannot tell you what lengths we went to and how much time we spent before we finally put a pigeon pastilla, the sweet and savoury Moroccan dish, on the menu in Shanghai. Secondly, I have to have eaten the dish in its natural environment, the country where it originated. It cannot come from a recipe book. And finally we never mix cuisines on a plate. Wasabi mashed potatoes are not on my menu. I may be an old-fashioned girl but those are the rules,' she said in a voice that would brook no dissent.

Garnaut had no capital to back up her vision for what was to become M at the Fringe. She had to borrow the cash to secure enough capital to buy her own shares, and her guarantee for the loan, should the restaurant fail, was a promise to go off to Paris to cook until it was repaid. She was extremely fortunate in choosing Michael Knock as her original partner, a man who not only won one argument with Garnaut by insisting that her own version of pavlova had to be on the menu (and today it is still hugely popular at Capital M), but has also allowed her to run the restaurants according to her vision ever since. The view Garnaut takes about her partners is that she runs the business and they are lucky to have her. Part of her vision, in fact, is a 'divide and conquer policy' towards her shareholders. 'There are about thirty in total and I am happy to listen to them but I won't take advice. I must not care what they think.' This large number of shareholders has had two main benefits: the first has been the large number of people spreading the word about her restaurants because of their financial connection with it, however small – a factor that was particularly important, she explained, in the early days of Capital M; the second is that it has given her the opportunity to dilute the shares, and even at one stage her own shareholding, to distribute

them to key members of staff, thereby binding them closer to her and to her restaurants' continued success. This arrangement, combined with her personality and philosophy, have inspired a loyalty towards Garnaut from her staff and senior management that is remarkable given the number of new hotels and restaurants that have opened in these rapidly developing cities. Espen Harbitz and his sister Elisabeth, who grew up in their family's hotel in Norway, have been at her side for over a decade, while Bruno van der Burg, the general manager in Shanghai, has worked with Garnaut for over twenty years. One long-serving former manager confessed that 'it was very difficult to leave'.

The success of Garnaut's restaurants lies also in her ability to read the market, to understand precisely what her guests are looking for. This talent was the reason behind a recent stopover in London en route to France. There, Garnaut was to sit on the jury for the Women's Initiative Awards sponsored by Cartier, the luxury French watchmaker. Since M on the Bund opened, the Bund had become a magnet for other bars, restaurants and top fashion brands. Just before Cartier opened there, she received a phone call from their vice president for Asia inviting her to lunch. Intrigued, she went along. He told her that the Bund was soon to become home to all the most exclusive brands, and her prices at M on the Bund were too low. 'This area is luxury,' he'd said, 'kindly double your prices.' Garnaut was polite but refused, explaining that it was crucially important for her business that people could afford to come as regularly as they wanted. 'It has been amazing,' she continued, 'particularly in China, to see so many young couples come along for dinner who have so obviously saved long and hard to do so because they share a glass of Champagne at the beginning, or a dessert at the end of their meal. The more marriage proposals there are in my restaurants, the more future customers there will be.'

While it is easy to see Garnaut as an extremely determined pioneer, I believe that a more accurate description of her impact as a restaurateur in Hong Kong, Shanghai and Beijing is as an educator. From the beginning she realized that she could never survive commercially if she were to serve Asian or Chinese food, so her menus have always been Western in style, albeit eclectic in their origins – a reflection of her most recent travels. It takes courage and good management to write, and deliver, a menu at Capital M that comprises a torchon of French foie gras; an Iranian dish of soft eggs, smoky aubergines and Persian feta; a Moroccan chicken tagine; crisp suckling pig; a mango jelly and fool; and a plate, described with complete honesty, as 'the best cheeses we can find'. It is not just the sourcing of these ingredients that has made executing such a menu difficult – and Garnaut did add that the current spate of cases of food contamination in China is a particular challenge – but explaining them and training the staff, many of whom have never tasted such dishes before, which has made her role so unusual. It is no exaggeration to say that the cooking, cocktail-making, wine and service knowledge of hundreds of young people in China would not have developed to the level it has without Garnaut's vision.

'When we opened in Shanghai, among the many ingredients we had to carry in by hand were all the good wines, coffee, sugar, saffron, vanilla beans, dried herbs and tons of other things. But there was great, and relatively cheap, caviar to make up for it.' Garnaut herself attributes her success to two apparently contradictory characteristics: the generosity and warmth of a Jewish mother and the frugality instilled in her as a trainee cook. The best flavours, she recalls being taught, are those left behind at the bottom of the pan. And now that she is in the position of hiring chefs she has learned precisely what to look for: someone who is smart enough to study medicine but has chosen to cook instead. Her most important mentor was a tiny, elegant, sophisticated restaurateur called Mietta O'Donnell who ran Mietta's restaurant in Melbourne in the 1970s. She was reserved, not particularly warm and never cooked, but said something that Garnaut has never forgotten. 'She said "Don't make it all about the chef" and that is a maxim I have always stuck to.' If it is just about the chef and he or she chooses to leave, then the business suffers. And if it is just about the chef, what is the role of the restaurateur?

Not everything she has attempted has been a success. An Italian restaurant she opened within M on the Bund was closed after eight months. 'Failure,' she explained, 'is the greatest teacher.' The plan had been simple: to create within a designated section of the restaurant a pizzeria that also served inexpensive rotisserie chicken, since the Shanghainese love chicken – this is one city where KFC is far more popular than McDonalds. But it lost its way in the period between planning and opening, and by the time it opened the menu had become too complicated, and the number of chefs required to execute it, and therefore the prices, too high. Having tried to ignore the problem, Garnaut realized she had to cut her losses, called a meeting and with immediate effect closed her foray into Italy, a country that has been a source of considerable culinary and artistic inspiration for her.

One rule that Garnaut has never deviated from is that she will not discount, ever. Nor will she issue the VIP cards that allow hefty discounts to the recipients and are extremely common today in China. This approach stems not just from the management problem of never knowing exactly who to give them to, but rather something that has been lodged within her since her Catholic upbringing. 'I want to sustain a long-term, full-time business, not go for broke, and that means not being overpriced to begin with and remaining good value.' She instead responds to economic vicissitudes with her own initiatives. The SARS epidemic of 2003 saw M on the Bund offering a glass of Champagne and caviar for the giveaway price of 10 Chinese yuán (just over £1.00 or $1.50), which drove the business out of trouble. When M at the Fringe was forced to close in Hong Kong, Garnaut decided to go out with a bang, so for its final twenty weeks, twenty of its most popular dishes were on the menu at HK $20 (£1.60 or $2.60), which is ridiculously good value. This is as much about the detail, she insisted, as the approach. 'During SARS I wouldn't let the waiting staff wear face masks because I wanted anyone who came to the restaurant to at least have the impression that life was going on as normal somewhere in the city. I knew that if we could survive that, we could survive anything.'

I asked Garnaut whether she could have chosen a more difficult career path. She laughed. 'Well, I suppose if it were easy then millions would do it. But I have now been in this business for over forty years and I have loved every aspect of it, although I've just had to spend a week back in the kitchens and I have to say it was hard work. I loved working behind a bar, I love interacting with the customers and I love hanging around the restaurants late at night. But it is a very emotional business, too. I have never taken any personal decision in my life without thinking about how it will affect my business and those who work with me.' Has she at any time wanted to give the whole thing up, particularly in the long delays she encountered before opening in Beijing? 'Oh yes,' she replied, 'but the loneliest time was undoubtedly before I opened in Hong Kong. Since then each opening has been relatively easy because there have been other ears to listen to the issues, other shoulders to share the burden. But then I was on my own, like a writer. I can still recall sitting on the floor polishing the old cutlery I had insisted on buying. It was impossible to find any staff because seven new hotels had just opened in Hong Kong. I was in tears when my old friend and business partner, Annabel Graham, came in and scolded me. "Pull yourself together," she said, "if not, it all falls apart." And since then we've been a team.'

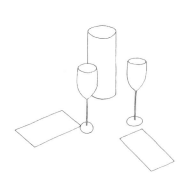

Symbiosis with the arts

Michelle Garnaut inherited her love of the arts from her mentor, the late Mietta O'Donnell. After the success of her first restaurant, Mietta's, in Melbourne, O'Donnell went on to open Mietta's Lounge in the early 1980s, where she held poetry readings, cabaret, chamber music, jazz and literary events. O'Donnell's counsel, Garnaut recalled, was that you should always do more than a restaurant. 'She was right. It's so much fun doing the extra-curricular stuff.'

For Garnaut and her team this now encompasses the literary festivals she has created in both Beijing and Shanghai, her love of chamber music, which she has also developed into an annual festival, and the extraordinary diary she has produced for the last ten years that sells for the equivalent of about £20 ($32) in Shanghai, Beijing and Hong Kong. Although it only just breaks even, she describes it as 'a labour of love'. The most recent orange 2012 diary was a thumping great collection of many of Garnaut's interests. There was a CD of chamber music, a fold-out model of a water dragon that roars, brief articles by Shanghai-based author Lynn Pan and Australian chef Gay Bilson, a list of targets for M restaurants in the coming year that focused on how the restaurants could reduce their environmental impact, photographs from the Village People Project (a series of poor rural villages in China her restaurants have supported), and some of her favourite Christmas recipes. Throughout the diary there are references back to her restaurants and what they do to support all these associations. This involvement with the arts is now so much a part of Garnaut's role as a restaurateur that she describes her working life as divided into four distinct aspects: putting the diary together, organizing the literary and chamber music festivals, working in the restaurants and looking out for new things to do.

In many ways this delineation is somewhat artificial, though. Any close association between the world of the arts and a nearby restaurant is likely to make the latter more successful. It is a symbiosis that can be hugely beneficial to the restaurant, the restaurateur and its customers. While the provision of an excellent cup of coffee, a glass of wine or a meal before or after the performance, as has been the custom for decades at Glyndebourne opera house in Sussex, obviously adds to the enjoyment of the visual performance, such an association also has other important benefits.

The first is that it makes the customer relax and therefore adds to their overall pleasure of what they are about to enjoy. Anyone going to the theatre, opera, a concert or with a timed ticket to an exhibition wants to be as close as possible to the entrance or their seats while they are having something to eat. Customers are watching the clock and any restaurateur and his team who can alleviate this anxiety is delivering a much-needed service. The second is that this proximity provides many restaurateurs with the opportunity to make their customers even more knowledgeable, even more receptive to what they are about to enjoy, by ensuring that their staff act almost as 'cultural ambassadors'. They can and should be trained to know not just when the performance starts but also when it ends, any changes to the cast list, and a brief knowledge of the plot so that the waiter appears to be as expert about what is on at the nearby theatres as he is at clearing restaurant tables. Being in a position to drop a broad hint that the stars of this particular show were in the restaurant for a late night supper earlier in the week is also something all customers like to know and talk about.

On another level, being involved within an arts organization brings unusual professional privileges, notably the opportunity to walk through parts of wonderful buildings the public never sees. In my restaurant consultancy role at the British Museum I looked forward to 9.00 a.m meetings because they allowed me and the interested restaurateurs I was showing round to walk through the magnificent Great Court and look at the ancient statues without the crowds. At the Royal Opera House in Covent Garden there is the added bonus of walking along the corridors and hearing great singers rehearse, or sitting in the staff restaurant watching the corps de ballet tucking into huge plates of food.

Michelle Garnaut

TREVOR
GULLIVER

PARED-DOWN
BRITISH STYLE
AT
ST. JOHN

Trevor Gulliver opened St. John restaurant in St John Street (just north of Smithfield, London's long-established meat market) in 1994 with Fergus Henderson as chef. They have remained steadfast partners, friends and eating companions throughout the intervening years. From what was then a derelict and neglected former smoke house (about which Gulliver recalls saying to himself the moment he saw it, 'Oh shit, this has got to be done!') the duo have created not just a restaurant that has come to define modern British cooking, but also one that has given many chefs the confidence to write their menus with a simplicity and directness that was hitherto never an option. St. John has become the first stop for many chefs, restaurateurs and restaurant-lovers on their visits to the capital.

This is a far cry from Gulliver's first career in the early 1980s, running a company that printed T-shirts for rock tours and concerts, which he later sold successfully. Orders for 250,000 T-shirts for Frankie Goes to Hollywood, Live Aid and Thomas the Tank Engine, as well as a staff of over 300, were his preoccupations in those days. But the experience allows him to stress how vital it is for any restaurateur to understand the principles of business: 'If you can't run a business or read a balance sheet, then you shouldn't be a restaurateur.' Even had a chain of unlikely circumstances not led Gulliver from the world of textiles to the life of a restaurateur, he certainly has the appetite of the world's best eaters. Short, broad and fit, his enthusiasm for food and drink are kept in check by a long career on the rugby pitch as a hooker and an ongoing passion for squash. His diary on the day we met had begun with an early morning meeting; a breakfast with me that lasted four hours; lunch with his bank manager; a game of squash and then dinner, with several other meetings in between. 'You have to enjoy your life as a restaurateur,' he explained, 'after all, you put enough into it.'

Gulliver is highly opinionated and equally loquacious, but has a tendency not to finish his sentences. His voice can often sound like a radio signal that comes in and out of its frequency, a characteristic that was most accurately described by chef Rowley Leigh: 'Speak up, Trevor,' he once exhorted him, 'you're cracking up.' At breakfast at the Goring Hotel (another great exponent of British culinary values), his arrival twenty minutes late began with his trademark bear hug (we have known each other a long time); a description of his first breakfast at home (a bowl of rolled oats); an order for yoghurt and fruit and a pot of silver tip tea; and an apology to the manager who looked somewhat crestfallen that he wasn't going to test the kitchen further. 'Please tell Chef I can't eat all the time,' he explained before turning to me and adding that even he eats less today than he once did. 'Chefs and restaurateurs are very hospitable to one another. I remember once in New York, Fergus and I snuck into Gramercy Tavern for a spot of brunch. We were recognized and the kitchen promptly sent out several extra dishes. We had to eat a little of each one so as not to upset them, and we left delighted but defeated.' Warmed up by the tea (Gulliver, fifty-eight, still crosses London on his scooter, which is emblazoned with the St. John flying pig logo, despite a major road accident in 2010) he launched into the principles of his restaurateur manifesto.

Firstly, restaurateurs must never compromise, a principle he demonstrated by saying that St. John had never served farmed salmon because it is tasteless in his opinion, or wild salmon or cod, on sustainability grounds. Being a restaurateur means recognizing that you are the Boss, and that you work for those who work for you. The benefits of this approach, he added, are not just more rewarding, but also more long term. 'Fergus and I make a point of dealing with every complaint we receive. It's our job to stand up and take responsibility,' he added. He returned to his original point. 'It is very easy to dilute what you're doing, to move away from your original principles. But once you do, it is very difficult to revert, impossible I would say, so you have thrown away what impelled you to open in the first place.' Gulliver chose to highlight this point commercially and aesthetically. Over the past decade, as chains (his particular bugbear) have opened throughout London's suburbs, it would have been very easy for them to open far more outposts of St. John Bread and Wine than the single one that exists in Spitalfields, east London. But he, Fergus and Justin Gellatly, their long-time, wonderful baker, feared the downside of dilution far more than they relished the potential upside of what would have been much higher revenue.

So to the white walls in their restaurants, which are devoid of any art. It's the quality of the space and the structure that should attract customers, Gulliver believes, not whatever art may be on the wall, which can create a theme and lead to confusion. He cited with pride the story of how Banksy, Britain's most highly respected graffiti artist, had painted on the wall of the restaurant during their tenth anniversary party, and how it had been covered over with white paint the following day. A gesture, he added, which even the artist had appreciated.

These principles emerged gradually after St. John opened in 1994 and once customers had begun to appreciate its unique appeal a couple of years later. The path that led Gulliver from the rag trade to becoming such an

Trevor Gulliver

unlikely iconic restaurateur incorporated various incarnations en route. The sale of his textile business had included a non-competition clause, which prohibited further activity in that field. A burgeoning interest in urban regeneration in Paris and Manchester followed, punctuated by a call from an old school friend who had created the very successful American-themed Break For The Border bar and restaurant on Charing Cross Road, to ask whether he would be interested in a diner project. They went off to do their research in the US, and the Fat Boys Diner they subsequently opened on a piece of wasteland in Maiden Lane, in then-rundown Covent Garden, was an immediate success. In 1989 he and Mark Yates, a fellow restaurateur who went on to great success with Livebait and The Real Greek, opened the Fire Station (in a former fire station) close to Waterloo Station, which they sold at the peak of its success. Next, there was a very personal attempt to change the image of Indian food in Britain with Pukka Bar, which moved from its original home in Sydenham, Kent, to Primrose Hill, north London, before closing. An association followed with the company that had built Putney Bridge restaurant on a difficult triangular site that had lain fallow for seventeen years, directly opposite the starting line for the annual boat race between Oxford and Cambridge universities. This ended acrimoniously and the site is now part of the Thai Square group. Finally, there has been the opening of the St. John Hotel in London's Chinatown, an area whose transition to gentility has not been as swift as many expected.

Linking all these unlikely outposts are two common threads: Gulliver's personal vision for what a restaurant ought to be and, more importantly in the period leading up to the opening of St. John, his growing reputation for unlocking difficult sites. There has also been the growing recognition among landlords and local politicians of the role restaurants can play in urban regeneration. Restaurants have formed a significant part in the development of many inner city areas over the past two decades, partly because in their many forms – bars, cafés, dining rooms and late-night drinking clubs – they can so easily adapt to the architecture available. Even more importantly, though, from a landlord's perspective, restaurants can bring life and light to a building for far longer than even the most respected retail name. The lights are switched on at 7.00 a.m in any busy kitchen when the first deliveries arrive, and they stay on in the restaurant until the last customer has left and the tables have been laid up for the following day's service, usually not much before 1.00 a.m. This is a security service many landlords relish.

The unlikely success of the first Fat Boys Diner in Covent Garden, then the Fire Station in Waterloo ('a lovely building,' Gulliver commented, 'which we converted into a restaurant for less than £100,000 [$150,000]') led to Gulliver becoming a member of Westminster Council and then working on urban regeneration projects in London, Manchester and Paris. He was particularly receptive, therefore, when a call came through from property developer Anthony Lyons to visit a derelict site in St John Street. What followed was a particularly convoluted property deal, but there was a determination, bordering on sheer bloody-mindedness (as there is with most successful entrepreneurs), which would not let him give up. 'It was a great space and revitalizing derelict buildings is what I do. It was obvious.' Although the expectation was that Gulliver would again appoint Dan Evans as chef, with whom he had worked at the Fire Station, he had by then been introduced to Fergus Henderson. The latter, ten years his junior, had graduated as an architect before turning to cooking and was then running a small restaurant above The French House pub in Soho to great acclaim. Gulliver remembers that John Humphrey, a supplier of good olive oil, Sol beer and Cava, was the conduit for their friendship, but not precisely where or when. Over a few lunches and dinners the fundamental principles of St. John were laid down. These principles were to produce the best seasonal British dishes based on very solid execution.

St. John is unquestionably a restaurant icon today, but its first two years of trading were far from successful. The whole place was very different from the norm: the setting, the simplicity of the menu, the lack of pretence. It was almost shocking. Gulliver can still recall how naive they all were, particularly when a booking for sixteen failed to show up for their Christmas lunch and no one, it transpired, had bothered to call them to confirm. There was no heating at all in the bar area which, along with the glass roof, meant that no one wanted to stay. On top of this, the Smithfield area was not yet 'cool'.

Three external factors began to change this. The first was a steady influx of customers from Soho for Fergus's cooking. The bar also became an attraction in its own right for the fashion crowd, as two fashionistas, Katie Grand and Luella Bartley, lived in one of the flats upstairs. Thirdly, St. John began to host the post-show parties for the increasingly influential White Cube gallery in Mayfair. 'Different crowds began to take it on,' explained Albie Ray, then its restaurant manager, 'and you could sense the change, the growing kudos of working there.' By this time Gulliver was

beginning to extricate himself from what was to prove a far less successful involvement in Putney Bridge. He had taken this on at the same time as St. John in order to spread his own personal risk and because the opportunity had presented itself for a new and exciting building. It failed, though, for a simple and basic reason that can ruin any business, let alone a restaurant that is open to continual public scrutiny: the partners, it transpired, had very different aspirations. 'It was an important and expensive lesson,' Gulliver observed, 'in choosing your partners well.'

Gulliver cannot hide his delight at having fallen into Henderson's company. 'We may be an odd couple, but we're not Morecambe and Wise or Gilbert & George as we are often portrayed. We are Fergus and Trevor.' They have not fallen out once in the past nineteen years – Trevor added that they are sufficiently challenged by their strongly opinionated wives to ensure that they form an unlikely working solidarity – and each is the other's best mate. Lunch, and its huge importance in their world, both philosophically and hedonistically, is also a magnet, most symbolically of all the first lunch they share on their return from their summer holidays (Fergus and family on the Isle of Tiree in the Hebrides, the Gullivers in France), which is celebrated with a roast grouse each and a bottle of red burgundy, at St. John, of course. This led to another of Gulliver's principles: 'Never have lunch with someone in a hurry.'

While the public manifestation of these shared principles is St. John's now well-known motto 'Nose-To-Tail Eating', they have been supported from the first day St. John opened by two physical manifestations in the kitchen. The first is that there is a butcher's block in each of the three kitchens. 'I'm very proud of these,' Gulliver admitted, 'because it means that we can buy whole animals, butcher them ourselves and do a hundred different things with them. It's more than just a metaphor because it means that our cooks learn more and, as a result, our kitchens are far more lively and interesting places for them to work in. And if we do our job well, when a chef comes along and says to Fergus or me that he believes it's time to move on, then we're delighted. It means that there'll be another good place to have lunch in.'

The second, under Justin Gellatly, has been their bakery. The popularity of the bakery at the back of the original restaurant led to their expansion into St. John Bread & Wine in Spitalfields in 2003, which has a more casual menu and an emphasis again on the local community. The underlying commercial principle was to create a place where residents and people working nearby could pop in for a glass of wine, a loaf of bread and possibly a bottle of wine on their way home. It was a location that shared two characteristics with Smithfield. Firstly, the street was then nothing other than a string of rather down-at-heel pubs. A good restaurant, Gulliver believed, would be the first step in its renaissance. And so it has proved, although today the management challenges are somewhat different: there are now forty different places to eat in the neighbourhood and the biggest daily problem is how to handle the number of buggies and prams. The opening was difficult, though. Bakeries operate on what many consider to be anti-social hours, starting very early in the morning, and this, along with the structural problems involved in installing the bakery in a nineteenth-century building, led to a serious dispute with a resident on the top floor. When St. John opened its much larger bakery in 2010 to cope with growing demand from other restaurants, it was in the seclusion of a railway arch.

Gulliver's demeanour only seemed sad once, when the topic of the St. John that never happened came up, because both he and Fergus believed it could have been the harbinger of political as well as urban regeneration. This was to be a St. John in the centre of Beirut, Lebanon. In 2005, Fergus had been introduced at a wedding to one of five sisters whose family palace was to be redeveloped. The omens were good. All the sisters loved food, the tie that binds so many Middle Eastern families; the property had great character as well as views of the sea; trips to Beirut had already introduced Gulliver to the pleasures of a restaurant simply called Le Chef, where he recalled eating the best hummus and flat bread he'd ever tasted. 'But it was not to be,' he sighed. 'It was sold to developers for a higher price.'

In 2007 an agent approached Gulliver with the details of Manzi's, just off Leicester Square in London. He was intrigued, not only by the prospect of another restaurant, but also for sentimental, commercial and idealistic reasons. The former concerned Manzi's history as one of London's most respected fish restaurants alongside the nearby J. Sheekey; it had been the venue for his first meeting with his prospective father-in-law. It was for him, therefore, an address that triggered happy memories, as well as the nobler motive of restoring it to its former glory. The commercial potential centred on the fifteen small bedrooms above the restaurant that would allow the kitchen to expand its repertoire. This would most obviously revolve around breakfast and afternoon tea, as well as serving the pre-theatre audience nearby. Finally, there was Gulliver's notion of a St. John hotel that conducted its customers safe and sound into the warmth in an area, sandwiched between Leicester Square and Chinatown, that was then far more squalid than it ought to have been. The W hotel chain were moving in next door and the landlords, Shaftesbury Estates, were most encouraging. Gulliver believed that once again St. John would be at the forefront of an emerging neighbourhood.

He could never have imagined that 2010 would prove to be such an *annus horribilis*. He was in a serious road accident and spent months on crutches; the renovation of Manzi's into the St. John Hotel went £1 million ($1.5) million over budget and finished a year late; it finally opened with legal disputes still running between his company and several of the professionals involved. One of the major contentious issues was the fact that the restaurant, which was originally projected as accommodating eighty customers, can in fact seat no more than fifty, leading to a probable loss in income of around £200,000 ($310,000) per year. This was partly due to naivety in the original estimate, as well as the fact that they lost space because the air conditioning for the floors took up additional space around the walls.

Gulliver also accepted that in the leap from restaurateur to hotelier he had been 'stupid and naive'. While this honesty is typical, so too is his determination to ensure the hotel is a success. 'You have to be patient in this business; if you're good enough, the customers will come. But only if you are properly funded. If you are prepared to sacrifice profits, and often your own wages, for the first couple of years. And then to be prepared to reinvest almost immediately. Be patient and delight in what you're doing.' These sentiments must be combined with flexibility, though, and this is an aspect of the business that has been lacking from Gulliver's game since he became a hotelier. Many other people were more cautious about the financial climate of 2010 than he was, and I also believe he has been too prescriptive about continuing the principles of St. John the restaurant into St. John the hotel; he hasn't created a pre-theatre menu, for example, which is what other restaurants around Leicester Square depend on in the early evening. But fortune does favour the brave. Although the hotel has not been an immediate success, the St. John bakery, which was his idea and a successful example of his commercial background fusing with his restaurant mind, certainly has. It now supplies many other restaurants and has a concession in Selfridges.

The challenge of the hotel has not held him back. Most recently, he has taken over a disused winery in La Livinière, in the Languedoc, south-west

France, which will not only make wine for the St. John restaurants, but will also act as a place where the staff can learn about wine, in the same way as the bakery teaches them about bread and the butchers' blocks about meat. Restaurants are a halfway house in vertical integration between farmers and wine-makers and their urban clientèle, but the ultimate satisfaction of St. John, he added, is that it belongs to the staff as much as it does to Fergus and Trevor.

I asked Gulliver what the job description was on his passport. 'Company Director,' he replied, 'just like James Bond. But what I think my principal role is as a restaurateur, is to make it look so easy, to wear it well. It never is, but that's my problem.'

A style of one's own

Every restaurateur has their own style – their own image of how they want to be seen by their guests, along with their unique vision of what they want their restaurant to be like, and how they want this to be interpreted by their staff on a day-to-day basis. Happily, these styles are radically different, even across relatively small areas such as central New York and central London, the two cities that in my opinion, contain the greatest concentration and variety of different restaurants. Maguy Le Coze's style at Le Bernardin, while formal and correct, conveys a certain distance between the restaurateur and the customer, and is in complete contrast with Drew Nieporent's style of service on display at Nobu 57, although the two restaurants are only separated by six blocks. His is more engaging and always includes a broad smile, and often an arm around the shoulder. In London, an even shorter distance separates the noisy, hectic atmosphere of Russell Norman's Polpo from the much calmer setting of Nigel Platts-Martin's The Square. In many ways this style is almost as readily determined by what the restaurateur does not want as what he does, and in this aspect Trevor Gulliver is typically forthright. 'I have never believed that our customers want to see me when they come to St. John,' he explained. 'They don't want me to come over and say hello and ask whether everything is all right. I love the notion that people have chosen to come and eat here, but once they have made that decision, they have the right to quiet enjoyment, to enjoy the business of having lunch or dinner.'

This is just one opinion, albeit very strongly held. Others have diametrically opposed views: restaurateurs who believe that they should do a tour of the tables at every lunch and dinner. In New York this approach is one of conspicuous importance, and there is widespread recognition in that city that Phil Suarez, who has masterminded the highly successful restaurants of French chef Jean-Georges Vongerichten, is the ultimate practitioner of this style, known colloquially as 'shake a hand, pat a back'. While widely appreciated, this approach can clearly be divisive, and can be misconstrued by those whose hand is not shaken by the restaurateur. Above all, it is an approach that depends very heavily not just on the tact and skill with which it is carried out, but also the consistency with which it is executed.

An inescapable fact of restaurant life is that, however detailed the planning beforehand, a great deal will change in the first six months of any opening. Suddenly, the customers are coming through the door and they are beginning to use the restaurant in ways that neither you, your experienced general manager nor your designer had predicted. Customers, for no apparent reason, may turn out not to like certain areas that looked so suitable on the plans, but prefer others that make life more difficult for the waiting staff than you had envisaged. They may want, for example, higher tables and chairs than the lower ones that you thought would provide just the place for a pre-dinner drink. The restaurateur has to adapt his or her style to this changing set of customer demands, or fail.

Success, and opening more restaurants as a result, promptly brings demands that show just how flexible any restaurateur has to be. The second restaurant is always the biggest challenge because it is the only time that the business will double in size, with all the implications that has for the administrative side of the business, as well as the challenge of looking after two sets of customers in two different locations. It is also the time when everything that is so attractive about opening a restaurant slips out of the restaurateur's personal control – forever. From the second restaurant onwards, it is no longer possible for the restaurateur to stand by the reception desk every lunch and dinner, to watch the service of the food and wine to every table, to choose the music in the evening, to lower the lights sensitively halfway through the dinner service, and to say goodnight as their happy customers leave the premises. All these elements now have to be shared with others, and the warmth and welcome received by the customer – the restaurateur's sense of style – has to be encapsulated and delegated to a trusted team. Creating a style and a vision for your restaurant, communicating them to, and instilling them in, your team, and working alongside the team to pass them on to an increasing number of customers in different locations is not easy. But this sense of style is an essential attribute that lies at the heart of every successful restaurateur.

Trevor Gulliver

SAM & EDDIE HART

SPANISH CHARM, BRITISH ELEGANCE

I hurtled through the revolving doors of Quo Vadis in Soho with relief rather than the usual excitement associated with walking into a very good restaurant. The sky outside was black. The roads were awash with water and umbrellas were ineffective in the torrent. The receptionist looked on as I tried to make myself look respectable and cleaned my wet, steamed-up and almost soggy glasses. Then she directed me to the club area on the first floor, where the three Mr Harts were waiting for me.

If hospitality is in the genes, then the prospects for future restaurateurs and, most importantly for their customers, are very good indeed. Sam and Eddie Hart have certainly inherited at least one characteristic from their father Tim that is, I believe, essential for a restaurateur: each smiles with a genuine sense of bonhomie. This smile never seems to desert them, whether they are on duty in their restaurants, or, as I have often bumped into them, off to sample what their competitors are up to.

With their dark hair and dark suits, the two generations often look similar, but today, while Sam and Eddie were wearing standard restaurateur outfits of dark suit, white shirt and, increasingly, no tie, Tim had travelled down from Hambleton Hall in Rutland, his highly successful country-house hotel, in more casual gear: pink salmon cord trousers, a white shirt and a tweed jacket with, of course, a white handkerchief in his breast pocket.

The unpredictable nature of the life of the restaurateur became evident early in the conversation, when Tim dragged up from the recesses of his memory the unexpected fact that his father, as well as being a successful merchant banker, had also had a share in Overton's in St James's Street (it is now L'Oranger), which fifty years ago had been one of the capital's most esteemed fish restaurants. 'The equivalent then,' Tim added with pride, 'of Scott's today.' Even more telling is the fact that although Quo Vadis is the third of the brothers' London restaurants, following on from the successes of their Spanish restaurant Fino and tapas bar Barrafina (illustrated page 125 and which has subsequently opened a second branch in Covent Garden), it is the one that has struggled the most. The fact that experience and a proven track record on the part of the restaurateur are no guarantee of the success of any future restaurant is perhaps one of the profession's few golden rules.

Tim, Sam and Eddie Hart have already accumulated almost sixty years experience in the restaurant business between them. It all began with a change of career which, although it now seems commonplace, was highly unusual in 1978. Tim, then thirty, had already followed his father into his merchant bank when an outbreak of the mumps led to two weeks of bed rest and the opportunity to reflect on what his career really ought to be. Oblivious to the mixed metaphor, Tim added, 'I kept thinking, what could I bring to the party?' His decision to join the then-emerging ranks of country-house hotel owners, a group that in the 1980s and 1990s included Paul and Kay Henderson at Gidleigh Park, the Skanns at Chewton Glen and Peter Herbert at Gravetye Manor, was facilitated by his father's decision to sell his bank, which provided both capital and a sense of freedom.

Hart settled on Hambleton Hall, which he bought for £110,000 ($175,000) – big country houses in the pre-Thatcher era were, as he described them, 'a drug on the market' – and renovated it for £440,000 ($690,000). Although these sums are ludicrously small by today's stand-ards, Hart leaned forward to emphasize one particular point. 'The sums were still quite scary then, but I was adequately funded from day one and that is very, very important.' Hambleton Hall is, and always has been under the Harts, an extremely plush, comfortable and quintessentially English hotel. The drawing room looks out on to a well-tended garden, the furniture throughout is extremely solid, and whenever you need something a member of staff is invariably close at hand. It is as close as one can get to staying in Downton Abbey.

Sam and Eddie were then aged eight and six, so the move to hotel life constitutes some of their earliest memories. 'I can still remember Nick Gill, Hambleton's first chef, living with us,' Sam recalled, 'and Angie, then father's secretary, working out of my parents' bedroom.' For Eddie, the initial memories were more hedonistic. 'I'm standing in the hotel's kitchen doorway with a glass of orange juice and a piece of shortbread,' he explained with an almost childlike grin on his face. Growing up as the sons of an hotelier was, not surprisingly, to influence Sam and Eddie, although their younger brother James has become a successful derivatives trader and a good customer. Tim explained, however, that he was adamant from the outset that they would not fall into one of the major traps of the business and 'eat off the restaurant'. Their home was not far from the hotel and Steffi, Tim's wife, used to entertain a lot there rather than at the hotel. 'Steffi grew up in Majorca and her instinct was always to involve the boys, to get them to take our guests' coats and to hang them up, to stir the pots and even to taste the food. The boys could see that I was enjoying myself and I wasn't travelling too much. They didn't see the obvious downside of what can be a very demanding profession, where you are on show to your customers twenty-four hours a day, seven days a week and a lot of the bonhomie revolves around the drinks cupboard.'

These childhood experiences had two long-term effects, as Eddie recalled. The first was that there was almost a competition between his parents as to who – their father at the hotel or their mother at home – could provide the better table, the more attractive garden or the more comfortable bed for their guests with the fluffier towel. Restaurateurs are always in competition, either with themselves, their partners or their neighbours, so this was a very early introduction into this aspect of the business. The second was that, if it is at all possible, holding onto a talented chef is always a recipe for success. Hambleton Hall has had only three different head chefs in its thirty-two years, with Aaron Patterson in charge of the kitchens for the last twenty. Sam and Eddie met French chef Jean-Philippe Patruno before they opened Fino in 2003 and they worked together for a long time on their various Spanish and British menus. Growing up so close to a hotel and good food did rub off on the boys, who recalled, aged fourteen and twelve, giving their first three-course dinner party for friends, complete with silverware, decorated tables and a *placement* (seating plan). They were then to go in very different directions before, at Eddie's suggestion, deciding to do something together.

Sam, with a degree in Spanish, decided he wanted nothing more to do with restaurants and headed off with Robin, his wife, to Mexico City to work for a foreign exchange dealer. The tedium of the job combined with the arrival of a friend lured them into opening Colmillo, a nightclub that struggled at first but then, on the back of the popularity of 'Cool Britannia' at that time, was soon turning over £1 million ($1.5 million) and had queues down the street at 2.00 a.m. Despite enjoying the good life, Sam quickly became aware of the downsides: life has to be lived from midnight to 7.00 a.m. and such a business is precarious, occasionally at the inexplicable whim of the police, who did in fact close it down twice.

Eddie left school after his A-levels – 'I'd had enough of failing,' he quipped – and allowed his father to put him through a three-year 'university of life course'. This began with a year on the lowest rung at Hambleton Hall, living in, paid £500 ($780) per month, and determined, he added, to prove himself. This was followed by a year in Madrid and a year in London with a design company. Most importantly, it was devoid of any pressure. 'No one expected me to go into the business, so I could just learn, particularly how to mix the perfect Martini,' he added.

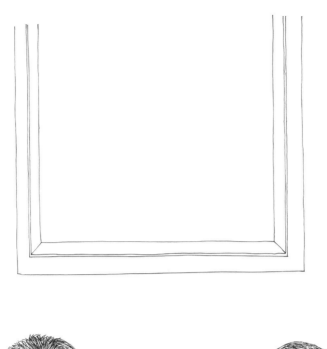

Sam and Robin, meanwhile, moved to Barcelona with the idea of running another nightclub, but promptly realized how much they enjoyed the sunshine. And here, like so many others, Sam was seduced by the restaurant Cal Pep. Close to the city's port, Cal Pep has had an extraordinary impact on chefs and restaurateurs all over the world, and for the past twenty years has been Barcelona's most iconic tapas bar and restaurant, its influence spreading in several different directions. Its straightforward layout, with the customers and cooks in close proximity across a long counter, has inspired restaurateurs to turn similarly small but compact spaces into buzzing places to eat, as the Harts have done with Barrafina. By not taking reservations, it has helped to spread this sense of informality, which has been a growing factor in restaurants over the past decade, particularly as customers have come to appreciate that if the food is as fresh and good as this, it is worth waiting for. The complete absence of pretension means that any customer can simply enjoy the key aspects of any restaurant: its food and wine. Most importantly perhaps, Cal Pep's reliance on a continually changing range of ingredients has meant that its menus are a source of great delight. 'Why can't there be a Cal Pep in London?' was Sam's question to himself.

It was just at this stage that Eddie called, leading Sam and Robin to return to the UK and to deliberate as to whether their future lay running tapas bars in London or a country pub. They even went as far as putting in an offer on one close to Colston Bassett, Nottinghamshire, before Robin put her foot down. 'She's a townie,' Sam explained, 'and said we would all go stir crazy in the country.' So London it was to be. Although Sam had already begun to modify his version of Cal Pep London – most significantly in that there would have to be tables and it would have to take reservations – he was not prepared for the complete disinterest the restaurant agents, who make their living letting licensed premises, had in them. In 2000 the restaurant market was very strong, Sam explained, they had no track record and therefore no covenant for a potential landlord. 'It wasn't a question of the agents not returning our calls – they wouldn't even take them. In almost eighteen months we never saw a single site.'

The Harts were to be the unlikely beneficiaries of 9/11. Demand for new restaurant sites promptly evaporated and they were shown a basement site off busy Charlotte Street, which, although it was the opposite of what they wanted in many respects, was nevertheless an impressive space with high ceilings, the very opposite of so many London

restaurant sites that could squeeze forty covers into a former town house with the kitchen in the basement. Here the bar could accommodate twenty-five, the restaurant ninety and a further ten at a counter opposite the kitchen. Eddie came up with the initial design, but the financing was more tortuous. Each brother had inherited £150,000 ($235,000), which they put into the building, with the balance of £800,000 ($1.25 million) coming from HSBC bank on the back of the surety of their house. To make life particularly difficult for themselves, they chose to open Fino on 3 March 2003, the first day of the Iraq war.

This was not their only self-inflicted obstacle. Their goal was to recreate a typical Spanish menu from which, rather than following a traditional sequence of first courses, main courses and desserts, customers would order a range of different dishes that would be served when they were ready. This was so novel in the UK at the time that Quadranet, the company that runs Fino's IT system, had to change all the buttons on the tills they had supplied to convey the orders to the kitchen. Nightmares inevitably ensued, and almost ten years later Sam can still recall one review that pointed out that their pudding was served before a squid dish and that the squid re-appeared after the dessert. He also remembered one service when there were six reviewers in the restaurant simultaneously, all at different tables. The burgeoning interest in new-wave Spanish cooking, which was soon to receive such a boost with the emergence of Ferran Adrià at elBulli, had brought in the reviewers, several of whom had first-hand experience of the Hart way with hospitality at Hambleton Hall. By the end of its third week, Fino was packed, taking over £40,000 ($63,000) per week, and the Harts were very short of sleep.

They felt encouraged, however, to return to their original idea of a Cal Pep in London. Sam was quick to admit that London in 2003 was simply not ready for what such an iconoclastic opening would have involved, and how relieved they were that a combination of timing and property availability had led them to open first Fino, the more formal Spanish restaurant, and then Barrafina, which would really take London by storm. Barrafina occupies sixty-five square metres (700 square feet) on Frith Street, Soho, which is unquestionably in the ideal location for a bustling tapas bar-restaurant. The numerous nearby media companies keep it busy at lunchtime, its proximity to so many theatres ensures a full house early evening and its culinary reputation, and the opportunity to watch the chefs close up, brings in the diners at night. Barrafina takes no reservations, does not even have a telephone and, Sam added with pride, 'nobody has ever jumped the queue'. Despite these apparent handicaps, the twenty-three seats around the counter manage to accommodate 1,400 customers a week with an average spend of around £45 ($70). Such figures would make any restaurateur, and any finance director, very happy indeed.

The theatre and ergonomics of Cal Pep, which the Harts have so successfully transplanted to Barrafina, are also great discipline for the cooks, Sam added, whose roles now incorporate taking the orders, turning around, cooking, then serving, which is far more than most are accustomed to. And the occasional piece of unexpected theatre, as I discovered when sitting at the counter one lunchtime, when a very heated exchange took place in Spanish between a cook and a waiter because the latter had allowed two customers in slightly after 2.30 p.m., which the former believed was the time for last orders. This salutary experience underlined the fact that, whatever the design, the perennial conflict between the kitchen and the front-of-house staff is every restaurateur's principal management challenge.

Barrafina, Sam and Eddie readily acknowledge, would not have been the success it has if they had not listened to Andy Martin, their designer. Their initial proposal had been to widen the working area for the chefs to make life easier for them but that, they now realize, would have reduced the customers' view. It was Martin, too, who insisted that the gap between the back of the stools where customers are eating and the queue of those waiting had to be as narrow as it is so that, as Eddie explained, 'you feel the hot breath of the hungry customers on your neck'. Their second site has followed the same principles, but comes with a basement essential for storage.

The success of Barrafina, far beyond the brothers' expectations, is also due to the optimal kitchen-design principles, which are entirely to do with flow: from the customers walking in, to the manner in which the orders are taken, then transmitted to the kitchen, and finally to the food delivered to the customer. The counter acts almost as a sandbank between the flow of customers on one side and the cooks on the other. The design here is at its most effective because the waiters stand next to the chefs. Once they have taken the order they have to travel no distance at all, not even as far as a computer terminal. They can simply turn and pass it to the chef in charge. There is no distance to travel, no space for any misunderstanding between customer, waiter and chef.

There is no correlation between the size of a kitchen and the quality of the food it produces – big kitchens are required for banqueting, for example, or in hotels with a wide range of menus – but the best kitchen layout ensures that a cook has to take no more than one step in any direction to reach everything they need. Small can be beautiful, and most effective.

In 2007 Sam and Eddie took a decision that appeared right at the time, but in retrospect was for all the wrong reasons: they took over Quo Vadis, a long-established Soho restaurant, which is like a rabbit warren constructed out of four different townhouses and spread over four floors, with the kitchens in the basement. Although Quo Vadis has been a stalwart for decades, its rather formal frontage and Latin name have made it appear more formal from the outside than it actually is inside. They did it, Eddie confessed, the wrong way round. They fell in love with the building, its charm and its history, took over the lease and then decided what to do with it. They made a mistake as experienced restaurateurs that they had never made before, even when they were starting out. 'One must always have the idea for the restaurant first, then find the most suitable building, not the other way round as we did here.'

Their style and presence did ensure that Quo Vadis got off to a flying start – what they referred to as 'several monster trading days' – but the frequency of these has declined since the financial crash of 2008. While Quo Vadis's rent is still below the ten per cent of monthly sales that is the trading norm, several other factors have hindered its financial performance. Firstly, because it is spread over so many floors, labour costs are harder to control: to serve 150 customers at Fino on one floor they need one runner, but here they require three each night. Secondly, by concentrating on simple but good-quality British ingredients, the food costs are less malleable than with Spanish dishes, as the dishes tend to be centred around a single piece of protein. On top of this, the local competition has grown almost daily. Eddie reckoned that in the past two years 1,200 extra covers have emerged within a five-minute walk. Quo Vadis was almost too posh for Soho, and may have prospered more readily on the other side of Regent Street in Mayfair.

During the second half of 2011 Sam and Eddie realized they had to take drastic action to turn round Quo Vadis's fortunes and began complex negotiations to lure the highly talented and demonstrative chef, Jeremy Lee, from behind the stoves at the Blue Print Café by Tower Bridge, where he had been for sixteen years, to become their chef and partner in the business. Although they had been spotted together on several occasions by journalists, including during one Eurostar trip to Paris, they managed to pull this off unsuspected, and made the surprise announcement of Lee's arrival just before closing for ten days over the New Year period. When they reopened in 2012, the interior of the restaurant was brighter and fresher, the menus had been cleverly redesigned to convey a sense of style and wit in keeping with Soho, Lee's ingenuity with fresh seasonal ingredients was there for all to see, and there was a strong, and relatively unusual, link between the management and the peripatetic Lee. The Harts also managed to pull off the equally difficult task of parting on good terms with their former chef.

Collectively, the Harts employ over 300 people: 120 in London, with the balance in the hotels at Hambleton Hall, Nottingham and a bakery in Exton, a small village outside Hambleton, which also supplies many local restaurants and is, family aside, Tim's pride and joy. They remain extremely comfortable in each other's presence and only interrupt one another politely. Both Tim and Sam acknowledge that Eddie is the natural restaurateur amongst them, the one they all defer to on questions such as the optimal distance between tables and the height of the salt and pepper pots. Eddie's response to this compliment was to say modestly, 'That's probably because I never like going to bed', another prerequisite for a successful restaurateur.

The bread at the Hart's four London restaurants is excellent. It is baked at Quo Vadis every morning, and its origins lie in a mother yeast that came down from their father's bakery, carefully cradled in his lap on the train. It is a striking metaphor for one of Britain's few restaurant dynasties.

Catching your chef

The relationship between the chef and the restaurateur is the cornerstone of any successful restaurant, but there is no blueprint and no formula for bringing the most sympathetic and talented individuals together. It is often the consequence of chance, chemistry or even love. The then-young Marie-Pierre Lambert fell in love with Michel Troisgros at catering college before moving to Roanne and taking over his family's restaurant. Joe Bastianich met chef Mario Batali while they were working on either side of the swing door at a big awards dinner in New York. Ferran Adrià came to work for just one summer at elBulli, was taken on and his subsequent partnership with Juli Soler has changed the way we look at food. In my case at L'Escargot, Martin Lam came to work some extra shifts on top of his full-time job, we hit it off and, happily, he stayed.

Restaurateurs can also work with the numerous executive search and recruitment companies to find cooks and head chefs. But while CVs and interviews can help fill the intermediate rungs, there is a perennial challenge in filling the highest position. Even if the candidate looks ideal on paper, how is the restaurateur going to put him or her through the ultimate test of eating his or her food? This is an ongoing problem because restaurateurs and chefs do fall out and chefs do move on, often to open their own restaurants. It is an unusual challenge, because while so much information about the restaurant business is widely available, this is one aspect of the business that has to be conducted in the utmost secrecy.

The chef in question will almost certainly be cooking elsewhere, possibly even for a competitor, and may well not have told his or her current boss that he or she is thinking of leaving. If the chef is good, his or her current employer is unlikely to let him or her go without a counter-offer and, if that fails, will almost certainly want to hold on to him or her for as long as his contract permits, which may, frustratingly, be after the new restaurant's proposed opening. The ideal process is to arrange for the chef to conduct a tasting of a range of dishes he or she feels proud of and believes will be suitable for the new restaurant. These take place regularly in any established restaurant whenever seasonal changes to the menu are due or for special events and dinners, and they often take place in the afternoon between the lunch and dinner services. If the proposed new kitchen is still home to a team of builders and the chef is employed elsewhere, then alternative locations will have to be sought.

A domestic kitchen is often the answer. Mark Sainsbury put his own kitchen at the disposal of chef Bruno Loubet to put him through his paces before they opened the original Bistrot Bruno Loubet in Clerkenwell. When I was consulting for The Roundhouse in Camden Town I made our kitchen available for chefs Josh Katz and Eran Tibi to serve a whole range of starters, main courses and desserts. I can add from personal experience that although this is a most exciting experience, professional chefs are used to having kitchen porters at their disposal and there is quite a lot of mess by the end!

For Fino and Quo Vadis, Sam and Eddie Hart twice lured away chefs from other restaurants, learning in the process an invaluable lesson about how best to do it. At the end of 2011 they announced that Jeremy Lee, who had been the chef and figurehead of the Blueprint Café by Tower Bridge for fifteen years, was to take over the stoves of Quo Vadis. Having been open for a couple of years, they had come to realize that to stand up to the intense competition in Soho their restaurant needed a chef with a wide range of skills: a strong personality, an ability to write seasonal and pithy menus, and someone who would appreciate the opportunity they were prepared to offer of a small shareholding in the business. That Lee also has a very good sense of humour, can hold his own in the bar and appears regularly in the media were all extra attractions.

Before they opened Fino the Harts had hired a French chef, Jean-Philippe Patruno, who was then cooking in another central London restaurant. The tasting was set for 2.30 p.m. and Eddie recalled what happened just before. Sam and he set off and then realized they were absolutely starving, so they stopped for a quick sandwich en route. The tasting went very well, and much better because they weren't hungry. 'You must never start a tasting when you're really hungry because,' explained Eddie, 'if you do, then everything tastes great – and that's always a mistake when you want to put a chef to the test.'

MAGUY LE COZE

Classic French

At le Bernardin

From Paris to New York

Maguy Le Coze has been the smiling, authoritative and glamorous restaurateur behind the success of the celebrated fish restaurant Le Bernardin since it first opened in Paris in 1972, alongside her late brother Gilbert, who was then in the kitchen. Today Le Bernardin holds the highest accolades: three Michelin stars, four stars from the *New York Times* and a reputation for being one of New York's most renowned venues for a power lunch. She was the driving force behind their move to New York, where Le Bernardin opened on 28 January 1986 on West 51st Street, and where it continues to prosper today. She handled the sale of the site of their former Paris restaurant in 1988 to the chef Guy Savoy, and she became the bedrock of the business after Gilbert's untimely death in 1994 – ably assisted ever since, she would be the first to say, by Eric Ripert, her executive chef and business partner.

These basic details give only the briefest insight into the emotional turmoil that has engulfed Le Coze's life as a restaurateur over the past four decades. After a morning spent in the lounge of the Hotel Lutetia in her beloved Paris talking about her life in restaurants on both sides of the Atlantic, Le Coze remarked that it had been almost like talking to a psychiatrist, 'but without the pain'. When she first sat down, though, pain was one of the first words Le Coze mentioned. She was very keen to recall the past forty years of her life, because she wanted to record the effort that it has taken for her to arrive where she is now.

For anyone embarking on a career as a restaurateur and wanting to reach the very top it is, according to her, a very, very long journey: 'Nothing comes overnight.' Yet despite the considerable distance she has travelled, Le Coze still remains firmly connected to the family hotel she grew up in, the Hôtel de Rhuys in Port-Navalo on the southern coast of Brittany, north-west France, half of which is her holiday home today. Here she first came into close contact with the sea, the leitmotif of Le Bernardin, where her grandfather (whose painting hangs prominently above the bar) was once a fisherman. The name Le Bernardin originates in part from a song, 'Les Moines de Saint-Bernardin', that her father used to sing to her and her brother when they were children.

Her life in the family hotel in the early 1950s was very different from the luxurious surroundings of Le Bernardin today. It was extremely hard, Le Coze recalled. The plumbing was so antiquated that the local firemen had to come three times a week to fill the water tanks so that the guests could have water in their bedrooms. From the time they were thirteen,

Gilbert was in the kitchen with his father, while Maguy (which is the Breton version of the name Margaret) worked at the reception desk and waited at tables with her mother. 'Our fun in those days was preparing the vegetables,' she remembered. As our tea arrived, she recalled an incident that shocked her parents. 'We went back to school after the holidays when we had been working in the hotel, and we were so exhausted we started falling asleep in class. The headmaster sent a note home to find out who had been supervising us and it was only then that my parents really appreciated quite how hard they had been working us.' These tough years allowed Gilbert and Maguy to reach two conclusions from which they would never deviate. The first was that they would escape from Brittany to the lights of Paris as soon as Maguy turned eighteen, and the second was that they would always work together. After a less-than-successful attempt at her baccalaureate (the French equivalent of A-levels or a high-school diploma), Maguy worked as a receptionist in a Paris hotel, although she would still go back to work in the family hotel during her summer holidays.

In 1972 Gilbert and Maguy opened their first restaurant, the original Le Bernardin on the Quai de la Tournelle, close to the banks of the River Seine in Paris. Backed by their own savings and contributions from friends, an uncle, their parents and the bank, they converted a former shop inexpensively into a restaurant that could seat twenty-five, and in which there would be room for Gilbert alone in the kitchen and Maguy and one waiter in the restaurant. The nearby abbey of the Bernardine monks (then in ruins but now restored) resonated with both of them because of their father's song, and led to the selection of the name Le Bernardin. The fact that they chose something other than their own name for the restaurant, in contrast with the practice of many chefs opening their own restaurants today, shows how much times have changed in chefs' favour. 'In those days, no chef would dream of opening under their own name, it just wasn't the done thing. Chefs were in their kitchen,' Le Coze explained. The restaurant where Michel Guérard was cooking was called Le Pot au Feu; Alain Senderens named his restaurant Archestrate; Paul Bocuse's name was not attached to his restaurant at the beginning; and even a little later, Joël Robuchon's restaurant in Paris was called Jamin.

It was certainly an exciting era in which to be running a restaurant in the heart of Paris, partly because they were not beholden to anyone or bound by any preconceptions. The main attraction was the enormous *plateau de fruits de mer*, a large tray of the very freshest seafood and shellfish

– far bigger than anything being served today by the same name – which allowed Gilbert to show off all he had learned from his father. The food was very simple, very plain, with the focus entirely on the fish. At the same time, the growing influence of *nouvelle cuisine*, then sweeping through French kitchens and removing as it did so the heavier elements of the cooking style handed down by the godfather of French cuisine, Auguste Escoffier, 100 years earlier, made experimentation much easier. Gilbert was keen to expand on the limited culinary repertoire he had inherited, their customers were receptive to new dishes, and business was very good, particularly in an era before credit cards were ubiquitous, when everybody paid in cash.

Suppliers were paid in cash too, brother and sister were living their dream, and their customers were leaving happy – until one morning, when, upon returning from the fish market, they discovered that Le Bernardin had been closed down. 'There was a sign in the window,' Le Coze recalled, 'offering ten tables and twenty-five chairs for sale, a coffee machine and all the kitchen equipment. It was our entire stock. There was a number underneath for any party interested in buying these items. I rang it straight away and a civil servant came round to my flat, where he explained quite how much tax and social security we owed. I had no idea of how to run a business, I was just too busy looking after my customers.' Happily, she was able to charm him, and he allowed the business to continue on the condition that they hire a financial controller. The arrears were quickly settled and Le Bernardin was soon successful and profitable. In 1976 it received its first Michelin star, in 1981 it moved to a much larger site in the rue Troyon, and in 1982 it received its second Michelin star.

This episode, which Le Coze recalled with some anxiety, is fascinating for two reasons. The first is a mistake that is commonly made (which I know because I did the same in my own restaurant) – being so busy at the outset chasing business and looking after your new customers that you turn a blind eye to the fundamental arithmetic of the restaurant business. The gross margins on the food and wine sales will inevitably get better as the business develops, but they do have to be fairly accurate from the beginning, or otherwise, as Le Coze put it, 'our huge popularity only meant bigger losses'. One of the financial controller's first moves was to increase their wine prices so that they would now make the standard seventy per cent gross profit on every bottle they served, rather than the fifty-five per cent she had settled for.

The second, and more unusual, consequence of this episode, and one that has affected many more restaurant-goers, is what would have happened

if Le Bernardin had been forcibly closed down. Certainly, the course of the Le Cozes' careers would have been very different, but so too would the history of French cooking in the US, and New York in particular. In the early 1980s the Le Cozes had moved their restaurant to a considerably larger and plusher location near the Champs-Élysées where, for the first time, it began to attract a more international clientèle. This was Maguy's initial encounter with Americans as customers; they were distinctive, she recalled, not just because of their accents, but also because of their habit, then quite unusual, of making their reservations one month ahead, before they set off on their European tour. James Beard, the celebrated American food writer, and Johnny Apple, a leading *New York Times* journalist and renowned gourmand, came to eat at Le Bernardin and praised it, and it was then that the idea of opening in New York began to germinate in Le Coze's mind.

Gilbert was completely opposed to such a move, a stand reinforced by a flying visit to New York in 1983, where he found an absence of top-quality fresh fish, no more than a handful of fresh herbs to cook with and iceberg as the only widely available lettuce. On top of this, he spoke not a word of English. Maguy, equally determined, only saw the absence of any other high-level fish restaurants as a major attraction – the only competition , she recalled, were one or two Greek restaurants serving grilled fresh fish with a baked potato and spinach – and she grew increasingly determined. 'I kept telling Gilbert that there are two of us, one for Paris, the other for New York. I even called him a coward,' she smiled ruefully. The advantage of being in the restaurant allowed Le Coze to talk the idea over with her customers – she tried a few times to get then to back the idea, but never succeeded – and to collect business cards for the time when her New York restaurant would eventually came to fruition. 'I was sure I would succeed,' she added, somewhat unnecessarily.

She persevered, with no idea that her dream would be realized so swiftly. In 1985 a friend introduced her to Ben Holloway, the US chairman of Equitable Life, who was responsible for the development of the brand-new Equitable Centre and was looking for three restaurants, one French, one American and one Italian, to animate the ground floor. The deal was swiftly concluded over a bottle of Dom Pérignon in his flat overlooking the Eiffel Tower. While there were several highly skilled French chefs working in the US at the time, most notably Pierre Franey, Jean-Louis Palladin and André Soltner, Le Bernardin was to be one of the very first transatlantic restaurant transplants. Le Coze was excited but overawed by her new home.

Le Bernardin New York occupies a third of a block – it is 1,110 square metres (12,000 square feet) in total, split equally between the ground floor and basement – and they had no trained staff other than themselves. Their maître d' from Paris was flown over with his wife and child and promptly turned the restaurant into a classroom in which to teach prospective waiters, while Gilbert tried to understand the ins and outs of the New York fish market. Before they opened, Gilbert was having little success at buying fresh fish of the quality he wanted. He had hired a German sous chef who spoke English, but he was at a loss as to the best suppliers. Gilbert turned to a fellow Frenchman, Christian Millau (of the famous restaurant guidebook, Gault Millau), for advice, and he in turn put him in touch with his good friend, Jerome Brody, the owner of the famous Oyster Bar at Grand Central Station. Brody offered to lend Gilbert his fish buyer for two hours at the Fulton Fish Market in the Bronx, and that's what he did. Early one morning the buyer spent two hours introducing Gilbert to several suppliers. After that, Gilbert was on his own. Their attempts to do things as slowly and professionally as possible were undermined by an enthusiastic article Franey wrote even before the restaurant had opened entitled, 'The Best Kitchen in the World', which had enthusiastic customers knocking on the windows. 'I was scared,' Le Coze admitted, but her New York restaurant was immediately successful and gave her no cause for concern. This lay back in their Paris restaurant and once again threatened to close the business.

She started shaking her head. 'We hadn't been to Paris for eight months, we were so preoccupied with New York, and then one day I got a call from a fellow restaurateur telling me that a cheque drawn on Le Bernardin had bounced. I flew back that night, walked into my office and the bookkeeper looked at me as though he had seen a ghost. I dropped my suitcase off at my apartment, went back to the office and he had vanished.' They quickly realized that he had stolen a great deal of money from the business. At the top-secret meeting the best French restaurateurs and chefs have at Michelin HQ every year, in which they discuss possible changes to the guide, she was relieved to discover that the restaurant's culinary reputation had not suffered. However, while they had 'their heads in New York' as she described it, their business in Paris certainly had suffered and so too had their standing in the French press, which was now more interested in the city's recent openings. They decided to sell, and Le Coze faced a new obstacle with her brother: he was now so happy in New York that he did not want to come back, even to cook the restaurant's farewell dinner.

At this point, Le Coze's voice seemed to falter. It had been quite a step, both financially and emotionally, to leave the first restaurant, the city they had been so happy in, their family and their country. Although the New York restaurant was immediately successful, it took an equally immediate toll. Gilbert lost fifteen kilos in weight, she recalled, as he combined his 5.00 a.m. visit to the fish market with lunch and the dinner services at the stoves (he was eventually to learn his English from watching TV during his afternoons off). For them both, the excitement of being in New York was almost enough, she recalled, and the level of success the restaurant achieved made her feel good and pushed the memories of her French life to one side. The size of the new Le Bernardin made her appreciate quite how much she still had to learn as a restaurateur, particularly in how, what and when to delegate to others. She knows how lucky she has been to have had the opportunity to start a new life, to be rejuvenated. Professionally, though, the most exciting aspect of all has been the opportunity to teach Americans how to enjoy fish and shellfish. They were serving raw fish long before Nobu and the other sushi chefs were doing so. 'It's part of the Breton repertoire, but nobody would try it. I used to have to say to customers, "Order it, and if you don't like it I will replace it with another dish free of charge." There were so many good raw dishes in his repertoire, and not just oysters. One dish of two sea urchins, one raw, the other barely cooked with warm butter was just fantastic; so too was another of scallops with truffles, and a tuna carpaccio with chives and olive oil.' Gradually, Le Coze managed to convert her customers to taste and then to enjoy these dishes, but it wasn't easy.

It was the originally reluctant Gilbert who decided they should open two other restaurants in Atlanta and Miami – 'we haven't come all this way to open just one', she recalled him saying – but in 1994, disaster struck. While working out, Gilbert suffered a massive heart attack and died aged forty-nine. This had been the episode I was least looking forward to discussing, but Le Coze sighed and ploughed on. 'Nobody expected Le Bernardin to survive, except me.' She knew she was lucky that Gilbert had taken on Eric Ripert, who had trained with Robuchon and Palladin, and that he had been handing over more and more to him, because he had already come to the conclusion that he could not evolve professionally any longer after thirty-six years in the kitchen. They needed new ideas and new inspiration, and Ripert had always had these. 'I took a month off, put some colour in my cheeks and said to myself, "the show must go on".'

And so it has, with Ripert, her second chef and business partner by her side, for the past eighteen years. The foundation for this longevity is simple. They don't always agree, but their guiding rule is that if one partner disagrees, and it doesn't matter what it is – a dish in a tasting, a charity that asks for support, or anything else – then they simply don't do it. They represent Le Bernardin together: 'we're the soul of the restaurant.' As well as modernizing many of Le Bernardin's dishes, Ripert has been instrumental in the restaurant's continued success through his books, television appearances and social media, a vital aspect of the business that Le Coze chooses to ignore. It was this approach to decision making that finally persuaded Le Coze not to retire as she had planned to do with her fortieth anniversary as a restaurateur approaching. Instead, they would jointly supervise a major redesign of the restaurant and sign a new lease for the next fifteen years with Equitable Life – now, ironically, part of the French company AXA. 'Eric came to see me and said, "why do you want to retire? We're still number one, and we can reorganize the management if you want to work less."' So she came back to Paris, renegotiated the lease on the New York restaurant and then went through the beauty parade of half a dozen leading restaurant designers and architects before they decided on Bentel & Bentel. It took eleven months from start to finish, but she is now confident it was the right thing to have done.

The main dining room, always renowned for its excellent acoustics and the generous space between tables that have made Le Bernardin such a popular venue for business lunches, is much warmer and slightly smaller, while the lounge area is bigger to accommodate those who want a quick and less expensive lunch. The portrait of her grandfather in his fishing outfit still looks very much at home. The biggest change has been the installation of a painting of a tumultuous sea that stretches right across the far wall. Le Coze and Ripert were tipped off about the seascapes of artist Ran Ortner just as the design was being finalized, and were greatly relieved to discover that this particular painting was precisely the same width as the wall. It seems to tie the new Le Bernardin to the kind of seascape that Le Coze would have seen off the Brittany coast as a child.

Le Coze seems most grateful to have enjoyed the various different stages of her career as a restaurateur, despite how hard some of them have been. They have included getting to know her customers in Paris, facing up to the much bigger challenges on the larger New York canvas, and now, as she grows increasingly weary of spending time in the restaurant, of the fascination of running the business side of a successful restaurant. Most significantly and most satisfyingly of all, she is the only female restaurateur to have run a restaurant at this level for so many years. 'That gives me a great deal of pride.' When she first arrived in New York she decided right from the start to keep a low-key approach. 'In those days many New Yorkers thought the French were very arrogant. Gilbert and I were here not just representing Le Bernardin, but also French cuisine, so we had to do our utmost to break down this prejudice. That was very, very important to me.' This is an approach that used to be the norm: to see and speak to the customers, but never to interrupt too much, and she carries on much like that today. Finally, she wanted to emphasize how tough a restaurateur's life can be. 'It's very worthwhile, but every young person must think twice before embarking on it as a career.' With that, this remarkable restaurateur headed off to spend a few days back in her native Brittany.

The importance
of a name

Gilbert and Maguy Le Coze may have been young and naive when they first opened for business forty years ago, but their restaurant began life with one great advantage: its unforgettable name, Le Bernardin. It is a name that meets all the criteria any restaurateur could want. It is short, easy to pronounce in either French or English, has an intriguing air to it, and is rooted in something more than just a restaurant (the nearby monastic order), as well as having the personal overtone of the connection to a song their father sang to them as children. As a result, this name has worked successfully on both sides of the Atlantic, a phenomenon that does not always apply to French names.

In two respects, in fact, the name Le Bernardin is even more fashionable today than it was to begin with. Names incorporating the definite article, such as The Modern in New York or The Wolseley in London, have become increasingly common, after a couple of decades during which this style has been neglected. Also, over the past decade or so the use of the word 'restaurant' in the title has tended to disappear, as it tends to convey excessive expense.

Restaurateurs spend a great deal of time thinking about the names for the businesses in which they intend to devote so much time and energy. The restaurant I took over had been called L'Escargot Bienvenu since it first opened in 1927, and I knew I had to change it. It was too much of a mouthful – 'the welcome snail' meant nothing to me and, I imagined, would mean even less to my customers. I wanted something that would convey the fact that this long-established restaurant was now under new and much younger management. A great deal of thought was put into lists of possible names, all of which were unsatisfactory. Then, as so often happens, my mother came good. I had gone home for dinner on Friday night, during which she suddenly said, 'Why don't you just shorten it to L'Escargot?' It took a few months for the brilliance of her suggestion to become apparent. Not only was this word much shorter and easier to pronounce, but I also realized that by reopening a long-established restaurant I could tap into an enormous well of good will that still existed in London for L'Escargot Bienvenu.

Equally important was the fact that the snail symbol was a striking motif for my designer, Tom Brent, to make a feature of. Not only on the carpets, but also on the bills, the match boxes (no longer an issue for restaurateurs, but I do recall having to order 10,000 at a time since they were manufactured in Japan), the business cards and even on the labels of our bottles of house Champagne and red and white wines.

The importance of my mother's advice only really struck home once we opened for business, though. L'Escargot was short, easy to pronounce, even for anyone without any knowledge of French, and followed a rule that I have since learned is incredibly important for anyone answering the phone. The name does not sound ridiculous or make the person answering the phone feel self-conscious. It should be snappy, relatively easy to remember, distinctive and, of course, not used by anyone else.

Many of the restaurateurs in this book have managed to find such names. The words Blue Smoke definitely convey barbecue; Eataly could only be about one particular country's food and wine; the capital letter 'M' has proved the unmissable, striking and successful logo for restaurants in Hong Kong, Shanghai and Beijing; Nobu is the equally memorable abbreviation of the chef's name as well as, subsequently, coming to represent a country's style of cooking; St John is a street with historic associations with nearby Smithfield Market, renowned for its meat; while Zuni, originally an Amerindian tribe, is today a corner building into which the bright California sun always seems to shine.

The other increasingly important factor for the most successful names is that they stand alone and don't need the addition of words such as bar, café or restaurant to explain what they are. This is partly because in order to manage increasingly high fixed costs, notably rents and business rates, these different guises are being absorbed within the same building, as breakfast gives way to a café, on either side of lunch, then it becomes a bar, and finally a place for dinner. It is also because today's customers want so much more from their favourite restaurants: a place to rest, to work and play, as well as to eat and drink well, and to be recognized and made welcome.

One short, easy-to-remember name that will do all this is not easy to find. But it is certainly worth listening to what your mother has to say, as well as, perhaps, trying to recall some of the songs your father sang to you as a child.

DES McDONALD

AFFORDABLE, CONTEMPORARY LUXURY

Des McDonald has spent thirty-seven of his forty-seven years working in kitchens or in the restaurant business, starting as a child of ten growing up in Northern Ireland, where his grandfather and father combined their role as farmers with a love of cooking and baking. McDonald washed up the pots and pans, 'some of which were bigger than me. It was fun.' Since then, McDonald has gone on to fill more roles in the kitchen and in restaurant management than almost anyone else in this book. His rise to the illustrious heights of being the CEO of the Caprice Holdings Group, which ran over thirty restaurants from the US to the Middle East, coincided with a time in London when wealthy outside investors began to take an interest in restaurants, as much for their prestige and publicity value as for their financial rate of return. His departure from that company in January 2012, after seven highly successful years alongside Richard Caring, its owner and chairman, reveals quite how precarious such working relationships can be when the company is owned by one wealthy individual.

At our first meeting one sunny morning at Scott's restaurant (illustrated page 155) on Mount Street in London's Mayfair, the first restaurant in the Caring-McDonald era, McDonald had looked every inch the CEO. He is tall and well built from years of rugby and skiing. In his elegantly cut dark suit and crisp white shirt, he had looked that day no different from one of the many hedge-fund managers who make up that restaurant's clientèle as he sat at a corner table sipping an espresso, playing with his smartphone and waiting for me. But when I went back to talk to him again after his circumstances had changed, his physical appearance seemed to mirror accurately the change in his situation. When we met on the first floor of the Arts Club, the private members club that opened, also in Mayfair, in late 2011, McDonald looked more like the restaurant entrepreneur he is determined to become. His hair was longer and slightly unkempt, his normally trim beard seemed a little longer, and he was wearing jeans. He was working on his tablet computer, and on the table in front of him were two smartphones, a pen and a notebook. 'Welcome to my new office,' he said with a smile. 'Although I'm spending so much time here it might as well be my home.'

Just then one of his phones rang and I listened to McDonald explaining that he could not make time to meet the caller that day. He had back-to-back meetings all afternoon with potential investors in what was to be his own restaurant business, followed by early evening drinks with someone else, then a business dinner. I got the distinct impression from overhearing this conversation that I would need to be swift and direct with my questions. This approach I knew would suit McDonald. In the fifteen years I have known him, our meeting at Scott's, which lasted over an hour, had been by far the longest I had ever managed. McDonald does not use two words when one will do, even in his emails, although he smiles readily and he has softened and mellowed with age and success. One colleague, who has worked alongside him for many years, confided, 'But you should see Des on the dance floor!' That spectacle has, however, so far eluded me.

McDonald's early apprenticeship as a washer-up kindled not only an interest in cooking, but also the awareness that such work could generate much-needed pocket money, particularly during half term. A growing realization that beyond this lay a profession that could harness these talents, provide a vocation and ultimately an income saw McDonald, after the family had moved to east London (much less fashionable then than it is today, he insists), enrol as a student at the renowned Westminster Catering College. Over the following decade, McDonald climbed the greasy pole that was the hierarchical structure in the kitchens of two of London's largest hotels, before becoming head chef in a busy City restaurant. While this era was to leave McDonald with one professional trait that he believes has served him and those around him extremely well – the ability, as he described it, to recognize immediately whether young chefs 'have cooking in them or not' – he was also to experience two aspects of kitchen life that he vowed would never be repeated if he were ever in charge.

The first was what McDonald described as 'a massive drinking culture', which was even in evidence among several chefs while they were working; the second, and equally invidious, was the long-established tradition of the older chefs bullying younger members of the kitchen brigade. Until about thirty years ago, cheap alcohol played far too large a part in many kitchens as a substitute for the poor wages many cooks received, while better bottles were a common form of bribery from suppliers to head chefs to ensure they held onto the business. Then, twenty years ago, drugs became a much bigger issue, particularly among the more macho chefs intent on working hard and playing hard. It is probably difficult, if not impossible, for anyone whose interest in cooking and restaurants has developed solely on the back of smiling, friendly chefs in today's smart open kitchens to appreciate quite how different and unpleasant these aspects of kitchen culture were only a few decades ago. Every restaurateur in this book, and many more besides, has been instrumental in consigning these aspects of kitchen life to the rubbish heap of culinary history.

McDonald was presented with the opportunity to put the management principles he felt were missing in the kitchens he had worked in – of being honest and fair, of nurturing and developing talent rather than squashing it – when he became executive chef at Caprice Holdings, the prestigious restaurant group created and then run by Chris Corbin and Jeremy King. Then, after Corbin and King sold their restaurants to entrepreneur Luke Johnson, McDonald was encouraged to cross the invisible, apparently narrow but in fact vast, divide between the kitchens and their restaurants' head office. 'Although I relished the challenge at the time, I do still remember the terrible sense of isolation,' he remembered. He went overnight from being responsible for a very noisy bunch of over thirty cooks and kitchen porters, and all the daily drama that this creates, to a quiet office with just a secretary for company. 'For a few months it was a very lonely existence, the recognition that the buck stopped with me. But I know now in retrospect that once I could generate the vital sense of commonality, our team's contribution to the restaurants' ultimate success would only improve.' It was a tough transition but ultimately an enjoyable one.

Our conversation was politely interrupted at this stage by Nigel Stowe, the Arts Club's general manager. He, like many in London's restaurants, had once worked under McDonald, and while extolling the skills of his new pastry chef, he also recalled that every service he had ever worked for McDonald had always begun with the latter firing off the same question: 'How many are on the book?' This question of how many reservations there are for lunch or dinner is one that rises twice a day from deep within every restaurateur's competitive DNA. As Earl Grey tea and cakes were served, I took the opportunity to ask McDonald which, of the many openings he had been responsible for, had generated the most professional pleasure. 'Scott's,' was his immediate response. 'It was an ailing brand. The investment – over £6.5 million ($10.25) million in 2007 – was enormous and technically it was very, very risky.' Before McDonald and Caring had applied their magic touch, Scott's of Mayfair had been a venerable but decidedly tired establishment. As well as planning the re-opening of Scott's, McDonald had been able to stand by its reception desk when the customers came in on the very first lunchtime because in 2005, Johnson had sold Caprice Holdings to businessman Richard Caring.

The latter's successful career in fashion and textiles in the Far East had led him to back his hunch that popular restaurant brand names could be taken around the globe as easily as those in other consumer fields that were already enjoyed and talked about by so many. McDonald stepped up to the plate and, as Caring went on a buying spree that encompassed the late Mark Birley's private clubs (Annabel's, Harry's Bar and George in London) alongside the various branches of his Soho House group, whose younger members Nick Jones had skilfully enthused, he became the Group CEO. This was an impressive career trajectory for a baker's boy, still aged only forty-three.

While the success of Scott's from the day it opened has been an obvious source of professional satisfaction, the very first days when McDonald stood at the front desk to meet, greet and seat were much more traumatic. 'It was as painful as the description my ex-wife used to give about giving birth to our daughter,' he added with a wry smile. Over the next four years, though, the size of the restaurant group under McDonald's stewardship grew threefold, employing over 2,000 people and with a geographical spread encompassing restaurants from the Middle East to the West Coast of the US. While in certain markets they would work with local partners, such as the Jumeirah Restaurant Group in Dubai, McDonald found himself spending a lot of time seeing and rejecting potential sites.

A key platform in the ensuing and immediate success Caprice Holdings had with their new restaurants stemmed from the strong working relationship between McDonald and his designer, Martin Brudnizki. Swedish by birth and an extremely dapper dresser, Brudnizki had cut his professional teeth with David Collins, the highly regarded restaurant designer, before setting up his own practice. Scott's was to prove such a success that it would not only immediately catapult Brudnizki into the ranks of London's most sought-after designers, but also establish what was to prove a successful modus operandi for Caprice Holdings' future openings. The principles of this approach never changed, wherever the prospective restaurant site was to be, whether in London, Miami or New York. Brudnizki and McDonald would look at the building and its profile. They would consider what would work best in each particular location and, if they reached the same conclusion, they would then test their own opinions against two unchanging criteria: was what they had in mind practicable and would it, ultimately, feel comfortable? If the answers to both were positive, then they would build to last in the two most important

areas: wherever the customer may look, however fleetingly, and, because of McDonald's background, the construction of the kitchen.

These peregrinations became even more frequent once the builders had moved in. McDonald stressed that as each day of the conversion progresses, it is absolutely essential, regardless of how big the investment may be, to continue to walk through the building in the same way that the customer eventually will, and to think of all the possible consequences of the new design as it begins to take shape. Their joint priorities as they did so were always to accommodate flexibility within the building and to minimize waste. Then, with the right lighting, it suddenly becomes glamorous and, according to McDonald, the best part of being a restaurateur gets under way. With a very broad smile he added, 'Then we can finally say, come to the party and have some fun.'

Behind the bricks and mortar of these restaurants, Caprice Holdings was also creating a marketing model designed to react efficiently and swiftly to the opening of any new restaurant and to their customers' different requirements. The aim was to elevate the role of the maître d's in the restaurants from mere meeters and greeters to that of brokers, McDonald explained. Their customers wanted introductions around the world and when it came to hospitality in its many forms, they saw it as their role, and a huge commercial opportunity, to supply this to them, to make their life easier and more fun. The company has the facilities to provide everything, whether a small dinner at home or a corporate event by their outside catering company, Urban Caprice. Across London the group controls twenty-five different private dining rooms, which are often hugely profitable when they are occupied, since food and wage costs are lower for what is usually a set menu. If the dining room the customer is interested in is booked, he or she would be immediately offered an alternative. Although each restaurant manager is encouraged to build up their own database, so too are all the clubs, which are featured on a website that bears the unassuming name of www.life.uk.com. This allows the company access to a source of customers that provide an immediate return and quality check on these capital-intensive restaurants. Once all these systems were in place, McDonald continued, it was crucial that he did not micro-manage. Each maître d' and general manager had to be left to satisfy their customers and to beat the budget.

Although today the internet supplies instant verdicts on any new restaurant, these are not really what conscientious restaurateurs are looking for. What they want most of all in the first few days and weeks is a controlled number of paying customers who, in addition to feeling privileged to be among the first to walk through the new restaurant's door, will, they hope, spread their favourable opinions far and wide. Nothing is more effective than a truly personal recommendation. Emails from Caprice Holdings to its database of over 300,000 people, plus the members clubs' websites, ensured that the group's second pizza restaurant, Pizza East in Portobello, west London, complementing Pizza East in Shoreditch, opened to full houses immediately (and pizza generates very healthy margins, too, with inexpensive ingredients – flour, water and a topping – that can be prepared and cooked easily and quickly). The overall marketing goal was never to create a homogeneous product, but rather to build on the subliminal links between their customers' desires and aspirations and then connect these to all the various entertainments that restaurants, and in their case, a successful outside catering business, make possible. In all these aspects, I believe that Caprice Holdings have set a business model that other large restaurant groups around the world will follow.

I was to encounter another manifestation of what this synergy involves, and the benefit it passes on to any customer, on the company's website. In pride of place was the offer 'Have a theatre drink on us': any pre-theatre customer could get a complimentary glass of Champagne on presentation of a valid theatre ticket for that day. As so many restaurateurs cut their pre-theatre prices to the bone to entice customers in, and then hope to see any profit from this early evening trade come from drinks sales, it was a demonstration of the group's clout that it could simply give this element away.

Even with so much experience, marketing advantages and talent do not guarantee a restaurant's success. During the last two years of McDonald's custodianship, Caprice Holdings made an extraordinary success out of the Dean Street Townhouse in Soho, from a site that had been languishing for thirty years when I moved in as a restaurateur two streets away. But they also had to close Le Caprice New York, which was in what looked like an absolutely safe and lucrative new home in The Pierre Hotel on New York's Upper East Side.

The Dean Street Townhouse is a good example of the role restaurants can play in urban regeneration. Soho Estates, the landlords, invested a significant amount of money, rumoured to be in excess of £12 million ($19 million), in what must have been a highly complex renovation judging from the number of times its opening was delayed, to drag this building into the twenty-first century. Then they entered into a management contract with Caprice Holdings to run the building. While Caprice Holdings brought the relevant expertise – Brudnizki on design, McDonald on the kitchen, bar and restaurant, and Nick Jones to make the bedrooms feel comfortable despite their rather pinched size – they also very astutely made the hotel and restaurant immediately attractive and accessible. They achieved this in two different but complementary ways. The first was to ensure that from the beginning the restaurant felt like a part of the Soho streetscape – despite their previous successes, there was no guarantee that this would be the case. Secondly, although their other restaurants were close by in Mayfair and Covent Garden, those neighbourhoods are very different. Each is not only distinct in how it feels, but also in how those who work in the area select in which of the many, varied places to eat and drink. They managed this by applying the principle of 'affordable luxury' to both the restaurant and the bedrooms. While it is relatively easy to fill any bar in Soho, restaurants are much more difficult because of the intense competition, while restaurants with thirty-nine bedrooms are a most unusual combination for this part of town. They were astute in pricing the smallest bedrooms at £95 ($150) per night initially, an accessible figure that not only ensured everyone talked about the Dean Street Townhouse as soon as it opened, but also that its restaurant and bedrooms were fully booked from the outset.

If the success of the Dean Street Townhouse was due to a precise, almost telepathic, understanding of the local market, this essential skill proved to be lacking in New York, where Le Caprice eventually closed its doors in March 2012. No restaurateur, however successful, is immune to the local working practices of any major city and on this occasion, upon talking to two different sources in New York it appears that Caprice Holdings may have failed to appreciate the importance of two crucial commercial facts of New York restaurant life. The first is the strength of the unions in many hotel kitchens, a situation that on its own is enough to put off many of the city's independent restaurateurs from taking over the management of many hotels' restaurants, however prestigious. The second is quite how competitive the New York restaurant scene is. As a well-placed insider explained, 'This city already has so many restaurants at this particular level, all aiming for three stars in the *New York Times*. I think the guys behind Le Caprice came in expecting we would be waiting for them with open arms. I don't believe they appreciated quite how assiduously they had to court the local media.'

McDonald seemed relieved to bring this chapter of his restaurant career to a close. When we first spoke after his departure from the Caring empire he told me that he was working on what he described as a 'killer concept'. This turns out to be taking one particular, and very well-loved, aspect of traditional British cuisine and giving it a much-needed patina of affordable luxury: a 'grown-up' fish-and-chip shop with vintage fittings that pays homage to the British café, and will serve potted shrimp, oysters and Dover sole, as well as a Martini while you wait. Such plans may see his travels restricted to domestic rather than international terminals, but he has high hopes that his own restaurants will become established widely across the UK. While McDonald is focusing on discussions with potential backers, he is keen not to stay away too long from what has been his unique strength as a restaurateur: his ability, based on his own years at the stoves, to understand and to motivate chefs. 'I talk their language, I understand their DNA, and when the chips are down I know all the right questions, and then most of the right answers, to be able to give them what they require to do their jobs properly,' he explained.

Like any good restaurateur, McDonald is in love with restaurants. Before we arranged to meet at the Arts Club, I had taken the precaution of asking him whether he was going to stay in the restaurant business. McDonald laughed. 'I've been in this business thirty-seven years, Nick. With a bit of luck I plan to be in it for another thirty-seven years at least.'

Getting on with your neighbours

As cities become increasingly crowded and the number of restaurants increases, the symbiosis between restaurateurs and their local residents – the people who live above, just behind or on either side of the restaurant's front door – has become much closer and, potentially, much more fraught. Managing this relationship is an important part of the restaurateur's role and goes far beyond simply putting the increasingly ubiquitous sign in so many restaurant windows that reads 'This is a residential area. Please be quiet and considerate when leaving the building.'

For any close neighbour, restaurants can be noisy, smelly and singularly unattractive. They are open long hours, often seven days a week; the deliveries can be annoying, from dripping carcasses of meat to the occasional wine spill from a broken case; there are several different sources of loud noise from the air handling units, the open windows of the kitchen and the customers. All that is before any music is played, which is a matter of personal opinion as to whether it is pain or pleasure for those living neaby. Finally, and perhaps most annoyingly, there are the smokers, over whom no one seems to have any control. Now that smoking, happily, is banned in restaurants, the location for smokers has moved to the restaurant's entrance and ideally under the entrance's canopy, which keeps them warm and dry. While this fug is a nuisance for any customer arriving or leaving, walking through it, at worst, is a nauseous but relatively brief encounter. For anyone who lives right next door, the smoke has to be endured regularly, particularly down wind.

The leverage that residents have over any restaurateur is, however, wide ranging and extensive, so much so that it can sometimes scupper the whole enterprise. Local residents often remain the biggest opponents to the granting of a new alcohol licence, and without this no restaurateur can prosper. Liz Southorn is one of London's most highly respected licensing solicitors, and her advice to any restaurateur at the outset is to ensure that the residents are always given the appropriate notification of any application. A neighbour's complaint can cost the restaurateur their licence, or mean the imposition of further conditions on the licence that can subsequently limit the ability to trade. Southorn's advice is always to make friends rather than enemies of the neighbours. From her experience, a cause for complaint can often be cleared up quite quickly if the restaurateur chooses to deal with the matter personally rather than delegating it to a manager. This is important, she believes, because although neighbours may exaggerate, restaurant staff can minimize or even deny to their employers the actual instances of nuisance to the neighbours. In particular, complaints of noise nuisance must be taken very seriously by the restaurateur, as there are many avenues of redress available to complainants. A modus vivendi, Southorn believes, is usually not too difficult to achieve. 'Neighbours do like to feel that they are being involved in the operation of the restaurant, and if this is handled sensitively, they can often become friends rather than enemies. I have had many instances of this with my own clients. Trading aggression for aggression does not help.'

When Des McDonald stood in the reception of the newly renovated Scott's in late 2006, a great deal was at stake. Most obviously, there were the millions that had been spent on bringing glamour and a brand-new kitchen back into the building. Then there were McDonald's and his chairman's reputations on the lines, as this was the first restaurant they had opened together, in contrast with the others they then ran, which they had bought as going concerns. Lying behind all this was one more critical and yet not widely discussed factor: how would Scott's neighbours react, those who lived in the expensive flats above and had got used to the restaurant being fairly quiet, with all that meant in terms of a relatively quiet kitchen, few early deliveries and not many bags of smelly rubbish being put out at midnight?

To ensure that their investment would not be in vain, McDonald and his team went to great lengths and considerable expense. All the kitchen equipment, most notably the fridges, were mounted off the ground so that their vibrations and any other noise could be contained within the kitchen. To introduce the air conditioning that customers demand today, two bore holes were drilled forty-two metres (140 feet) below the building into the water table to access cold water. This added an extra £500,000 ($800,000) to the conversion costs but, on the evidence of Scott's subsequent popularity and peaceful relations with the neighbours, it has proved to be money very well spent.

DANNY MEYER

THE ESSENCE OF NEW YORK

When I last had lunch with Danny Meyer, New York's – and possibly the world's – most respected restaurateur, I wasn't sure if we'd chosen the right restaurant. I would have felt the same way had we agreed to meet at any of the numerous and varied restaurants that the Union Square Hospitality Group, which he founded in 1985, now operates with such exuberance. Lunch at Union Square Café, his first restaurant, would have been fun, as would a return visit to the Gramercy Tavern (illustrated page 169), which is such a fascinating expression of American cooking; I would certainly have enjoyed the grilled tuna burger with ginger at the former, and the braised lamb with bok choi at the latter. My family has always had great fun at Blue Smoke, Meyer's barbecue restaurant, although perhaps my fingers would have become too sticky to take decipherable notes. And while the bar at The Modern, his restaurant inside MoMA, New York's Museum of Modern Art, is always an exciting location due to the juxtaposition of the garden, the art, the food, the wine and the smartly dressed clientèle, it would probably have been too noisy, whereas even a corner table in the much calmer restaurant next door would have been too conspicuous. So too would have been lunch at Maialino, his Roman trattoria overlooking Gramercy Park.

This last point was the root of my concern. Meyer is now so well known throughout the city, and so conscious of the importance of greeting, however briefly, the management, staff, guests, doormen and security guards at his restaurants, as well as anyone he recognizes and the many more who recognize him, that I wondered whether one meeting would be long enough. Sure enough, no sooner had we strode across the bridge that leads into the Whitney Museum on our way to breakfast at Untitled, the café he runs there, than Meyer was off. His first handshake was for the security guard, who gave him a warm smile in return. As he ran down the stairs there was a big hello for the cleaner, and then, once across the threshold and into his own territory, he seemed to step up a gear. He reached out his right hand to give warm handshakes and high fives to the two young women working behind the coffee machine, at the same time asking them which breakfast pastry was special that day. Next there was a hug for Jill Cabral, the café's general manager, to whom he offered his congratulations on the fact that they had managed to serve 360 customers each day over the previous weekend without any reservations and despite the café not really having a reception area. This was a tribute, Meyer made sure I heard quite clearly, to the good job that Cabral, the chef Chris Bradley, and their teams were doing.

We finally made it to our table, where Cabral recognized my trademark red socks from my first visit six months earlier. Meyer, on the other hand, ran his finger across the top of the wooden counter next to where we were sitting and inspected the result. He promptly shook his head: there was too much dust for his liking. This attested to the maxim that for the most conscientious restaurateurs it is the little details that are the most important, and that nothing is ever quite good enough. As our waiter approached, Meyer realized that they had not met before and that he was therefore a new member of the team. 'I'll see you at the new-hire meeting later today, won't I?' Meyer asked, and received a prompt affirmative. This, I learned, is a seventy-five-minute session at which Meyer meets, talks to and takes questions from that month's new recruits, of which there are usually about fifty, as well as enthusing about the restaurants, setting out his personal view of hospitality and, most importantly, establishing a personal connection between himself and all those who work with him. It is something he has done since before the Union Square Café opened, and in the early years no one could work a shift before they had this meeting with him. Now that he employs over 2,500 people he has had to adapt it a little.

I was delighted to be meeting Meyer at Untitled because I knew I would get an excellent breakfast: cheesy scrambled eggs with grits, sourdough toast and a Stumptown Roasters cappuccino, while Meyer gleefully tested the sausage, egg and cheese in the breakfast roll. And the Whitney is also the perfect illustration of one of the most distinctive aspects of Meyer's approach to restaurants. Most of the restaurants that USHG currently operates are in other people's buildings: the cafés and restaurants in MoMA and the Whitney; Maialino on the ground floor of the Gramercy Park Hotel; and Shake Shack, the phenomenally successful hamburger operation, began life in the park at the heart of Madison Square, and its popularity has helped transform the area. Shake Shack now also has outposts in Citi Field, where the New York Mets play baseball, and at the Saratoga Springs horse racing track, as well as in a dozen more locations across the East Coast and several in the Middle East. Although two of Meyer's earliest restaurants, Union Square Café and the original Blue Smoke, are leaseholds, and the company owns the freehold on Gramercy Tavern, his three most recent openings (further outposts of Blue Smoke, Shake Shack and the latest departure, North End Grill, a bar and restaurant inspired by the grill restaurants Meyer encountered on a trip to

San Sebastián, north-west Spain) are in a building developed by Goldman Sachs in their Battery Park development in the city's financial district.

The move by so many restaurateurs to open in arts organizations, above or on the ground floor of major office buildings, or within sports venues, rather than on the high street, has been one of the most fascinating changes in how restaurants are perceived and how they have developed over the past decade. It is an area with which I have been closely associated myself as a consultant to numerous arts organizations in the UK. For the landlords, such a liaison, when successful, can bring happy customers and significant income over the duration of a reasonably long lease. For the restaurateur the deal can be even more attractive. The building is likely to be in good condition and architecturally striking; there is the possibility of a capital contribution from the landlords, thereby saving some of the restaurateur's limited funds; it is often possible to negotiate a rent-free period that takes pressure off the business in the crucial first few months; and the rent is usually an agreed amount per square metre or an agreed percentage of sales (whichever is the higher), in which case both parties can share in the restaurant's prosperity. And that is the major inducement. Meyer's cafés and restaurants have their own attractions, but they certainly benefit from the crowds that these partners can bring in. 'We really love it when there is a blockbuster exhibition on here or at MoMA, or the Mets are playing well, or when the sun is shining at Saratoga. Whenever they do well, we do well.'

Such associations can also be fraught, however, because restaurateurs are somewhat less independent, a role they may have to learn to adapt to. They have to learn to be flexible. 'It is as though we are guests in their home and we have to look after their staff, from those who sit on the Board of Trustees, to their executive team, to the cleaners and security guards, and we have to make them happy that we are here. It is effectively like having another stakeholder in our business, and this type of working relationship goes far beyond the four walls of this café. I always impress on our staff here, for example, that while USHG pays their wages, they are actually representing the Whitney.' At this point Meyer looked up at the high ceiling and his usual disarming smile momentarily left his face. He had noticed that the bulbs in several lights in the ceiling were not working properly and added, 'That's another downside of being in someone else's home: I can't get things fixed as quickly as I would if this were my own building.'

Meyer's ability to introduce the most appropriate level of food, drink and hospitality into so many different organizations is one of his most remarkable achievements as a restaurateur. This is an intuitive talent, based on his own passions, travels and a voracious appetite. I am not alone in believing that the cafés, bar and restaurant in MoMA are the most impressive I have ever seen or enjoyed anywhere in the world in an arts organization, particularly considering the volume of customers and staff they serve. I suspect this talent is one that would have made him extremely successful in any field he chose to put his mind to. Meyer himself admits to having 'good antennae and good pitch', two hugely important traits in a city like New York, where so much power, influence and money is so tightly concentrated. This intuitive sense for judging just what, how and where New Yorkers want to eat has brought him a remarkable strike record in opening a diverse range of restaurants (with only Tabla, his Indian restaurant, closing in 2011 after a twelve-year run); kept together a talented executive team that includes Paul Bolles-Beaven, who began as a waiter at Union Square Café in 1986 and now oversees all the restaurants once his colleague Richard Coraine has managed their openings; and seen the successful development of Hospitality Quotient, a sister company that teaches the generic principles of hospitality to companies that are not restaurants but feel that their own field of healthcare, charity work or retail would benefit from better customer care.

These antennae are so well tuned that I often feel in Meyer's company (and I have known him well for the past fifteen years) that I am in the presence of a consummate communicator as well as a consummate restaurateur. I was alongside him once on the opening morning of one of his restaurants, and, while he made a point of meeting and shaking the hands of every single member of his team, I also noticed how he seemed very briefly to lock eyes with them, wishing them luck but at the same time subtly convincing them that the restaurant's future success rested on their shoulders. It was rather like a politician leaving the impression with every single voter he or she shook hands with that his or her success at the polls depended on their very vote.

In fact, it was only Meyer's dread of taking the entrance exam for law school, which thirty years ago was the necessary prerequisite for a career in politics (his original chosen career path), that led to him turning his emerging love of food and wine into a career as a restaurateur. 'On the night before this exam I was out for dinner with my uncle and aunt.

I wasn't drinking and I must have been looking pretty miserable because my uncle asked me what the matter was. I explained my dread of spending any time at law school and he responded by saying that I should really pursue what interested me, as I would spend a lot longer dead than alive. It still didn't really click so he spelled it out. For as long as I have known you, he said, you've only been interested in food and restaurants. Why don't you open a restaurant? It was something that had never occurred to me. Back then it simply never seemed a legitimate career path for a college boy.'

He bade farewell to law school and became a successful salesman, an episode that allowed him to accumulate some capital and enrol in a management class at the New York Restaurant School. Finally, in early 1984, he took the job of assistant daytime manager at Pesca, a seafood restaurant. Destiny or good luck meant that during his eight-month stint there he met Audrey Heffernan, an actor and waitress who subsequently became his wife, as well as Michael Romano, recently returned from cooking at Michel Guérard's renowned restaurant in France, who has been his executive chef and partner ever since. East 22nd Street, Pesca's former location, also introduced Meyer to the part of the city he now lives in, and around which he has opened several successful restaurants.

Other traits have played their part. Meyer, despite his slim frame, has an extraordinary appetite ('worked off in the gym,' he hastens to add) and an iconoclastic approach to food. Like a top chef, he seems capable of looking at a range of dishes, dissecting them and then coming up with ideas to replicate them authentically in the case of Maialino, more elegantly in the case of The Modern or on a much bigger scale as at Shake Shack Madison Square, which can feed 1,500 people on a sunny day. The ability to scale up, to handle large numbers of customers every day, seems to be a particular trait among American restaurateurs – an extension of their management skills, and perhaps also a reflection of the work ethic of a large workforce from Mexico and South America.

These achievements, his restaurants' continued success and the publication of his memoir and professional manifesto, *Setting the Table: Lessons and inspirations from one of the world's leading entrepeneurs*, led to a significant change in how Meyer perceives his role within the company. 'I made the leap then from being a restaurateur to being the leader of a restaurant group,' he explained. Despite this change he believes he has to stay close to two fundamental principles. First, his role is to build relationships between his staff and the guests, and within his own organization. For him, this is crucial, because while most people focus on the inanimate factors in a restaurant – the menu, the wine list, the art on the wall – he believes it is the human beings who animate the space, who bring everything to life and who determine whether a customer will return or not. 'It's the receptionist, the barman, the waiter, the pastry chef who alone, and collectively, can do this and I simply cannot leave this to chance. If my staff are good enough, the customers will return,' he said, although he looked somewhat vexed that a lone diner had just left without being thanked by anyone. 'How did that happen?' he wanted to know. 'The road to success is paved with mistakes well handled,' is a maxim he learned at dinner, sitting next to retailer Stanley Marcus of Nieman Marcus stores, and it's one Meyer believes has to be a top priority: how to handle mistakes to win back disappointed customers is as crucial for restaurateurs as it is for any other business. He then summarized his roles in order of priority: the care and feeding of his staff; then of the guests; then looking after the hosts whose homes USHG operates within; then the communities the restaurants are part of; and finally, their suppliers.

The second is having a specific vision of what every restaurant ought to be, although even Meyer finds it difficult to be too detailed. 'It's a question of harmony, of striking in the customer's mind the right balance between the pleasures of going out – to be seen, to eat and to drink things you couldn't prepare in your own apartment – and at the same time the sense of coming home, of being welcomed, looked after, cared for. Food is obviously the principal driver of the first sentiment but it is the gestures of hospitality that I hope my staff will be making that govern the second.' He loves the challenge of playing with this equation, although it can be much harder in a more formal restaurant, where the setting can be austere and the plates so big that generating that sense of hospitality can be extremely difficult.

These approaches, coupled with a good sense of humour, have seen Meyer through some difficult episodes. The success of Gramercy Tavern in the 1990s led to a split with his chef and former partner Tom Colicchio. They parted company to pursue their own interests independently, at which both have subsequently prospered. This was an episode he took to heart when agreeing, somewhat reluctantly I gleaned, to the sale of the highly successful Eleven Madison Park to its chef, Daniel Humm and its general manager, William Guidara. His experience with Colicchio had shown him that if what seem to be irreconcilable differences between the restaurateur and the chef appear, it is best to find an amicable solution sooner rather than later, even when this means the parties having to go their separate ways.

Tabla, the Indian restaurant that Meyer opened next to and at the same time as Eleven Madison Park, is also testimony to the unwritten rule that even the most successful restaurateurs never get it completely right (in London, Chris Corbin and Jeremy King had to close St Alban despite the popularity of their other restaurant, The Wolseley, nearby). Tabla was a courageous attempt to bring exciting Indian food to the heart of New York in a site that made this proposition even more taxing: it was on two floors with the kitchens on the first floor, which immediately led to higher labour costs as there were no economies of scale. A meal at Tabla seemed to be the one luxury New Yorkers could do without: whenever there was a downturn in the economy, Meyer noticed, Tabla suffered before any of his other restaurants and took longer to recover than any other. In September 2010 Meyer announced that Tabla would close at the end of the year, allowing time to say thank you to its customers and to help the staff find jobs within his company or elsewhere. He held a Jobs Fair at which he brought in chefs who had formerly worked for his company to interview his staff. It was an important experience to have handled well, Meyer confessed, as was the scrutiny to which he subjected the list of restaurateurs interested in taking over the site on behalf of the landlord, which was a necessary step in the assignment of the lease. He examined all the prospective buyers because at the time he owned Eleven Madison Park next door, and he continues to own Shake Shack in Madison Square itself, so he wanted an individual or company that would share his vision for the neighbourhood. The selection of the Peruvian restaurant La Mar will, he believes, be an exciting addition to all those who live and work near Madison Square.

Meyer acknowledges his good fortune – and not just at avoiding law school. He arrived in New York from St Louis in the 1980s when the norm in restaurants across the city was to be as stiff and formal as he has been hospitable. When his first restaurant Union Square Café had been open for just six weeks, a lighting track came away from the ceiling, swung down and missed the head of a female diner by no more than five centimetres (two inches). This could have ended his career as a restaurateur before it started, he recalled with great relief. Most importantly, though, he knows he has fallen into a business that has brought out the best of other personal strengths. His father's travel business allowed him to travel around Europe at an impressionable age, but its financial demise only reinforced his determination to succeed. 'I love winning, the joy of doing something great. But I don't think of it as a competition, a zero sum game. The busier the restaurants are, the happier the customers will be and that is good for all of us,' he enthused. Early in his career he lived in an apartment above The Gotham Bar & Grill, and each morning when he set off for work he could see from the number of empty bottles outside their front door that they were selling more, and better, wine than his restaurant was. This sight alone was enough to make Meyer want to do better, and he embarked on a programme for establishing wine lists that are now among the best in the US.

'What I love most about this business is that I enjoy people enjoying food. It's an obsession. And when it goes wrong, I enjoy turning it around.' We got up to leave, and as we did so Meyer's last words came back to haunt him. He spotted an elderly couple eating buttermilk pancakes and interrupted to check that all was well. He stood, somewhat crestfallen, as the couple explained that all was not, in fact, well. They were on a return visit from their home in Nantucket and had already sent a note to the kitchen saying they were back for what they thought were the best pancakes in the world. But this serving was not as good as the pancakes they had enjoyed the first time around. Meyer's smile returned in seconds. The plates were taken away, their coffee cups refilled and a fresh order was under way. After he left I couldn't help but notice how thrilled this couple were to have been treated in such a fashion. It was another striking example of the fact that the road to success is indeed paved with mistakes well handled. Meyer had shown that the art of the restaurateur lies not only in what you do, but how you do it.

Supporting charities

Danny Meyer has been on the national board of SOS (Share Our Strength) since 1992. SOS is a charity founded in 1984 to end global hunger, and it has proved highly effective in raising funds as well as uniting people in the hospitality industry across the US to donate their many talents to this worthy end. Meyer is not alone in this respect, either in his own country or in the rest of the world. Many restaurateurs are aware that their profession puts them in a position in which they can help those less fortunate than themselves, and, along with their chefs and colleagues in the wine trade, turn their unique skills to altruistic ends.

These can take many forms. The most common are the numerous requests to donate a free dinner for two as a prize in a charity auction. It is hard to calculate exactly how often such requests are made, but I would guess that the most popular restaurants receive such a request every two or three days. As a result, most restaurateurs now have a well-defined policy for how they will respond. Meyer explained: 'We ask each restaurant to create an annual budget for giving away gift certificates that may be used for not-for-profit organizations to auction off to raise money for causes we hold dear. Chief among those are hunger relief and public parks.'

Over the past decade, as restaurants and chefs have achieved an increasingly high profile, there have also been very successful fundraising activities that have taken professional chefs into private homes in return for very high bids, with the considerable proceeds going to charity. The most successful exponents of this in the UK have been chef Peter Gordon and restaurateur Chris Corbin, both of whom in 1994 had first-hand experience of leukaemia. Gordon donated bone marrow to his sister, while Corbin was diagnosed with the disease himself, from which he has since made a successful recovery. As a result, they joined forces in 1999 to inaugurate the first 'Who's Cooking Dinner?' event, which has since raised over £4 million ($6.25 million) for the charity Leuka, which aims to cure leukaemia this century.

The dinner, which is sensibly held on a Monday night (most restaurants' quietest night of the week), takes place in the kitchens of a West End hotel, into which twenty top chefs crowd along with assistants, equipment, food and wine to serve a four-course menu to a table of ten people. Once the 200 guests have arrived, their hosts' names are drawn out of a hat and each one is paired with a chef. Who will be cooking for whom remains a surprise until this moment. After the dinner, the chefs are auctioned off to the highest bidder, the prize being a dinner for eight people cooked in their own home by the chef. Sums of around £20,000 ($30,000) change hands for personal appearances by Ruth Rogers from the River Café, Richard Corrigan of Corrigan's Mayfair and Angela Hartnett from Murano. These are occasions that money usually cannot buy.

Restaurateurs have many opportunities to turn their altruism to society's advantage because the staples that they deal in - food and wine – can so readily be turned to charitable advantage. One aspect of this is any restaurateur's close association with the wine merchants who supply him. Wine merchants probably receive more requests for charitable donations each week than even the most successful restaurateurs, but it is the combination of good wine with food that is really exciting. At charity dinners around the world, the generously donated wine and the skills of a talented chef, restaurateur or hotelier have jointly led to significant amounts of money being raised at auctions held towards the end of the evening, once the needs of the charity have been explained to an audience that has eaten well and enjoyed excellent wines. This is particularly the case when several of the tables are occupied by competitive bankers who really do want to spend a week at an exclusive hotel off the coast of Zanzibar.

The other great advantage for restaurateurs, on top of their proximity to the ingredients that can persuade people to donate so generously, is the relative ease with which charitable arrangements can be put into practice: it does not need to be an elaborate dinner to have a significant impact. Mary-Lou Sturridge, William Sieghart and Nick Emley created StreetSmart in 1998, which is a simple mechanism whereby £1.00 ($1.50) is added to every bill at the 500 participating restaurants across the UK during November and December. It has so far raised over £5 million ($7.75 million) for the homeless. Pret a Manger, the sandwich business, does something similar with an automatic donation of 25p (40¢) on a couple of their sandwiches during the Christmas period, and last year this alone raised over £150,000 ($235,000), also for the homeless. Today, many restaurateurs consider it an equally valuable part of their role to look after those who cannot afford to be their customers.

Danny Meyer

dREWNIEPORENt
FROM TRIBECA CHIC TO NOBU
WORLDWIDE

11

Drew Nieporent – who has opened thirty-five restaurants around the world over the past twenty-seven years, including the original Nobu restaurants in New York (illustrated page 183) and London – and I have enjoyed numerous good meals together, several bottles of equally good wine and even the odd Cuban cigar on both sides of the Atlantic. Instead of restaurants, though, our conversations in the past have usually started with Bruce Springsteen. Nieporent is a massive fan and has been fortunate enough to listen to him play in very intimate settings on several occasions. Normally, it has been a discussion of Springsteen's most recent concert or album that has taken up the first ten minutes when we get together.

But not on this occasion. 'I'm really glad you're writing this,' he said with his usual broad smile. 'We restaurateurs are a dying breed. We're the dinosaurs of the industry, being wiped out by the chefs.' He explained that over the past few years restaurateurs have also been their own worst enemy because they have not stood up for the profession. 'We've never collectively explained what we do. For example, I will go on a TV cookery show and later in the day someone on the street will recognize me and call over saying, "Hey Chef." We're all chefs to these guys, and even if we both had the time to stop to let me explain just what a restaurateur does, they wouldn't want to understand. But restaurateurs supply the vision, that's at the heart of everything we do.'

Even if, in this brief summary of his life's work, Nieporent comes across as someone with a hint of a professional inferiority complex, it is nonetheless an accurate reflection of this ebullient man and successful restaurateur. This is partly down to the overshadowing effect of the partners with whom he has been involved since his first restaurant, Montrachet (which now trades as Corton), opened in 1985. Robert de Niro became his partner in Tribeca Grill in 1990 and the first Nobu in 1994, all within a few hundred yards of each other on New York's Lower West Side. While a partner with such a reputation as de Niro's has been a great draw for the restaurants, it is inevitably de Niro the actor rather than Nieporent the restaurant director who has attracted all of the media attention. They are always far more likely to be referred to as de Niro's restaurants than as belonging to any of the other partners, even the one who actually ensures that the restaurant runs smoothly.

That was before the emergence of chef Nobu Matsuhisa, to whom de Niro introduced Nieporent after eating at his first sushi bar in Beverly Hills in 1988, in the hope that one day they would open something together. Nieporent could have had no idea that the first Nobu, then the London opening, as well as the move into Nobu Next Door and uptown to Nobu 57 in New York, would unleash such a phenomenon onto the restaurant world. In the intervening years Nobu the chef has come to represent not only a style of cooking, but also a whole country and its cuisine, a cuisine that before 1994 was often difficult to comprehend, expensive and exclusive. Nobu has simply demystified Japanese cuisine and showed it is fun, healthy and accessible to all (their good-value set lunch menus have been important in this respect). One of the consequences of the worldwide success of the Nobu restaurants has been that Nieporent and his management company, Myriad Restaurant Group, have not been involved with any Nobu restaurant beyond these four (and there are now twenty-two Nobus worldwide).

Nieporent has also suffered from having to compete for the extensive coverage that restaurants have enjoyed in the media for the past twenty years with his contemporary Danny Meyer, not just in New York but also across the US. In a city that so obviously values size and success it is perhaps inevitable that many of the awards, headlines, accolades and votes should go first to Meyer. Even Nieporent recognized this when he talked at his usual speed, and with his enthusiasm undimmed by the years, about the time when the James Beard awards finally got round to establishing an award for the best restaurateur in the US, long after they had handed out similar awards for the country's best chefs, sommeliers and pastry chefs. Or, as Nieporent put it, 'they finally threw the restaurateurs a bone. And in its first year it went to Danny, quite rightly.' For a man of Nieporent's age (fifty-seven), experience and involvement in so many restaurants that range from world famous to the far less successful, it may seem somewhat naive that he still displays such emotions so conspicuously on his sleeve. But these traits are also an integral part of Nieporent the restaurateur.

He certainly looks and behaves every inch the restaurateur. He is broad, plump, sports a beard and loves a party: a definite Father Christmas figure. His current frame betrays the once-slim figure I saw in a photo crossing the finishing line of the New York marathon back in 1983. Before any trip to Europe he will invariably pump me for restaurant information and gossip, and whenever we have eaten together he has shown an enthusiasm for food and wine that I have rarely seen equalled. Nieporent the restaurateur has, however, had an extraordinary impact on several areas of the restaurant world that many customers now take for granted. The first, which has directly benefited his fellow New Yorkers, has been the transformation of Tribeca, the part of the city in which he has concentrated so many of his openings. When he initially opened there in the early 1980s, Tribeca was neglected and unwelcoming. New York food and wine writer Eric Asimov recalls his first visit to Montrachet in 1984 and described the restaurant appearing as 'a beacon of light in dark Tribeca'. Today, Nieporent laughingly refers to himself as the Mayor of Franklin Street, home to his restaurants and head office, a justifiable recognition of the role he and his restaurants have played in Tribeca's regeneration over the past two decades.

His approach to the wine list at Montrachet has led to another large improvement that can be felt and enjoyed right across the US. Many believe it was the combination of Nieporent's vision and the talents of his original sommelier, Daniel Johannes, that initially attracted so many wine collectors to the restaurant and then kick-started the city's vibrant wine culture. From the outset, Montrachet offered a sixty-bottle selection on its list, which was printed on every menu so that every customer could see it, an approach that makes it so much easier for anyone afraid of wine, as so many Americans were then, to relax and enjoy whatever was recommended. Montrachet's success has, in turn, trained many young sommeliers who subsequently went off to preach, and put into effect, this far more customer-friendly approach to wine in the wave of new restaurant openings that followed.

Nobu has had a similarly profound effect on how many of us now perceive and enjoy Japanese restaurants. Nobu heralded fundamental changes: there were to be no clichés of Japanese design, no shoji screens or tatami rooms; there was a far more democratic arrangement of the seating that involved banquettes, booths and freestanding tables; and, perhaps most significantly, Japanese dishes began to be served family style, in the middle of the table, so that customers would be encouraged to share and taste what for many at that time were still quite unusual dishes. Before Nieporent and Nobu, none of these were standard practice in a Japanese restaurant. Today, they most definitely are.

Nieporent's love of all that happens inside his and other people's restaurants emanates from the romantic streak in him, the years he has spent working his way up through many different restaurants, initially on cruise ships around Scandinavia and then in New York. Most of all, though, from growing up with his brother and business partner, Tracy,

in Peter Cooper Village in New York's Lower East Side. Their mother, Sybil Trent, a well-known radio actress and casting director, certainly gave Nieporent a sense of the theatrical, and their father worked for the state liquor authority. As a result, from an early age the Nieporent boys frequently went out to eat at the city's best restaurants, whether Chinese, Italian or French, and naturally were afforded the best service. The restaurant's alcohol licence was far too important to lose.

Nieporent got the bug. 'I used to come home from school, make my own lunch – I loved flambéing hamburgers – and then eat them watching cookery shows on TV: Julia Child and Graham Kerr, the Galloping Gourmet,' he recalled with relish. In 1972 he got a job with McDonald's a block away as a grill man, preparing quarter-pounders. This was a great experience during which he learned a lot about systems and quite how important they are in running any restaurant, an episode that has stuck with him and has proved essential. A place at the Cornell School of Hotel Administration followed, but it was an advertisement for waiters that was to have the biggest and most long-lasting impact on the future restaurateur. 'Six Waiters Required For Scandinavian Cruise' the advert read, and despite the fact that he had never worked in a dining room before, Nieporent was taken on. 'It was the most extraordinary learning experience.' The restaurant seated 600 and was the size of a football field. The kitchens were on the floor below, serviced by an escalator. He learned to carry a tray on three fingers; how to serve dishes *à la Russe* (in other words, from a large tray with a fork and spoon onto the customer's plate); and after he had completed fifteen different cruises he had learned the entire French classic culinary vocabulary. 'It was just like learning to ride a bike,' he smiled – only this lesson was to prove far more commercially valuable.

We were sitting at the corner table in the Tribeca Grill, which afforded Nieporent the best view of the entrance into, and exit from, the kitchen (precisely the same position that Joe Bastianich had chosen to sit in at Esca), when he decided we should eat. 'You must try the octopus braised in red wine,' he said, calling a waiter over. He suggested starting with a cup each of the soup on the daily menu, just to make sure it was as it should be, then the octopus, then he asked me what I would like to follow. Intrigued, I plumped for a dish of *gigantone*, or thick pasta tubes topped with braised short ribs, ricotta and basil. It was a really excellent combination.

Then we were back to New York in the late 1970s, when Nieporent worked at two of the city's busiest restaurants, Maxwell's Plum and Tavern

on the Green, right by Central Park. Maxwell's Plum, on 64th Street and 1st, boasted an Art Deco interior, Tiffany lamps, and during its heyday from 1966–88, a frenetic bar scene and restaurant that could attract up to 1,200 customers a day. While the building that once housed Tavern on the Green is still there, right by Central Park, it is now a shop after its glory days as one of the city's largest and most glamorous restaurants came to an end in December 2009. Working as restaurant director at Maxwell's Plum on $300 (£190) a week brought him face to face with a menu of 160 items, a room full of 950 customers on Saturday evenings and exposure to serving such great bottles of wine as Château Margaux and Petrus 1961. Tavern on the Green, in that era the largest-grossing restaurant in the city, exposed him to some of the industry's excesses, most cruelly the damaging effects that can result from such easy access to alcohol. But they also introduced Nieporent to Warner LeRoy, a restaurateur with extraordinary vision.

Warner LeRoy, whom I met once at The Russian Tea Room (in which he invested far too heavily in his attempt to revive it in the 1990s), was the son of film producer Mervyn LeRoy, who made *The Wizard of Oz* with Judy Garland. Part of LeRoy's farsighted approach included giving Nieporent and a colleague $2,500 (£1,600) and telling him to go off and investigate ten of the three-Michelin-starred restaurants around France. Memories of meals at La Tour d'Argent in Paris; Fernand Point at La Pyramide, Vienne; Paul Bocuse at Collonges, Lyons; and Roger Vergé at Le Moulin de Mougins came flooding back, as well as the realization that this style of cooking, at a more approachable level, was just what was missing in New York. Back in the city, Nieporent worked at what he referred to as the 'Le/La' restaurants, then the city's most admired – Le Périgord, La Regence, La Grenouille – to get close to the people he wanted to become regulars at his own restaurant. He saw at first hand how the Bronfmans, the Hiltons – the future customers and future investors, he imagined at that stage – wanted to be treated. It was an invaluable experience.

Although Nieporent's first restaurant failed after a financial disagreement with his chef, a morning jog on the cobbled streets of the area now affectionately known as Tribeca but much neglected in the 1980s, brought him to his first site in the area that he and his restaurants have done so much to revive. His entire savings of $50,000 (£32,000) were matched by those of an old school friend, and to this mix were added the culinary talents of chef David Bouley, who went on to have a very successful career with Nieporent, and then with his own restaurants.

Montrachet was born, and so was Drew Nieporent, the proud and independent restaurateur.

Retreating from his usual expansive style, Nieporent recounted two stories of how his extensive apprenticeship had proved useful in his own restaurant. The first was when the food writer James Beard, at the beginning of his first dinner there, ordered a Manhattan neat, which is an unusual way of drinking this popular American cocktail. On his second visit, no sooner had Beard sat down than Nieporent approached him and asked whether he could bring him a Manhattan neat. 'The expression on his face was unforgettable.' So too was the observation that Craig Claiborne, then the highly influential restaurant editor with the *New York Times*, made, and which Nieporent has since passed on to all his waiters. 'Claiborne once said that he always knew that if he removed the swizzle stick from his cocktail, and the stick was immediately taken away by a waiter, he knew that he was going to get very good service. That became a golden rule.'

Another element of the restaurateur's profession that has always excited him is how to recognize talent and not to let it slip through your fingers. This, he believes, is best effected by engaging with people and appreciating what they need to be effective, something Nieporent can identify with because he started out as a waiter. 'There is no doubt that the most powerful and influential chef-restaurateur in New York today is Daniel Boulud with Daniel, Bar Boulud, Boulud Sud and several other places. And I don't think it is any coincidence that he used to work for Sirio Maccioni (legendary restaurateur of Le Cirque), from whom he will have learned a great deal.' As a restaurateur, Nieporent is particularly proud that he was able to launch the careers of David Rockwell the architect; the chefs David Bouley and Traci Des Jardins, who was the chef at Rubicon, San Francisco, and has now gone on to open Jardinière; and chef Mark Edwards, who has been at Nobu London ever since it opened. Then there are the now stellar wine careers of Daniel Johannes, formerly with him at Montrachet and now with Boulud, and Larry Stone who ran the wine programme at Rubicon. 'Wine was then almost the ugly duckling of American restaurants, but we've certainly changed that,' Nieporent explained, looking around his restaurant, whose shelves are lined with the very best of the empty wine bottles his customers have enjoyed. Supported by this talent Nieporent was able to go global from the mid 1990s onwards, aided also by the realization that chefs, until then restricted to their own kitchens – apart from the occasional guest appearance in a top hotel – were becoming international icons. London and San Francisco were, however, to prove diametrically opposite experiences.

Nobu, on the first floor of London's Metropolitan Hotel by Hyde Park Corner, has been extraordinarily successful by any measure. Its annual turnover is close to £9 million ($14 million). It won the highest professional recognition from all guides and reviewers and enabled Nieporent to become the first American restaurateur to win a Michelin star, since at that time Michelin did not publish a guide in the US. In the process it became an example of how one style of cuisine can seduce the world. Nieporent did recall, though, how difficult it was at the outset. 'First of all, Nobu just didn't want to go to London at all. I tried to persuade him, but initially to no avail until the offer of a Concorde ticket finally changed his mind.' Nieporent travelled economy, they met in London and it was all agreed virtually immediately. Then there was the much more difficult and subtle process of changing the public's perception of Japanese food. At that time the experience of going out to Japanese restaurants was not one that the public found either easy to enjoy or to understand. Nieporent's role was to change that through myriad details including, contrary to the prevailing opinion at the time, not having a bar at the first Nobu in New York because he wanted it to be taken seriously as a restaurant, rather than for the bar scene.

Three thousand miles in the opposite direction, Rubicon was to close, despite a plethora of great reviews and accolades, as Nieporent finally appreciated, as all restaurateurs have to, the challenges and peculiarities of each locality. 'Lots of us restaurateurs support numerous charities, particularly Citymeals-on-Wheels in this city, but San Francisco is the biggest charity I ever gave to. I loved being a restaurateur there for fourteen years but it is the city that is the hardest place to make a profit in of all the cities I have ever worked in.' The rents were high, and the wine country and the farmland were so close that every customer knew the cost of everything. The customers were very price resistant, and in the end they just could not continue.

The aftermath of 9/11 dealt a devastating blow to Nieporent's restaurants because of their proximity to the World Trade Center. They were all forced to close for two weeks while Nieporent turned his kitchens over to feeding the emergency services. Once they reopened, he lent his forceful personality to the 'Eat Downtown' campaign that ultimately

186

proved so successful at persuading New Yorkers and tourists to venture downtown. His restaurant openings since then have been fewer, although the only disappointment he expressed was that his proposed deal to reinvent the Rainbow Room at the top of the Rockefeller Center was not successful. He has, though, gained great satisfaction from the success of Crush, his wine store on East 57th Street.

Nieporent's passion for all that restaurateurs represent and create burns as brightly as it ever did. The first issue for any restaurateur, he believes, lies in choosing the correct layout for the raw space, thereby solving the major problems from the beginning. 'The key has to be to maximize revenue, and the difference between whether there are ultimately eighty or eighty-five seats in the restaurant can be as much as a million dollars over a busy year. And that's the only way to make money,' he added with a smile. Then, once open, the restaurateur's job is to minimize the number of times any customer hears the word no. 'That's not what they come for and we are there to ensure that word is used as infrequently as possible. Say a customer comes in and wants to eat at a table on the roof. The correct response is to say, "One moment please, I'll just see whether it's possible," and then come back and say, "I'm very sorry – not today, but I can get you a table quite close." You've got to err on the side of the customer.' Restaurateurs also have to stand up for their customers against chefs, or anyone who doesn't want them to be allowed to make substitutions in certain dishes, who doesn't want them to take photos of their finished dishes, or who is obsessed with different styles of presentation, introducing plates that are too small, or more frequently, far too big. 'You have to be in your restaurants and you have to be constantly vigilant.'

The best, most enjoyable and ultimately the most successful way for any restaurateur to do this is by 'working the door': being at the front desk and meeting, greeting and seating. That way a restaurateur can directly set the policies that the restaurant is to be run with. At this point, Nieporent's tone turned more philosophical. 'I always thought of a restaurateur's role as akin to that of a film director, someone who is responsible for all the ingredients of a great film, the lighting, the cast, the script, the editing.' But he has come to believe that just as film stars today have become more powerful than most directors, so too have chefs become more important than restaurateurs. 'Potential backers go directly to the chefs now, bypassing the restaurateurs without appreciating the difference we can make. Restaurateurs are the taste-makers, we're the first line of defence and we are the customers before the food ever gets to the customers.'

Nieporent's succinct analysis explains his love of restaurants and what they can bring to the lives of so many. He also wanted to emphasize an early lesson that has stayed with him, that came from Vance Christian, a professor at Cornell University. 'Why do you think you're here?' Christian had asked his students. Then he had pointed to his wallet and said that the keys to its future growth lay in professional knowledge and confidence. 'A bulb lit up in my head,' Nieporent recalled, 'and since then I've spent my life learning about this business and building on the confidence that this knowledge has instilled in me.' That is why, it turns out, he called his restaurant group Myriad. 'Because restaurants involve myriad decisions that are endless, countless and know no boundaries. And that is the joy of it all.'

Working the door

Drew Nieporent has been successful at opening restaurants in so many different locations because as an enthusiastic newcomer he learned to work the floor and the door. While the former involves looking after your customers once they have been seated, working the door is the front line of the restaurant business, more confrontational than any other department. This is not just because first and last impressions are so important, or because those who arrive are hungry, late, may have often forgotten who they are meeting, or sometimes even forgotten to make the reservation that they were so looking forward to. It is much more complex than that.

The challenge for any receptionist is that, unlike the waiting staff or even the chefs in the kitchen, they cannot control the flow of customers through the front door. Whereas the maître d' can manage the flow of his or her customers by diverting some into the bar, and can then stagger taking the orders so that the kitchen is not overwhelmed at any one time, the receptionist has no such room for manoeuvre. Certain times of the day, usually just before 1.00 p.m. and then again at 8.00 p.m., will bring a large influx of people, some behaving rather grumpily. As well as coping with this, the receptionist has a crucial role to play in any restaurant's profitability, most notably by converting walk-ins into satisfied customers. This area is absolutely vital because one common fact of everyday restaurant life is that even if the reservations list looks absolutely full, with no room for even the most regular customer calling at the last minute, someone is bound to cancel, meaning lost revenue for the night – revenue that cannot be replaced unless the receptionist fills the table either on the phone or by saying yes to any walk-ins.

The most memorable description I ever heard of what every receptionist in any busy restaurant has to manage came at 5.30 p.m. from Roger Raines, maître d' of Maialino, Danny Meyer's busy Italian trattoria in the Gramercy Park Hotel. He was standing next to his receptionists as they pored over the bookings list. I wished him luck, to which he replied memorably, 'Thanks. This is like dealing with a moving jigsaw puzzle.' Happily for both restaurateurs and their customers, there are many people who find the rhythm and challenge of a busy lunch or evening service exciting and rewarding, particularly in the winter when there is the added bonus of tips from handling the coats.

To discover precisely why I sat down one afternoon with Kerry Held, who for two years worked the door at Blue Smoke, a busy barbecue restaurant on New York's East 23rd Street. There is a jazz club in the basement and the restaurant will often welcome 500 customers a night. Held is tall, blonde and armed with a ready smile – essential prerequisites for this job, although her original career path would have taken her onto the stage. Instead, she made the restaurant's front door her stage. Initially she was very nervous. 'At first I didn't like it, but I was working with someone far more experienced than me and gradually my confidence grew. I slowly realized that this isn't open-heart surgery and that I could take some risks that would benefit the restaurant and have some fun.' What she most enjoyed was the sense of welcome, of being able to express her passion for the restaurant to strangers. The definite pluses for her were the adrenaline rush before each service got under way, the fact that no two nights were ever the same, and that there was a start and finish to every shift, a cycle that fuelled her sense of having achieved something great. This was the case no matter how early in the morning she left the restaurant, and however tired she felt on her way home.

There was also, she enthused, the challenge of figuring it all out, of dealing with so many different people in a fair and considerate manner, which allowed the rest of her team in the restaurant to look after them all.

Along the way she learned some valuable lessons. Firstly, and most importantly, she realized that although it is the restaurateur who pays your salary, the receptionist has to appear to be on the side of the customer. And, secondly, how one conveys the message is crucial, even the often unwelcome news that there may well be a two-hour wait for a table. 'How you say this will affect the customer more than anything else. Never say no and never seek solace in the computer screen. Smile and just try to be as sympathetic as you can,' she continued.

She recalled with a laugh the tricks customers would stoop to in order to get a table, such as pretending they were personal friends of the owner (whose name they usually mispronounced), or that they have made a reservation that has somehow got lost. In this latter instance, her goal was not to try and teach the customer a lesson, however appealing this tactic may seem, but to try and find a solution. 'We're there to be the agent for the guest, rather than the gatekeeper. We have to be seen and heard to be advocating for the customer. It's that simple, and that hard. And I really do miss it.'

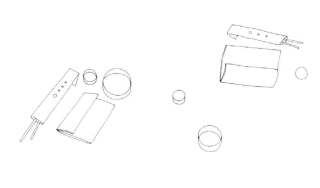

RUSSELL NORMAN

BUSTLING INTIMATE BARS

WITH SMALL PLATES

Russell Norman is the chameleon of restaurateurs: a man who changes not only his demeanour, but also his complete style of dress to blend in with the restaurants he once managed and those he now owns and runs. When he first appeared on the London scene in 2002 as general manager of Zuma, the contemporary Japanese restaurant in Knightsbridge, which is still one of the city's highest-grossing restaurants and which rose like a phoenix from the ashes of a former failed restaurant, Norman looked every inch the dapper gentleman. He wore smart suits, perfectly knotted ties, and the ends of his crisp white shirts were adorned with a pair of shining cufflinks. This was how Londoners got used to seeing Norman, whether he was in charge of the floor at Le Caprice or Zuma, or later when he glided between the floors of The Ivy Club, which he opened for his then boss, Richard Caring. One had little doubt about where or how he spent his money or days off.

Today, his dress sense is completely the opposite, and to describe it as casual would be an understatement. In the last three years he has branched out on his own to open Polpo, a Venetian *bacaro* or wine bar; Polpetto, a smaller branch of the same concept; Spuntino (illustrated page 199), a small American bar-diner where all the action revolves around a bar that seats twenty-six; the first branch of da Polpo ('son of Polpo'); and Mishkin's, a Jewish deli with cocktails in Covent Garden. The first three are located cheek by jowl in Soho, and Norman's dress today reflects that bohemian quarter – jeans, a less-than-crisply-ironed shirt, and all he needs from his office stowed in a knapsack hanging diagonally over his chest. One hand is permanently attached to his phone, which he consults frequently to show off his two families: his wife and two daughters on the one hand, and his five restaurants on the other.

The key to Norman's ability to change guise so readily, and to inspire the staff who work around him, lies in his unlikely past: he used to be a teacher. But the years he spent in this underrated profession, which depends on getting the right information across as effectively as possible, were also enhanced by the fact that he taught a discipline that affects the world of restaurants every time a customer walks in. Norman used to teach drama.

Although he had acquired a bug for bar work while travelling around Greece in 1990, he went on to teach English and drama from 1994 to 1998 at Bentley Wood High School for Girls in Stanmore, Middlesex. He recalls that era with great pride. 'I was the youngest male teacher there. I managed to increase the class size, and by the time I left I was Head of Drama.' Norman's face darkened when I asked if he could remember his final salary.

'Precisely,' he said. 'It was £26,000 ($40,000) a year.' This was, however, supplemented by the £100 ($235) per week he earned from his part-time job as maître d' at Joe Allen's in Covent Garden on Saturday evenings. This relaxed basement restaurant, a sibling to the one in New York, has long attracted a bustling crowd, particularly on Saturdays when the theatres and Royal Opera House close by are so popular.

As I envisaged Norman multi-tasking with hungry and impatient customers and the joint jumping, I recalled Sian Cox, who had been the quintessential receptionist in my own restaurant. Cox was also a teacher, with three children, who often used to work on Friday and Saturday nights, not only to supplement her income, but also because the glamour of London's West End provided excitement that may have been lacking after a week in the classroom. Cox had the most wonderful manner about her, which almost certainly came from spending most of her working life with children. A name that was not on the reservations list? Somebody's coat was missing? The phone was ringing while she was helping a lady on with her coat and a party of twenty was walking through the front door for the private dining room? Somehow, Sian could cope, and always with great charm. Sadly, she too left the world of teaching for a permanent and much higher-paying job as head receptionist at the Oxo Tower restaurant on London's South Bank, a restaurant so popular that its six receptionists receive over 1,000 phone calls a day.

It was the pressure of working in such large, constantly busy restaurants – for Rainer Becker at Zuma, alongside chef Mark Hix, then executive chef for The Ivy Group, and later for Richard Caring when the building above The Ivy was transformed into The Ivy Club – that finally persuaded Norman to go it alone. 'It was not just that I was burned out,' he explained, 'but also I felt it was finally the time to pursue my own dream.' Norman's long-cherished ambition was to open his own *bacaro* in London, to import into the narrow, waterless streets of Soho a version of the small, intimate wine bars that are such a compelling reason for visiting Venice. Dotting the banks of the canals, they serve cups of espresso to gondoliers, and their menus are a long list of *cichetti* (pronounced chi-ket-ee), or small Venetian snacks similar to Spanish tapas. He even had the great good fortune of finding a site for the first Polpo that bears on its exterior wall a blue plaque announcing that Canaletto, the great Venetian painter, once stayed there.

There are physical and financial factors common to Norman's varied restaurants, as well as the fact that Richard Beatty, his oldest friend,

Russell Norman

is a partner in them all. Beatty is a fellow marathon runner and a Mr Fixit
behind the scenes – he concentrates on ensuring that Norman's plans
and visions can be put into very best practice. He is always on the lookout
for restaurants that have failed in popular areas, and is happy to pay
a fair premium for a site that already has an established kitchen, even if it
needs a major overhaul. He will never spend a lot of money on the interior,
preferring to work with antique and second-hand dealers to create a lived-
in atmosphere. The high tables at da Polpo are made from re-purposed
chemistry laboratory benches. The original Polpo cost £140,000 ($220,000),
Spuntino £160,000 ($250,000) and da Polpo £200,000 ($315,000). This last
comes with a view of the tower of Corpus Christi church next door, which
gives it an extra layer of Venetian authenticity. The sixty-seater Mishkin's,
at over 158 square metres (1,700 square feet), cost the most at £300,000
($470,000) because it required a brand-new kitchen. But this is considerably
less than many restaurateurs spend (a minimum of £1 million ($1.5 million)
is often cited as the start-up cost today) because Norman believes that
designing and sourcing the material for one's future restaurant is one of the
joys of being a restaurateur. He described his company's evolution
graphically: 'At the beginning, with very limited funds available, I thought
of us as rather like a hermit crab, looking for a shell, a home, we could fit
into. Now, with good cash flow, we can afford a little more luxury.'

Since all his restaurants, apart from Mishkin's, serve their own
versions of small plates, financial success depends on serving as many
customers as efficiently as possible. But Norman admits that when he first
opened Polpo he did something that almost ensured its immediate failure.
'At the beginning I decided to take bookings, a policy I abandoned after
a few weeks. It was entirely inappropriate for the relaxed, informal place
I was desperate to create and, of course, there were no-shows that really upset
those who were waiting patiently for a table. I just threw the reservations
book in the bin.' Since then, business has prospered. Polpo serves 400 from
sixty-six seats on a busy day, Spuntino around 230 from twenty-six seats.
And the fact that customers will wait thirty to forty-five minutes for a table
generates a buzz in the air that not only reinforces the belief of those who
are already there that they are in the right place, but also acts as a magnet
to anyone walking by.

It's at this stage that Norman's previous career comes into its own.
'It's all about role-playing, and when I was a drama teacher I never allowed
anyone to be an observer. Even when someone came into the class to observe

196

either me or my pupils, I would never let them just watch. It didn't matter whether it was the headmaster or someone from the school inspectorate. They had to join in. I apply the same principles now whenever we train our waiters. If you like,' he smiled, 'I will find a role for you at our training session next week.' I readily agreed.

When I walked past da Polpo, where the training was due to take place, on the morning of the session, I was reminded once again of the many unexpected challenges in the life of a restaurateur. The whole of the street in front of the restaurant was being dug up: there were workmen and diggers everywhere. The already narrow pavement had been cut in half by a protective fence and the noise of a steamroller filled the entire street. Restaurants are only too frequently at the mercy of roadworks and general improvements to our city centres, but these do come at a price. Obscuring the restaurant's front window will not put off too many regulars, but it will certainly reduce the number of walk-ins, who may think, unsurprisingly, that the restaurant is closed. When scaffolding goes up around the building, it not only obliterates the view of the ground floor, the sign and the entrance, but also induces any but the most committed customer to keep on walking. Situations like these can cause a loss of as much as twenty per cent of revenue for as long as they persist, and I have never heard of a landlord who was prepared to offer any compensation.

When I entered the restaurant, most of the sixteen new recruits were standing on the left-hand side, but four were seated around a table, facing a waiter taking his first order. Norman and his restaurant manager were sitting close by, watching and encouraging whenever they could. The roleplay had begun. For the next hour I witnessed the surreal experience of a restaurant meal without food, wine or even a bill, although there were plenty of carafes of water, used here to welcome the guests and as a stand-in for wine. These wannabe waiters were at the beginning of their immersion into Norman's thirty-two-point sequence of service, a sequence he was confident would have them responding successfully when the new restaurant opened in a week's time.

Each time the people playing waiters and guests switched places, Norman encouraged the guests to begin by asking a difficult question. 'What comes with olives?' was one he suggested, because he knows from bitter experience that it is right at the initial stage that a waiter can develop a fatal bad habit. Jumping down off his stool, he turned to face his audience and explained: 'Sometimes, when you get an unexpected

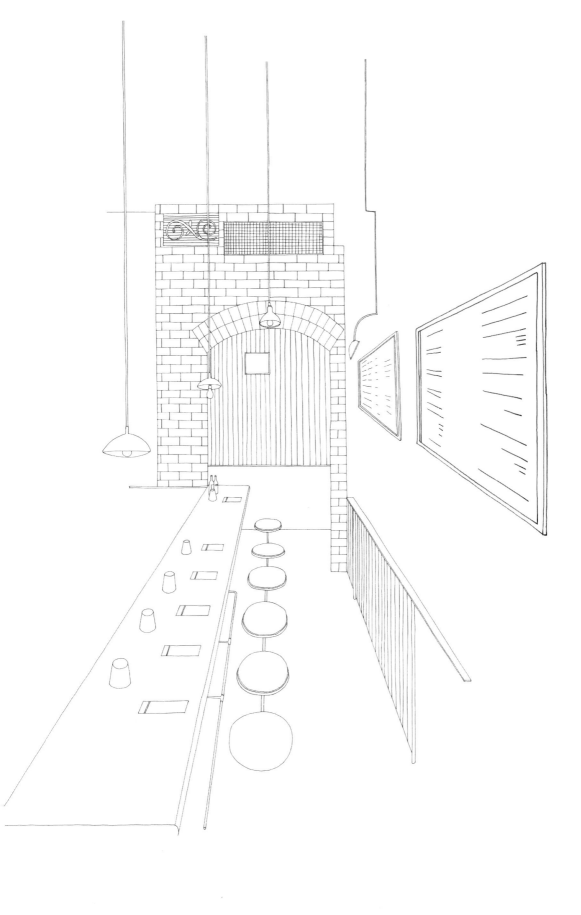

question, your mind can go blank and you're tempted to make up an answer. Never do this, please. Never, ever make it up. Don't be a hero,' he pleaded. 'Give the customer a smile, say you don't know but that you will find out for them right away. In time you will find your own phrase.'

The detailed sequence of service, which Norman has kindly allowed me to reproduce here, demonstrates forcefully that even in a relaxed, inexpensive restaurant there has to be a structure to the way every customer's order is taken and processed. But Norman emphasized, 'There is no party line. What I want is that my staff start to learn all this and then embellish it, to be creative in how they treat their customers.' He added to this one other golden rule: 'We never force anyone to eat or drink something they're not enjoying. If they don't like something for whatever reason, we change it.' At this point he saw a young waitress walking back to the bar, having just cleared a table of all its plates. He smiled and shouted, 'Good carry!'

Just after 5.00 p.m., Norman called it a day and asked them all to be back promptly the following morning. He had a brief chat with Robin Parish, who was going off to manage Polpo that evening and who explained that he would miss the freshness of these new recruits. Norman wished him luck with what was promising to be another busy evening. Before he too set off on a circuit of his restaurants, Norman revealed that his biggest challenge is finding good staff, although it does become slightly easier as the number of restaurants in his group increases. He offers a signing-on fee for anyone on the current team who introduces a new member of staff of £150 ($235) for the first three months and another £150 if they stay a further three months. As I was about to say goodbye, Norman was keen to add a final observation about the profession that has captivated him for the past fifteen years. 'Quite recently, I was voted Restaurateur of the Year in the *Tatler* restaurant awards, which was a very nice compliment for me and all those I work with. Then two things happened that were not quite so lovely. First, of all I had to deal with the biggest complaint I have ever had to deal with since I started on my own. And then something broke in one of the kitchens and at 3.00 a.m. I was up to my elbows in sewage. Quite humbling, really.'

To make sure there is consistency, we all need to follow the same sequence of service. This should be the same every time, whether customers are dining at the bar or in the restaurant.

1

Customers enter. They are greeted by the manager if possible, the bartender if not, and then whoever sees them first. *We must all look out for people entering.*

2

The manager seats the customers at a table or at the bar. Remember that menus are printed on the place mats, so there is no need to offer menus.

3

The section waiter or bartender should approach the table or bar counter with a bottle of tap water and pour water into the glasses. Use this opportunity to say hello, welcome and ask how they are. Hand the drinks list to the customer. One list per table.

4

Offer drinks to the customers. If they order drinks, enter these into the computer system. Also enter 'New Table' and the number of covers for the kitchen.

5

Collect the drinks from the bar and take them to your table. Use a tray. There should be no longer than two minutes between ordering and receiving drinks.

6

If there are any verbal specials, inform the customers of them at this point. Also inform them if any dishes are off the menu.

7

When your customers have had a few minutes to look at their menus, approach the table and ask if they are ready to order.

8

If they are not ready, inform the manager and neighbouring waiters or bartenders quietly with 'Not ready on Table five'. This stops the customers being continually bothered.

9

If your customers have not ordered drinks yet, they might order wine at this point, in which case enter the wine order into the computer.

10

Collect the wine from the bar and serve it to the customer, offering a taste first to the person who ordered the wine. You must offer a taste in a fresh glass to the person who orders for every subsequent bottle, too.

11

When your customers are ready, take the order using a waiter pad and pen.

12

Since Polpo's is a sharing menu, we recommend at least two dishes per person. Remember that the *cichetti* are small single bites. Advise your customers if they have ordered too little or what seems like a lot. You should *not* say 'That's not enough' or 'That's too much', but instead say 'Are you very hungry? That's quite a few dishes' or 'That's quite a light lunch/dinner. Let me know if you want to order anything else later.'

13

Enter the dishes into the computer, using course dividing lines if appropriate. Put the white copy on the tab rack and put the yellow copy on the pantry spike.

14

Take any extra cutlery to the table if required (a spoon for a dish with lots of sauce, for example), and place an empty side plate in front of each customer.

15

When the food comes to the table, make good eye contact to make sure you are there if the customers need you. Everyone is responsible for taking food to tables, not just the section waiter. If the pantry chef gives you food to take, please take it, whether it is your table or not.

16

Remember to call away courses if you have used them. (In a normal restaurant, an important element of any waiter's job is to call away the main course from the kitchen when the customers are finishing their first course, so that there is no delay between the two. Polpo does not follow a traditional course-based pattern, but when customers order a lot of food the waiter won't want it all to come at once, so he or she separates their order into several courses. When the waiter does this he or she must remember to tell the kitchen to send the next lot of dishes. Norman has organized the system to allow any number of courses, which depends on the waiter calling each of them away.)

17

It is important to practise good table management: Top up water and replace with a fresh bottle if necessary. Take away empty plates and put them in the bus area (the place where waiters put dirty crockery, cutlery and glasses to be taken to the washing-up area).

Take empty glasses back to bar.
Replace dirty napkins with clean ones.
Top up wine and offer more when finished.
Keep track of what dishes have been ordered
    and what has been served.
Smile.
Make good eye contact.
Do *not* ask if everything is OK. This suggests that OK
    is good enough. Please say: 'Is everything good?'
Smile some more.

18

When all dishes have been finished, clear the empty
plates and place in the bus tray at the back. At the
waiter station, load the cleaning cloth with anti-bac
and wipe down the table. Remove the place settings
and offer the small dessert slips.

19

Remove the salt and pepper.

20

Go back to your table for a dessert order.
Offer coffee at the same time.

21

Remove the dessert menu and place the order into
Tevalis (the electronic point-of-sale system).

22

Go back to your table with appropriate cutlery for
dessert, and/or place a sugar bowl on the table if the
customers are having coffee.

23

We serve coffee at the same time as dessert unless
the customer specifically requests it afterwards.

24

After desserts have been finished, clear the plates and make good eye contact. The customer may ask for the bill at this stage.

25

If not, continue to practise good table management as above.

26

When the customer asks for the bill, print two copies. Staple one to the duplicates in the tab rack and present the other one to the customer, stapled to a bill slip.

27

Take payment (either credit card or cash – we do not accept cheques) and process it. If taking a credit card payment, ensure you initial our copy so it is obvious who took the payment. Signed payments also need a duplicate copy printed, which states the signature has been verified. Ask your manager how to do this if you are unsure.

28

Take the payment with second copy of bill to the bartender and leave it on the spike if a credit card payment, or hand to the bartender if cash (particularly if you need change for the customer). You must wait for your change.

29

Any cash tips go into the pot and are shared at the end of the shift amongst floor and bar staff.

Russell Norman

If customers ask whether service is included, the
politest response is: 'Yes it is. Thank you for asking.'
The best response when they ask if service goes
to the staff is: 'Service charge and tips are shared
amongst the staff.'

When the customers leave, help them with their table,
smile and say goodbye. Even if you miss them leaving
at the table, try to say goodbye at the door. Customers
want to say goodbye!

Set up the table ready for the next sitting as quickly
as possible.

Restaurateurs have to be excellent communicators, whether in formal
restaurants in which the maître d', complete with the reservations list,
will brief all the waiting staff half an hour before the first customers arrive
for lunch or dinner, or in the more casual restaurants that Norman has
now made his home. But there is no doubt that any meal in any restaurant will be far more enjoyable for the customer if they too make their
intentions clear from the start. Waiters can do a better job if they know as
clearly as possible what their customer wants. And although it applies to
every restaurateur, Russell Norman highlights this challenge well because
his restaurants demand two different sets of communication skills. In the
four restaurants that serve small plates, customers often order too many
dishes as soon as they sit down, whereas at Mishkin's, where each dish
is much larger, customers may order too many dishes, and their meal will
be immediately out of balance.

The response to each situation, Norman teaches his staff, has to be
different. For those serving the small plates, the waiter has to explain as
politely as possible that the food will come quite quickly, so the best policy
is not to order everything at once. More challengingly, at Mishkin's it
is important not to convey the impression that the waiter knows best, or
to deprive the customer of the dish they are longing to eat, but it should

be communicated that ordering a little less will result in a lot more pleasure. Norman undoubtedly relishes this challenge, particularly now that his five restaurants will serve 900 customers per day on average.

I asked what changes he had noticed when he moved from the organizational hierarchy of running some of London's most prestigious restaurants to owning his own. 'I definitely work longer hours than I used to and I am a much harder critic of myself than any of my former bosses used to be, however tough they appeared at the time. It's my reputation at stake, so the potential for failure pushes me even harder. My standards are more demanding and I want everything to be right from the day we open. But I wouldn't have it any other way,' he ended with a smile, 'I love coming to work.'

On a broader scale, what is perhaps most fascinating about Norman's emergence as a successful restaurateur is that this obviously confident and fluent communicator has made his mark in London's Soho, the epicentre of the UK's communications industry. He is a restaurateur who has studied, memorized and learned to speak his lines very well indeed, and knows how crucial it his for his team to do so equally fluently.

Russell Norman

To book or not to book

Taking a reservation by phone is one of the most enjoyable aspects of the restaurant business. It is a real pleasure to talk to someone who wants to spend time and money in your restaurant – more fun, I would imagine, than simply reading the growing number of bookings that now come in silently via the internet. It is the first step towards generating happy customers. But how restaurants operate their booking policy varies enormously. No ambitious or expensive restaurant can survive without taking as many bookings as possible, usually leaving only one or two free tables to give to regular customers at the last minute. Mid-priced restaurants, on the other hand, may only take bookings for fifty to sixty per cent of their tables, particularly on busier evenings, as this allows the manager and receptionist maximum flexibility to 'turn tables', and thereby generate the highest number of customers, which in turn means higher sales and more tips.

Then there is the distinction between lunch and dinner. It is possible, but almost certainly not in the restaurant's best interests, to adopt a no-reservations policy at lunch. This is unlikely to be appreciated by most customers. Lunch is for business meetings, and they want to be sure of a table and an agreed time to meet. The evening, by contrast, is for pleasure when time is less pressing.

Neither approach is without problems. Not taking bookings is commercially the riskier strategy of the two, but taking bookings requires considerable work by the receptionists to ensure the reservations list is as accurate as it can be. This involves not just taking the bookings, but also the practice, now virtually standard in many restaurants, of calling every customer who has booked that day to confirm that they will indeed be coming. This can be a significant expense.

Russell Norman moved from being a general manager of large restaurants, which took reservations as a matter of course, to open the much smaller Polpo, and understandably took this policy with him. He soon realized the error of his ways. 'We got some great reviews at the outset, which meant that we received a huge number of bookings that we obviously took with some relief,' he explained. 'But then on top of that we had lots of people walking in looking for a table whom we couldn't accommodate. These were the people living and working nearby, who were obviously going to be our long-term customers – and we were turning them away!' Norman decided to change tack. He honoured all the bookings they had already, but after an agreed and well-publicized date, he decided that they would take no more bookings in the evening. He expected the dip in trade that ensued as his customers learned to live with this change, but it was much briefer than he had feared. Since then, business in the evening has been even better. Bookings are still taken for lunch, and also in the evening at some of his restaurants, but there are no receptionists. Instead, the manager is responsible for all the bookings and is equipped simply with a clipboard and seven or fourteen sheets of paper, depending on how far in advance reservations are taken.

The policy of no bookings at Polpo has caused Norman and his team to face the new challenge of queue management, and this has led to significant changes in the layout of the restaurant to ensure that they keep hungry and thirsty customers happy and on the premises. The first change was to create as much space as possible for people to wait in. After a year, Norman decided that the private room in the basement would have to be decommissioned to make way for a Campari bar for waiting customers. The second was that it became absolutely crucial to produce a limited food menu to be served in the bar along with the drinks list, so that no one becomes too drunk before their table is ready. And, from his own experiences in 'inoteca, Freeman's and the Waverly Inn in New York, he added shallow shelves wherever he could, to hold customers' drinks and plates.

It is down to the restaurateur to make the necessity of waiting for a table in to the most pleasurable experience possible. Having a few drinks before dinner is a very sociable activity, and Norman has watched with pleasure how often two couples, unknown to each other at the beginning, start talking to each other and then become a table of four in the restaurant. This is an outcome, a smiling Norman concluded, that leads to happy customers – and an equally happy restaurateur.

Russell Norman

NEIL PERRY

AUSTRALIAN STYLE, SUBSTANCE AND CONFIDENCE

Neil Perry strode into the private dining room on the first floor of his Rockpool Bar & Grill, in the heart of Sydney's business district, at 10.30 p.m. on a Monday evening looking every inch the successful restaurateur he has become. He had just come from presiding over a charity dinner that had raised over AUS $1 million (£700,000 or US $1.1 million) for OzHarvest, a national organization that takes the food the supermarkets and food manufacturers consider superfluous – produce that used to end up in landfill – processes it and delivers it to the homeless. The scene he walked into delighted him. Around the long table were the judges from the prestigious annual Sydney Wine Show, and in front of them were the remnants of what they had enjoyed for dinner. There had been platters of two different breeds of Australian beef that Perry dry-ages at the restaurant, alongside a string of empty red wine decanters that not so long ago had held magnums of Jaboulet's Hermitage La Chapelle 1990, Brokenwood Graveyard Shiraz 1998 from the nearby Hunter Valley and the even more sought-after 1996 Wendouree Shiraz. The rest of the table was covered in glasses. Perry also felt the internal delight that, however difficult his years in the restaurant business may have been, his empire of seven restaurants, which stretches from Melbourne to Sydney and then east to Perth, is currently thriving. His restaurant group has an annual turnover of AUS $78 million (£53 million or US $83 million) and employs 520 people, and an eighth restaurant, his first venture into Italian cooking that will generate a further 110 jobs, is planned for Melbourne in autumn 2012. For a restaurateur who has had more than his fair share of failures over the past thirty years, this must be a source of considerable satisfaction.

From New York, restaurateurs Joe Bastianich and Drew Nieporent manage restaurant businesses across distances as large as those Perry deals with; Maguy Le Coze has epitomized France, her home country, in America, her professional home, for almost as long as Perry has been cooking. But there is no other restaurateur, in my opinion, who has come to personify the changing, dynamic and always surprising face of a whole continent's restaurants in quite the same way that Perry has for Australia. Since my first visit in the early 1980s, I have always been struck by the vibrancy of Australia's restaurants and by the ability of so many of its chefs to turn the culinary techniques of Europe to their own advantage while at the same time uncovering, respecting and adapting their continent's extraordinary produce. As a restaurateur myself, I was the beneficiary in London of numerous itinerant and highly talented Australian chefs and waiters who then went back and became successful in their own right in their own country.

No one in Australia has experienced the highs and lows that Perry has. No one else has established restaurants that have contributed to the transformation of what were at the time rather run-down areas of Sydney into what are now unmissable tourist destinations, as Perry has done with Rockpool (illustrated page 219), which has re-energized The Rocks since it opened in this most historic part of the city in 1989. No one else has turned a vast and once neglected building, originally designed as a banking hall in 1936 Art Deco style, into the kind of restaurant that would make any restaurateur green with envy, as Perry has done with Rockpool Bar & Grill, which he opened in 2009. Or taken what was once a large basement directly underneath a former storage facility, and simultaneously opened a second restaurant, Spice Temple, devoted to the cooking of six different regions of China.

These last two openings finally marked Perry's transition from chef to restaurateur, although even in his mid fifties he still has the energy to put in a number of strenuous shifts in his kitchens every week, as well as fulfilling his role as TV chef and food columnist. No other restaurateur, perhaps again displaying the very Australian characteristic of openness, talks about the good and bad times with such ease or rapidity. The following lunchtime we met again at Rockpool Bar & Grill, and Perry, sporting his signature ponytail, was carrying a white T-shirt for a photoshoot immediately afterwards. We sat at a table facing the long open kitchen that stretches along the entire right-hand side of the restaurant, generating columns of steam that rise languidly to the ceiling. Once he'd helped himself to one of the two mini-burgers the waitress promptly put on our table, muttering that this was his breakfast, he was off – although not, initially, about what I had wanted to talk to him about. Instead he recalled that he had once sat at a dinner table with Thomas Keller, the renowned American chef and proprietor of The French Laundry in California and Per Se in New York, who had asked him what his 'exit strategy' for his restaurants was going to be, how one day he intended to realize their financial value. Perry's response was that now that his daughter Josephine was in the restaurant business, his goals were very different, that he was focused on leaving as successful a business as possible for her and her two younger sisters, if they were to show the same interest, to take over. He dreamed of coming into their

Neil Perry

restaurants at a ripe old age, hoping to be well fed, watered and looked after by their staff.

While he was still relishing the success of the previous night's charity dinner, he also wanted to express his continued surprise and delight at how the role of the internationally acclaimed chef today can unite so many people from the worlds of politics, the arts and business to support such causes. Dinners in Sydney with Keller and Britain's Heston Blumenthal had not only proved hugely beneficial for the Starlight Children's Foundation, the charity that aims to provide dying children with their final wish, but also provided lots of fun for everyone in the restaurant. There was then a momentary lull in Perry's rapid fire, and I was able to ask him about the influence that the book *The Great Chefs of France* has had on his career. Written by the late Quentin Crewe over thirty years ago, with striking black-and-white photos by Anthony Blake, for the very first time it documented the professional lives and achievements of all the three-Michelin-starred chefs of France, and has also been a significant influence on my desire to write this book. Perry smiled even more broadly. He could still remember buying a second-hand copy many years ago, and how it inspired him to do the best food he could, to focus all his passion and energy into cooking. 'Reading it was as though a light bulb went on in my head. I've just handed it over to my daughter and I hope it will have the same effect on her.'

This strong French influence, though, came on top of a very Australian upbringing. His father Les was a butcher who knew his meat and was more than happy to pass on this knowledge to his interested son, as well as his love of fishing, tending vegetables and his enthusiasm for the food then being cooked in Sydney's Chinatown. Perry absorbed a love of cooking based on the principles of catch, kill, prepare, cook and eat. Although in retrospect he can see that he was destined for a career in the kitchen, he decided to take what he now describes as the 'long path' to this goal. It was a path that was to yield unanticipated professional advantages that were to make him more customer-focused. Aged eighteen, Perry started work as a waiter, and this began to instill in him an appreciation of the detail that has to go into the success of any restaurant. 'It is the interconnection between the kitchen, the floor of the restaurant and the customer that is crucial. Had I just been cooking in the kitchen I would not have had the opportunity to appreciate all this at such an impressionable age.' There was one further advantage. As a waiter in busy restaurants, Perry earned far more from his tips than his counterparts in the kitchen, and it was to be the start of his burgeoning interest in wine, which has played such a part in his restaurants' profitability. In Sydney in the early 1980s, public appreciation of wine was finally emerging, thanks to a strong dollar at the time and to an increased appreciation of the best French wines. Perry recalled the kindness of two wine sales people in particular, Gill Hurley Gordon and Kate McKillop, whom he described as generous teachers and who introduced him to some wonderful bottles. 'There was a period,' he added with relish, 'when we would have a bottle of Dom Pérignon every Sunday lunch.'

The close proximity to chefs that resulted from his work as a waiter, combined with what I can only imagine was a natural cockiness or conviction that he could do even better than those he was watching, finally propelled Perry into the kitchen. During the early 1980s he moved swiftly through a series of the best restaurants in Sydney and Melbourne, describing himself at that time as 'a wandering minstrel soaking up as much as he could.' According to winemaker Michael Hill-Smith, this was not as relaxed a strategy as it might appear. 'Neil cleverly chose to work with and learn from all the best chefs at the time: Stephanie Alexander, Tony Papas, Stefano Manfredi and Damien Pignolet at Claude's, which was a really influential French restaurant at that time. He was very focused.' This period was not only instrumental for his grounding as a chef, but also for his approach. There was a feeling in the air among the better Australian kitchens of that era that, far from Europe, anything and everything was possible and that, as these new restaurants prospered, business would only get better and better. In a phrase I could not imagine any other chef repeating, Perry described this era as a time when 'if you were a keen cook, you just needed to tie up your horse outside and come on in and cook.'

Perry shot to recognition as a chef in his own right when he took over at Barrenjoey House, Palm Beach, a forty-minute drive north of Sydney, where he received a seventeen out of twenty review from Leo Schofield in the *Sydney Morning Herald*. In 1986 he moved on and opened the seminal Blue Water Grill on Bondi Beach, a restaurant that singlehandedly changed Australian cooking. Perry described this restaurant as significant for him because it marked the first step back from fine dining in his nascent career, and at the same time he lamented that he had not retained it's evocative name. Barry McDonald, fellow Sydney restaurateur, Perry's closest friend and best man at each of his three weddings, described its influence as far more significant and long lasting. Before the Blue Water Grill, he explained, Australians only saw their grilled fish or meat smothered in sauces or butter. After Blue Water Grill, people realized that this practice served only to mask the main ingredient's inherent freshness and flavour. 'We all began to follow Neil's lead in serving precisely cooked dishes with something really striking like an Asian salad or a South American salsa on the side. It was the start of what came to be seen as our very own style of cooking. It was great food in a great location at very good prices.'

Blue Water Grill lasted only three years before it succumbed to the external pressures of being an extremely busy restaurant in a heavily residential area, with all the associated problems of noise, traffic and waste disposal upsetting the neighbours, an outcome that brought a touch of sadness to Perry's voice. More sadness might have ensued for far more Australians had Perry then accepted an inviting proposition to open a restaurant in New York, which he was weighing up against opening what was to become the original Rockpool. A flight back to Sydney to sort out visas and work permits was to make the decision for him. He recalled a glorious morning as the plane circled over the city; he looked down and saw the Harbour Bridge and the Opera House and the whole bay covered in sunshine. 'I realized that I am an Australian and that I had spent my whole life cooking the freshest Australian produce, so why would I want to move to New York?' His decision to stay in Sydney was made before the plane had even touched the ground.

While the opening of Rockpool was to transform an area best known until then for its opportunities for pub crawls, and simultaneously to bolster Perry's and Sydney's culinary reputation, it was the partnership he entered into at the same time with his cousin, Trish Richards, that was to form the financial foundation of his restaurant business. Richards had just successfully sold her own business, and now stepped in to provide Perry with all the financial advice any burgeoning restaurateur demands. Many years later, Perry still cannot hide his delight at this turn of events. 'Trish is the rock of the business. Because we're family, she provides me with the kind of financial advice that money simply cannot buy. It's a great relief for me to know that this increasingly complex side of the business is so well covered by her and her team.'

In 1997, the success of Rockpool led Qantas, the Australian airline, to appoint Perry as catering consultant for their first and business-class customers on board and in the airport lounges, an arrangement that continues to this day. Unlike the more common practice, whereby well-known chefs propose recipes and dishes to their national airline, Perry's

role is much more involved, and he currently employs six full-time chefs whose role is solely to source the right produce and train Qantas and their catering companies' staff to ensure that the dishes served in the air are as close as possible to those created on the ground. This arrangement has taken Perry's profile around the world, and the solid financial deal behind it has also helped underpin a business that, however popular the restaurants may seem, has not always been quite as profitable.

This certainly proved to be the case in the years immediately before and after 2000, when Perry was forced to close a series of recently opened high-profile restaurants. Wockpool, XO, Bistro Mars and Rocket came and went, losing him in the process AUS $2 million (£1.35 million or US $2.15 million), and his business came close to the professional precipice. 'We could have put the company into liquidation, walked away and reopened six months later. But the money was owed to people who had become friends and I didn't want to behave like that. I decided we had to trade our way out, however long it would take, however painful the process,' he explained. With hindsight he is quite clear how and why things went so badly wrong. His single biggest mistake was human: he began to believe in his professional infallibility, that he could do no wrong. Most importantly, he now recalls with acuity, he never stopped to ask himself the simple question: what if the proposed restaurant doesn't work? There were also several external issues, such as the hype leading up to the 2000 Olympics in Sydney, the commercial lull afterwards and a change in the treatment of tax benefits that severely affected business lunches, but Perry is now mature enough to acknowledge his own failings. It's vital when you plan a restaurant, he believes, that you are confident and optimistic of success. 'But I simply got carried away. I thought that once they were open, everything would be all right, that the customers would come.' Now he knows better: the advantage of experience is being able to see what can go wrong and know your limits so that you can walk away before it's too late. 'It's crucial not to be sucked in, as I was. If it's not going to work, let it go.'

In true Australian fashion, Perry had a sporting analogy for the challenges of running restaurants. 'I love skiing but we never get much snow here, so you've got to learn to ski on what is not much more than ice.' With tough labour laws, red tape, high running costs and relatively small populations in even the biggest cities – Sydney and Melbourne only have just over four million each – there is a much smaller pool of potential customers, a fact that many overseas restaurateurs have failed to appreciate.

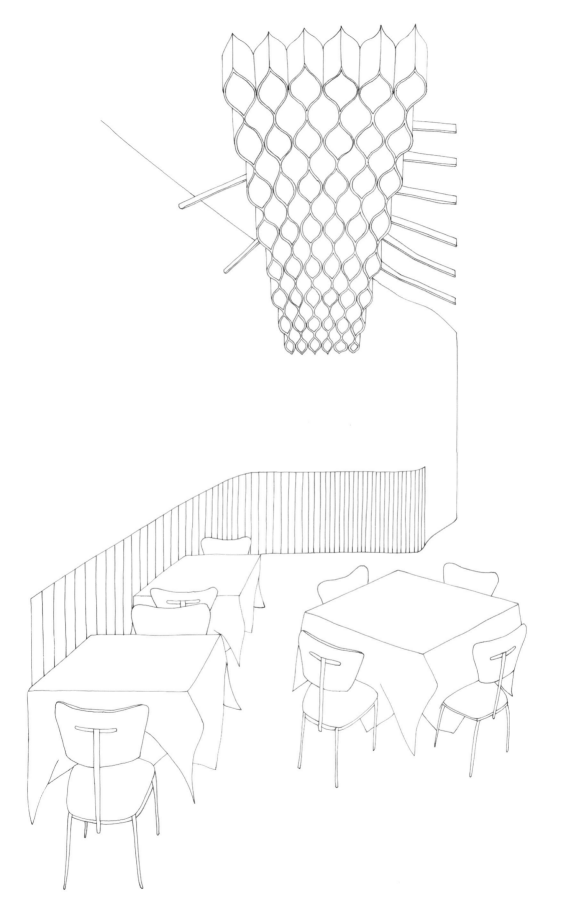

'That's why I've seen so many come here and fail, sadly. I reckon if you can master it here, you can master it anywhere, but the reverse is not true.' As Rockpool began to emerge from what Perry described as 'the financial shit', his business was transformed by the most unlikely combination of partners and backers. The instigator was James Packer, son of the Australian media mogul Kerry Packer, who was beginning to develop the Crown complex of casinos and hotels in Melbourne. Advised by John Alexander, a publisher and a highly influential figure in the development of Sydney's restaurants, Packer approached Perry with the site, confident in his expertise. As soon as he walked in, Perry said, he knew that it would be an ideal home for the steak house he had long dreamed of, one that focused on the best produce and a great wine list. Since he was determined to build the Rockpool brand, a Rockpool Bar & Grill was the obvious next step. The first of what have now become three classic steak restaurants in Melbourne, Sydney and Perth, complete with prints of hefty cattle on the walls and cellars full of red wine, was born.

This new development also saw the entrance of American tycoon David Doyle as an equity partner, in many respects the kind of financial fairy godmother any restaurateur would wish for. Having made a fortune in his dotcom business, Doyle had used the proceeds to indulge his passions for good food and great wine, building up a significant wine cellar in the process, and had met Perry at Rockpool, where common interests had sparked a friendship. Perry approached Doyle to take a significant stake in his business, not just because he did not want to repeat the mistakes of the past, but also because, although he had always enjoyed Melbourne as a visitor, he knew that commercially it was a very different city from Sydney and bringing in a new partner allowed him to minimize the risk. This new structure allowed Perry not only to open Rockpool Bar & Grill in Melbourne, but also Spice Temple, a Chinese restaurant, next door, and then The Waiting Room just across a lobby as an homage to the cocktail bars Perry had enjoyed on his travels. Their locations close to one another, along with the allure of the casinos, which quickly came to attract sixteen million visitors a year, assured the restaurants' success.

Doyle and Perry went on a trip to San Sebastián, north-west Spain, where the attraction of the local fish restaurants such as Extebarri and Elkano that specialize in large grills inspired them to plan to replicate something similar in Sydney (a visit by New York restaurateur Danny Meyer to the same part of the world prompted him to open North End Grill in January 2012).

On his return to Sydney, Doyle contacted property agents requesting sites with views of the harbour or in Bondi. Shortly afterwards, Doyle phoned Perry with news he was not expecting. 'You've got to come and see this,' Doyle enthused, 'it's got Bar & Grill written all over it.' Although today Sydney's Rockpool Bar & Grill exudes glamour and excitement, the location was not at all like that when Doyle and Perry first saw it. It occupies the ground floor and mezzanine of 66 Hunter Street, a building constructed in an elegant Art Deco style as the headquarters of a big insurance company, but subsequently severely neglected. Its 1,300 square metres (14,000 square feet) were full, Perry recalled, of office dividers and fake palm trees and it cost AUS $60,000 (£40,000 or US $65,000) just to clear the space of rubbish. When this was completed, Perry recalls phoning Doyle in Las Vegas to tell him that what they had taken over was in fact 'a cathedral'.

Today, with its ten grand columns, 3,000 customers a week, 7,500 Riedel glasses displayed hanging over the bar and in several locations throughout the dining room, and views up to the tables on the mezzanine, Rockpool Bar & Grill exudes culinary excitement. Perry recalled, though, that the sheer size was initially terrifying. He remembered showing a friend round as the AUS $10 million (£7 million or US $11 million) refurbishment was under way and he was very dubious. 'He kept saying, this is the business district in Sydney, it's not the Crown complex in Melbourne. Who's going to come here? We walked out at about 8.00 p.m. and I remember looking around and there was no one on the street. I didn't sleep for a month.'

The design of Spice Temple in the basement of the same building, Perry admits, owes a great deal to Hakkasan in London, and has succeeded because, despite its lack of both natural light and view, both factors so synonymous with Sydney, it has created a distinctive, somewhat sepulchral ambience, providing sufficient reason for the customer to want to be in the space. And that, in his words 'is always the trick'. While Rockpool Bar & Grill has many of the natural and architectural advantages, it has also created a particular commercial one. Restaurateurs around the world aim for a 70:30 ratio of food to drink sales by value and are continually trying to ensure that the drink proportion never diminishes, as it is the easier source of profits. In this restaurant, however, Perry admitted that the sales split can sometimes be 50:50, the considerably higher drinks sales resulting partly from Australia's notorious thirst, partly the exceptional wine list, much of which comes from Doyle's cellar, and also from the highly unusual and attractive display of so many top-quality wine glasses. Anyone coming in for just a quick business lunch will find themselves tempted to order something to drink once their eyes roam. It is a hugely effective, clever and subliminal boost to business.

For this Perry gives full credit to Grant Cheyne, his designer on this and on several other restaurants, whose approach from the outset was to pay homage to the original building and to interfere with it as little as possible. Perry continued in the vein of a singer introducing the rest of the band, describing himself as 'the mouthpiece of a brilliant organization' that encompasses not only all his staff and Cheyne, but also photographer Earl Carter as well as Fiona Brand and David, her late husband, as graphic designers. As though speaking on behalf of restaurateurs everywhere, he continued to explain that what he finds remarkable is that because they are in the restaurant business dealing with customers all the time, it is an organization steeped in humanity. 'And that is why I always stress my care philosophy. We're here to care for our suppliers, the space we work in, one another, our customers and our ultimate profitability. And profit must never be a dirty word.' Every restaurant, he went on, needs to be buoyant and reinvent itself, to replace continually cutlery, glasses, carpets, to reinvest for the company's future and, most importantly of all, for those who work for it. 'Maintaining the restaurant's patina, its sheen, is crucial, not just because it is what the customer sees, but also to make the staff feel proud about where they work.'

Perry let slip two final insights into his career. The first was personal: that the most significant change and improvement in Neil Perry the restaurateur over the past fifteen years, as failure has given way to success, has been his growing ability to understand people, to select, motivate and instruct them for the increasing benefit of his customers. On that note, he wanted to recount a recent highly satisfying experience. In another of James Packer's Crown complexes, Perry had opened his third Rockpool Bar & Grill in Perth, Western Australia, in January 2011, to a hugely enthusiastic response as that city's economy booms on the back of its commodity exports. He had just received a letter from a couple who had dined there and were effusive about everything they had experienced, in particular the waiting staff, who had made them feel like royalty, as though 'we were the only people in the restaurant'. Perry had made a point of reading the letter out loud at a staff meeting and had asked them all to remember it every time they approach a table. The memory of this, and the pleasure his cooking and his team had obviously generated, brought yet another smile to his face.

Nurture your suppliers

'The cornerstone of good cooking is to source the finest produce.' This quote from Neil Perry has appeared in the top left-hand corner of every menu he has written since the original Rockpool opened in 1989. While this ingredient-focused philosophy is now common among today's chefs and restaurateurs, it remains very close to Perry's heart, and not only because it has been a constant factor in his approach to cooking and to his success. Freshness, Perry believes with a passion, is in fact the 'sixth taste' in the food we enjoy. On top of salt, sweet, sour, bitter and umami (which is sometimes described as savouriness, is prevalent in Japanese food and has been recognized much more widely by Western chefs over the past decade), it is freshness, in Perry's opinion, that adds

the vital extra dimension of verve and life to whatever the customer orders, and will be a major factor in whether they return.

To ensure your restaurant receives the freshest produce, and to compensate for producers' hardships and modest financial rewards, it is incumbent on chefs and restaurateurs, Perry believes, to promote their suppliers' names to the public and the press. Chefs cannot be selfish and keep these individuals to themselves, and that is the principal reason the menu at Rockpool Bar & Grill lists certain suppliers by name: Bruce Collis supplied the King George whiting and the fillets of flathead; David Blackmore bred the dry-aged Wagyu beef; the oyster beds of the Clyde River are the source of the five-year-old Sydney rock oysters. 'I know from my own experience that to line-catch a fish, kill it humanely and prepare and deliver it swiftly so that it arrives at the kitchen door as fresh as possible may generate a forty per cent premium for the fisherman. But this process is at least ten times more difficult than the norm. I know that without their commitment I would not have had the success I have had. These suppliers are my heroes.'

There are several other reasons why it is important to look after your suppliers. The most obvious is that any menu or wine list is in many ways a reflection of their skills, whether at sea, on the farm, in the orchards or in the vineyards. Over time, as the restaurant's reputation spreads, there is the sense of reflected glory that many suppliers feel at seeing their produce or wines listed at well-known restaurants. I have seen supposedly tough-skinned Australian

Neil Perry

wine producers almost purr with delight as they scan the wine lists of some of London's best restaurants, 20,000 kilometers (12,000 miles) from home, and see the fruits of their labour exposed to view. The pleasure is even greater if they see customers at another table actually drinking their wine with their bottle prominently on display.

Suppliers are also conduits of very practical information. Many provide timely emails to the kitchen about when certain ingredients are about to come into season, so that they can be incorporated into the menu and, just as importantly, when they are close to the end of their natural cycle so that they can be taken off the menu before they disappoint or become too costly. In the UK, knowing exactly when the asparagus season is going to get under way, in order to take full advantage of what is always a hugely popular ingredient, can be a significant boost to a kitchen's gross profit during the short but glorious six-week season. While the best suppliers are usually careful not to disclose too much about what they see or hear at another restaurant's kitchen door, they do – like everyone else – enjoy a good gossip, and this can be comforting. If a series of public holidays has led to a quiet month's trading, a report from a supplier of any restaurant's most basic purchases (such as milk, cream, butter or vegetables), that all his or her customers are experiencing the same downturn can bring some relief. Where this mutually beneficial relationship can, and often does, go wrong, is when the restaurateur, accountant or finance director, treats their suppliers as a source of credit as well as goods, and unilaterally

extends the agreed payment terms by an extra thirty days, or even more. Wine merchants, in particular, tend to be the victims of such brutal treatment.

Suppliers also play one other vital role in the life of a restaurateur. While restaurateurs tend to be urban animals, their suppliers are not, and this invaluable connection to nature can give the restaurateur both a sense of fresh air, and of his or her role in passing it on and providing culinary pleasure to so many people every day. The late Bob Baxter used to supply me with his renowned Morecambe Bay potted shrimps twice a week. They were shipped down directly from the coast of Lancashire because, served with brown toast, lemon and a green salad, they were a constantly popular dish. He used to visit the restaurant a couple of times a year, impeccably dressed in his double-breasted suit and tie, and would call me once a month, never to sell but always for a chat. He had a broad Lancashire accent that I never had any trouble recognizing on the phone, although it was always a source of wonder to him that I did. Whenever we spoke, I was immediately transported to that part of the English coastline where the tiny shrimps were caught before being cooked to a secret recipe and topped with a thin layer of butter (the 'potting' that preserved them) by a team of women he always referred to as 'his girls', although they had spent all their working lives potting shrimps. Just by talking to him I was suddenly no longer in central London but on the coast, where the wind blew off the sea and the air was bracingly fresh. Although, sadly, never for very long.

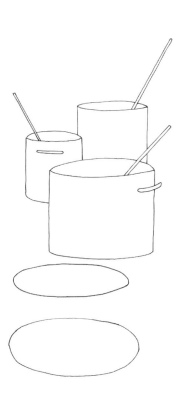

GILBERT PILGRAM

ZUNI: FLAVOURS OF THE WEST COAST

Chez Panisse in Berkeley, California, and Zuni Café on Market Street, San Francisco, are two of the most influential American restaurants of the past forty years. They share several features in addition to proximity. Each has been conceived of and inspired by a remarkable female chef: Alice Waters at Chez Panisse and Judy Rodgers at Zuni Café. Their menus showcase the fresh seasonal ingredients that have come to epitomize Californian cooking, and are so replete with tempting dishes that choosing what you want to eat is far more difficult than in most restaurants. On the many occasions I have been fortunate enough to eat at Zuni Café, I have always intended to order their signature roast chicken dish, but somehow something else even more appealing has always intervened. Both restaurants have a policy of working closely with farmers, growers and winemakers across the Bay Area to create a symbiotic relationship that is the envy of many chefs and restaurateurs, not only in the US but also in the rest of the world.

Both restaurants also have Gilbert Pilgram in common. This one-time manager of a San Francisco law firm, who switched careers to learn how to cook and then became a chef and finally a restaurateur, held a significant share in Chez Panisse for many years before he sold it in 2006 to take on a new challenge as the co-owner of Zuni Café alongside Rodgers. And this all came about because thirty years ago Pilgram was deeply envious of the fact that his partner, Richard Gilbert, used to come home happy after his day's work as a lawyer.

When I met Gilbert Pilgram for breakfast at St. John Hotel in London, one of the first things I noticed was his darting gaze. In any restaurant, however well designed, there are always places where customers and staff intersect: where customers walk back from the lavatories alongside waiting staff carrying trays of hot food, where customers are signalling for something, and where the receptionist is keen to know how soon the next table will be vacated. It is hectic in the thick of a very busy service, and one pair of eyes is never enough. Like many of his best fellow restaurateurs, Pilgram has grown adept at maintaining eye contact during a conversation while simultaneously watching the entrance to the restaurant and observing who is coming to sit down at one of the tables nearby – even if he is sitting in someone else's restaurant. As I was later to learn from his comments about the way staff meals should be served, he was also observing how the chefs and waiters around us were performing.

The layout and structure of Zuni Café allow Pilgram's wandering eyes to roam with ease, since its two floors are bathed in more natural sunshine than most, and this of the bright California variety. It occupies a triangular corner site on downtown Market Street. The tall windows on each side of the building, together with the wooden interior and the piano close to the front door, give it the air – to me at least – of a proud ship about to set sail. With a long bar, an open kitchen around whose chimney are stacked loaves of sourdough bread, and its very own oyster bar, walking into Zuni Café as an occasional customer (it is conveniently located close to the freeway to the airport for the first or final meal of any trip) is an uplifting experience. The name Zuni, which is that of an indigenous American tribe, dates back to when it was a café attached to a cactus shop and specialized in south-western American food.

The building dates back to 1913, shortly after the city's devastating earthquake, and although it is a delight to eat in, it presents its owner with daily ergonomic challenges. Rodgers once confided in me that her labour costs are forty per cent higher than they would be if the restaurant were on only one floor, and that architecture students have visited to learn how not to design the interior of a restaurant. Pilgram, however, certainly appreciates how fortunate he is to be able to walk in there every morning as its co-owner. 'It's a wonderful building, there's nowhere like it in the city and it looks great whatever the weather, sun, rain or cloud. It's dramatic but not played with.' The building doesn't seem to age or look dated, and both he and Judy know that part of their role as restaurateurs is to act as custodians of the building for future generations. In describing this stroke of daily good fortune, Pilgram mentioned two important but very different aspects of how the building any restaurant occupies has a significant effect on the restaurateur as well as the staff.

Obviously, when planning a restaurant, the vision has to be of it teeming with customers all having a very good time. That way lies financial salvation. To deliver this, though, any restaurateur must spend a great deal of time in the space when it is empty, long before the first customers have arrived, when the laundry bags are being delivered along with the wine and produce, and the place is being cleaned and prepared. How does the building feel when it is empty? How will you feel about it when you have to get out of bed at 5.00 a.m. because the alarm has gone off and the other keyholder is on holiday? If that feeling of empathy between you, the prospective restaurateur, and the building that you are thinking of taking a lease on for the next fifteen to twenty-five years is not there, it may not be the right leap to take, either personally or professionally.

Secondly, while the most common complaint among restaurateurs worldwide is the difficulty of finding good staff, the question of whether the building under consideration can provide any advantages to your staff's future wellbeing is worth bearing in mind from the outset. Any chefs who have had the rare privilege of working in a kitchen with natural light rather than in a basement for eight or ten hours at a stretch will tell you that as well as making them feel better, it probably allows them to cook better, too. At Zuni Café it is not only the owners, waiting staff and customers who feel the benefit of the natural light that streams through the tall windows, but also the chefs. This may be one unspoken reason why their food always tastes so good.

For Pilgram, of course, that is what restaurants are all about: cooking great food. Without stopping in London, he was off to the Bund in Shanghai. 'Have you seen the restaurants there?' he asked. He observed that there is so much white Italian marble everywhere that he cannot imagine how the owners will ever recover their investment. 'They are not principally about food, and that's what matters. Although seeing places like that upsets me (and there are plenty in the US designed along these Vegas principles), I have to say that I love travelling as much as I love working in a restaurant, and that travelling makes me a better restaurateur.'

The lynchpin of Pilgram's unusual career on both sides of the swing door is the two-year Masters in Finance course he took at The Golden Gate Business School in 1979, and the analytical approach this has allowed him to adopt at both restaurants he has been involved in. His initial career in law had only led to professional unhappiness, and a conversation with his partner that he recalled as though it happened only yesterday. He was looking at offers from other law firms when Richard said, 'Why don't you stop talking about your love of cooking and do something about it? I'll support you.' And that was how he started. His first steps were tentative: working on Mondays in the kitchens at Zuni Café, when the restaurant is closed, making pickles and sauces, and a half day on Tuesdays. Although unpaid, it was a less expensive route than a full-time course at a cookery school, and Pilgram is very keen to repay this professional debt. He has always been highly supportive of the intern programmes at Chez Panisse and Zuni Café. 'Both kitchens over the decades have been factories for training and producing lots of good chefs. It's something Alice, Judy and I have been very proud of.'

Pilgram then transferred his allegiance across the Oakland Bridge to the kitchens of Chez Panisse, where he worked for the first year for nothing, before graduating to an opening wage of $6 (£4) per hour. From there he climbed the slippery slope, working his way up as a cook in the café to a chef (and therefore responsible for much more than just what he cooks) in the restaurant, and then as a manager. Finally, he was rewarded with a significant number of shares in a restaurant that was world famous, continuously busy but, incredibly, barely profitable. Along with the shares came the instructions, Pilgram added bluntly, to 'straighten the restaurant out'. Chez Panisse has always been an unusual combination of the most clear-sighted vision for the food it serves with rather confused socialist business principles that reflect its location in Berkeley and an era when profit was a dirty word. All the staff are given a share in the business after they have stayed for a certain period, which can delay effective decision making, and well-intentioned practices had come to be abused over time. During the interval between the first and second sittings in the ground-floor restaurant, the custom had been initiated of all the chefs sitting down to eat the same four-course meal as the customers, a policy designed to allow them to share in the customer experience. To this expensive practice was added the luxury of the chefs choosing from the cellar whatever bottle of wine they thought most appropriate, regardless of cost. Added to this, Pilgram explained, was a casual approach to how timings were taken for reservations, which meant that only the last couple of tables really generated any profit from a restaurant that was packed every night. Although he would not disclose precise numbers, the profitability of what was then one of the world's most revered restaurants was so low that he was able to increase it by more than fifty per cent very quickly. He realized that this period of 'butting heads', as he described it, was not going to work in the long term for those who considered him a 'monster', hell-bent on turning Chez into a corporate restaurant. In 2006, Pilgram decided, it was time to sell up and move on.

But, he began to wonder, to what? He wanted to stay in the restaurant business but he was approaching fifty. It would have been physically impossible for him to open somewhere on his own, and unfair on any younger partners. 'I simply didn't have enough energy for that route.' Then he heard that Judy Rodgers' original partner at Zuni Café wanted to retire, and they managed to settle on a mutually satisfactory deal very quickly. There were only two disadvantages. Firstly, he and Richard ate

at Zuni Café so frequently that Judy complained she would be losing two of her best customers. Secondly, Richard had always enjoyed eating at Table 1 because it has the best position in the house. But now that Pilgram is a co-owner he can't be seen to be sitting there, ever. 'So the rule is that Richard only eats at this table if he's in the restaurant without me. Otherwise, it would be like cooking at home for your friends and helping yourself before you serve them. You just can't do that.'

This is one of the many tacit rules that restaurateurs have to live by, rules that Pilgram believes that many outside the business simply don't appreciate. 'I think every adult wants to be a restaurateur at some stage in their lives, just like every boy wants to be a policeman or a fireman. But they don't have the foggiest idea of what's involved, they believe that all we do is wear clean shirts and fancy suits, walk around talking to customers and get free food and drinks whenever we want.' Pilgram admitted that even his partner had begun to question quite how difficult a restaurateur's role can be, despite weekly tales of the ice machine breaking down, the sump in the basement failing and occasional power cuts that can lead to them having to close Zuni Café for the entire evening. '"How hard can it be?" he used to say,' Pilgram added, before explaining that Richard was at least present when the restaurant suddenly developed its very own waterfall. His face turned ashen as he continued. 'It was a Sunday night and we were having dinner with some friends at Table 69, which allowed me a very good view of the section of the restaurant we call A Back. Now I remember thinking I'd had a fair bit of wine to drink, but when I looked over to the far wall I didn't think we had ever installed a waterfall feature in the restaurant. But there certainly seemed to be one now, with water gushing down the wall. We evacuated the area, got up on the roof and found the cause. We spent the rest of that night and all Monday working to patch it up temporarily so that we could open again on Tuesday.' They knew just how lucky they had been. If it had happened when the restaurant was empty, it could have been devastating.

Pilgram is highly unusual among restaurateurs in that he can execute, with consummate skill, 'both ends', as he calls it. Although most of his time is spent patrolling the floor, he does step into the kitchen from time to time in a variety of roles, including that of writing the daily menu. One of the principles that Rodgers has established for Zuni Café is that she, the head chef or Pilgram will always sit down and write the menu for the following day, which will include sixteen new and different dishes.

Certain seasonal ingredients will often appear more than once, but this almost masochistic principle is what Pilgram and Rodgers believe makes Zuni Café special and their jobs so fascinating. They really do start with an almost completely blank sheet of paper every day, apart from a few signature dishes such as cured anchovies with celery; any of a dozen different species of oyster; bowls of polenta with mascarpone; gnocchi with chanterelles; pizza topped with a local hard cheese, sorrel and thyme; and a whole roast chicken for two, which comes with a warm bread salad, mustard greens and pine nuts – a dish that has become synonymous with Zuni Café. The other dishes they invent. Most restaurants have a menu with a few daily specials, but here it is the reverse: a few specials around which they create a menu. Pilgram described the process thus: 'We plan out the proteins every week so that we know that we have allocated, let's say, a pork chop to the grill station on Thursday. A chef acts as the menu writer every day, following tested recipes that have all been approved by us (mostly by Judy, since a lot of it happened before I joined Zuni Café). I am the chef every Tuesday and write the menu for dinner. I know what my proteins are, and I make a point of going to the farmer's market on Saturday and Sunday to buy produce as needed. On Monday night I spend no more than an hour reviewing cookbooks to refresh my memory. I get to the restaurant at around 9.30 a.m. and do a visual inventory of the walk-in fridges and stores, and I also know what has been ordered. I then decide on a theme, let's say Italian with a touch of North Africa, or a wider one would be farmhouse European, and let my mind wander to come up with dishes. I try to introduce one or two new dishes every week, and they are added to the repertoire.'

Behind the front-line action there is inevitably a certain amount of politicking and conflict resolution, to which roles Pilgram brings not only experience, but also a calm and measured manner. 'Cooks believe that waiters do nothing but pick up plates, make a lot of money, and occasionally screw up the orders to make their lives as difficult as possible. Part of my job is to let them know that waiters are human after all, that they can make the odd mistake and that certain customers can be quirky, too.' Running the floor is not straightforward, either. Under Californian law, the service charge that is apportioned to every bill belongs in principle to the waiter who has served that table. In practice, no waiter would dare not to pool their tips with the busboy who clears the table and serves the water, the barman or the receptionist. If they didn't share them, the consequences would be dire for all concerned: the barman may ensure that this waiter's customers would have to wait an inordinate amount of time for their drinks, while any upset receptionist could wreak her vengeance by sending no tables to their section, or three or four bookings simultaneously, thereby ensuring that the waiter could not give proper service. Pilgram clearly sees one aspect of his role as minimizing animosity, and another as ensuring that factions never emerge that can undermine the customer experience. There are, he added, people working in the restaurant whom he does not like, but he was proud to say than neither Judy nor Richard know who they are.

It is widely accepted that restaurants are theatre, but the corollary of this for Pilgram is that he must do everything in his power to maintain the sense of spectacle in the customer's eye or consciousness. It was this mission – never to let anything intrude to break this sense of theatre – that led to Pilgram hauling a series of serving platters back from a trip to Oslo for the staff to take their staff meals from before the service starts. When he started at Zuni Café he wasn't very happy with how the staff meals were served. The food was dished up out of roasting trays and several of the kitchen staff could be seen eating from the restaurant. 'I put a stop to that. And when I saw these platters in Oslo, I bought them because they were distinctive, they wouldn't be available at the local discount store and that this would make the staff feel good,' he explained.

Zuni Café is open six days a week, employs ninety-eight people (under California law it is far more expensive to employ over 100), has an annual turnover of over $7 million (£4.5 million), and generates a great deal of pleasure for its many customers. And happily, for Pilgram too. Pleasure is important to him and he feels very fortunate that he can be involved in it professionally twice a day. 'Some of it, and quite a high proportion I believe, is really only an extension of what you would do at home for people you care about. When I am cooking I check the flowers before my guests arrive. I put the main-course dishes in the oven to warm them up so you don't serve hot food on cold plates and I put the salad dishes in the fridge so that they are not too warm. That's all pretty straightforward.' Where he believes that being a restaurateur is so special is that it is one of the very few crafts that remain in a world in which crafts are disappearing so quickly – it is the only one left that is affordable and so good for everyone involved. By describing the work of a restaurateur as a craft he means that it is like making bread or building furniture: you have to have the disposition and personality to do it well. If you are not a social person, forget it. The steps for making it work, Pilgram believes, are basically quite simple: the lighting and music have to be right; there have to be constant inspections of the room for cleanliness (which is not glamorous at all); and there has to be eye contact with guests, including visiting every table at some point and starting a brief conversation. This is something only the owner can get away with – he can make jokes that a manager cannot so that the guests feel part of the whole event. He also finds it important to dress the part, so the guests know that attention is being paid to detail. 'I don't think it is an art: anyone who really wants to do it can do it, the only gift necessary is that you have to like being social. Anyone who is good at giving good parties at home can do it. It's just like the simplicity and deliciousness of the broth in that wonderful Japanese film, *Tampopo*. Being a restaurateur is life-enhancing.'

Looking after your regulars

When Gilbert Pilgram made the decision in 2006 to take a share in Zuni Café as a partner and restaurateur alongside Judy Rodgers, its chef-proprietor, one significant consequence was that the restaurant lost two of its best regular customers – Pilgram and his partner. That is sad news for any restaurateur anywhere. It is difficult to overestimate how important regulars, the customers who come once a week or even once a month, are to any restaurant's business, and, just as importantly, the restaurateur's self esteem. They are part of the reason for being in the business. Their presence represents one of the main reasons that any restaurant comes into existence: to serve as a comfortable location where people can work, rest and play, and where the restaurateur can display the qualities that were attractive about the profession in the first place.

Regulars are, of course, very good for business, and not just because of their frequent visits. They take pride in the restaurant's progress and can often provide the same service as the far more expensive, and more anodyne, mystery diner schemes that can monitor restaurants. Regulars want the restaurant to prosper, and are invariably quick to offer advice. Of course, this may not initially be welcome. I remember on several occasions being taken to one side by one of our regular customers as they were leaving after lunch to be told that a fish dish on the specials menu had not been as good as it should have been, that a particular waiter's personal hygiene needed improving, or (and this was the most annoying but at least the quickest to remedy), that he, as the host, had had to wait too long between asking for and receiving his bill. Regulars act as the restaurateur's spies, passing on the useful information that a restaurateur can never glean, because should you choose to eat in your own restaurant then, naturally, the food will always be first class and the service impeccable. Regulars provide the restaurateur with a vital sanity check.

An ever-expanding group of regular customers is also highly beneficial commercially. Because they already use the restaurant, it is bound to be among their first choices when they contemplate organizing a larger event, which may fit nicely inside the restaurant's private dining room. This will, in turn, bring in their friends and guests who will be impressed by how the restaurant looks after its regular customers. They may want to become regulars, too.

Today, however, it has become simultaneously more difficult to identify those who want to become regular customers, and easier to look after them. In previous decades, before new restaurant openings were followed with such attention and by so many, a restaurant would over time establish a gradual following from which the regular customers would emerge. Today, such a huge influx of customers can result from even one or two immediate internet reviews that any general manager, however skilful, can be swamped by bookings, to the detriment of those who work nearby, as Russell Norman discovered at Polpo, and may eventually become those valuable regular customers. Norman got round this problem by not taking bookings. The presence of a bar area in a growing number of restaurants, in which a complete or shortened version of the full menu is served and for which reservations are not taken, also provides an opportunity for any restaurateur to accommodate those valuable customers who may not want to spend too long in your restaurant at lunchtime but, to both parties' mutual benefit, would like to call in two or three times a week for a quick lunch.

Although I have had invaluable experience of quite how important it is to establish, cultivate and listen to an enthusiastic group of regular customers at my restaurant L'Escargot, I have had no experience of being a regular customer at any one restaurant today – as a restaurant correspondent with a weekly column I am not allowed that luxury. If the kind of restaurant I would like to become a regular at were to open nearby, though, this is the strategy I would adopt. I would call in and ask for the general manager. I would hand over my business card and wish them the best of luck in their new venture. I would add that I will return to eat at the bar and as soon as the opportunity presented itself I would be contacting them for a table in the restaurant. And I would gauge the reaction. I would look for a genuine sense of welcome and interest in me as a fellow human being. I would expect some curiosity, without being intrusive, about where I work or live (if it is a neighbourhood restaurant), to establish how they could make the restaurant as useful for me as possible.

Regulars are a vital part of any successful restaurant and at its best this is a mutually beneficial relationship, one that brings ongoing pleasure to the customer, and a continuing sense of professional satisfaction to the restaurateur.

Gilbert Pilgram

CLASSIC

NEIGHBOURHOOD

RESTAURANTS

15

Nigel Platts-Martin has had an unprecedented success rate over the past twenty-five years with restaurants in five very different locations across London. The first, and at the time the most unlikely, was in Wandsworth, south-west London, which he and his first chef and partner Marco Pierre White made a culinary destination with the opening of Harvey's in 1987. Upon White's departure in 1993, Platts-Martin showed his deftness even as a nascent restaurateur by plucking Bruce Poole from the kitchen of his second restaurant, The Square, and persuading Poole not only to take it over, but to lend his name to its new incarnation. Since 1995 Chez Bruce (illustrated page 247) has been one of the capital's most highly regarded restaurants.

In 1991 Platts-Martin took over a restaurant on a corner site in St James's Square, Mayfair, which had formerly traded under the name of Silks (the interior decoration included jockeys' outfits and horsewhips, he recalled). He changed its name to The Square and saw it through the extremely difficult trading conditions of the early 1990s before master-minding the complex negotiations with its landlord, Prudential Assurance, that allowed it to move to its current location on Bruton Street. Platts-Martin and Poole then worked their magic on two other suburbs around the capital, opening The Glasshouse, close to the entrance to the magnif-icent Kew Gardens, in 1999 and then La Trompette in Chiswick in 2001. Finally, in 2005, he converted a former pub in Notting Hill Gate into The Ledbury, the startling success of which, Platts-Martin believes, has changed the way his restaurants are viewed.

All five restaurants have justifiably won numerous accolades from the Michelin, Zagat and Hardens' guides, as well as recognition for the three chefs who have been responsible for their success. Philip Howard and Brett Graham hold two Michelin stars at The Square and The Ledbury respec-tively (Howard is also a partner in The Ledbury), while the three restaurants Platts-Martin and Poole run together, Chez Bruce, La Trompette and The Glasshouse, each hold one star. As a result, Platts-Martin has acquired the reputation during this period of being 'the restaurateur's restaurateur', a professional who has won the respect of his peers, as well as an MBE, not only for the standards his restaurants have set, but also for the manner in which he has established the restaurants' and their chefs' personalities far more strongly than his own. Platts-Martin is one restaurateur who definitely prefers not to be in the limelight.

This is partly down to a very English upbringing – an upbringing, he confessed over lunch at Jason Atherton's Pollen Street Social in Mayfair, that seemed to rule out a future career as a restaurateur. He was born in what was then West Germany: his father was an officer in the British Army stationed there. He went to boarding school, to Oxford and then into the City, 'so until I was twenty-seven the only food I encountered was pretty institutionalized, nothing exciting at all.' In many respects, though, these years were the ideal background for the working relationship that Platts-Martin has managed to establish so successfully with such a diverse array of talented chefs. Cooking is not his forte, he is the first to acknowledge, but it is theirs. His strengths lie in the business management of his restaurants; his love of wine, which was the trigger for the risky career change from banker to restaurateur in his late twenties; his determination to see just what a restaurant should offer while on his extensive travels as a merchant banker and then as a restaurateur; and, finally, the experience of spending three years at the front desk of The Square when it (and he) were still young, which has left an indelible mark on him, and informed his approach as to how restaurants should be managed for their customers' benefit.

Platts-Martin is quintessentially English, from his double-barrelled surname to his style of dress. Over the years this has relaxed somewhat from a suit and tie to a tweed jacket and open-necked shirt, but his manner is always formal and correct. It is this strong Englishness that has also contributed to a marked disregard for publicity. The best way to find out about him, and all that he does as a restaurateur, he firmly implies, is not to ask too many questions, but to go and eat in one of his restaurants. To this inbuilt modesty must be added another factor, which is that when Platts-Martin began his career as a restaurateur in 1987, and although certain chefs had begun by then to attract significant media attention, the restaurant profession had not. He still finds this change of emphasis in the profession that has preoccupied him over the past twenty-five years somewhat baffling, and is equally surprised by the success that he, his restaurants and his chefs have achieved. Particularly as all this success emanated from an encounter with a single glass of red wine thirty years ago.

Not surprisingly, he recalled the bottle and the occasion with very happy memories. He had been driving through Burgundy in 1982 en route to the south of France. He stopped for lunch and ordered a bottle of 1979 Savigny Les Beaune 1ère Cru Marconnets from Simon Bize. 'I was stunned, not just by the pleasure this one bottle could impart, but also by the realization that here was a whole world that at this stage in my life I knew nothing at all about.' Driven by a desire to learn more, Platts-Martin

returned to Burgundy the following year, although he still lacked the
confidence to call in at growers' cellars to taste their wines. On his return to
London he determined to enjoy whatever red burgundies he could afford
and to eat in as many good French restaurants as possible. He was fortunate
that his flat in Clapham was close to Battersea and a particularly strong
concentration of what were then some of the capital's best French restaurants, most notably L'Arlequin, Lampwick's and Chez Nico. Six years
with the merchant bank SG Warburg were to provide the vital foundation
upon which to build his restaurant business because they allowed him
to develop a logical, transactional approach to each opening and the
challenges each new redevelopment presented. By 1985 he was in love
with food and wine, and only too keen to make his future career in restaurants. He promptly quit the bank. It was not until 1999 that he was to
earn the same salary as a restaurateur.

In June 1986 Platts-Martin put together a group of fifteen shareholders
to buy the lease on Harvey's, a down-at-heel wine bar on a corner site
opposite Wandsworth Common for £170,000 ($265,000), with no very clear
idea of what he was going to do with it. A growing friendship with Marco
Pierre White, then cooking at Lampwick's restaurant, was to convert this
from a risky gamble to an almost immediate success. Many would argue
that the restaurant was instrumental in changing the image of London's
restaurants, as well as the manner in which young British chefs were then
perceived. This was because it served classic French food cooked by a young
chef from Leeds with an attitude that fascinated journalists – and all of this
was happening not in the West End or Knightsbridge, then the traditional
home for such restaurants, but in Wandsworth, south London. Harvey's
won its first Michelin star a year after opening in January 1987, and a second
in 1990. This was an unprecedented beginning, and one that seduced Platts-
Martin. The restaurant won a reputation for its food and the wine list that
Platts-Martin put together, and also for White's behaviour, particularly
towards customers he took against. It was run on a principle that was all too
common then, especially in the more expensive French restaurants: that
the chef knew best. Platts-Martin and White parted company in 1993.

By that stage, Platts-Martin was standing by the reception desk of
his second restaurant, The Square, in the heart of St James's, an extremely
wealthy area of London, but at that time predominantly composed of
gentlemen's clubs, auction houses and art dealers. There were very few
restaurants in the area. He undertook this role for three years, during which

244

he was preoccupied with minimizing its trading losses during a recession while formulating a much clearer role for himself and what his current, and future, customers would want from his restaurants. 'I spent all that time standing by the reception and answering the phone. I got to know how a restaurant works, rather than being just an investor as I had been at Harvey's, and I began to appreciate how our customers wanted to be looked after,' he explained. Very close by were the offices of two major executive recruitment companies, who used the restaurant to conduct their interviews. 'Now these could go either way. The interviewee could either be no good, in which case the host would be signalling to have their bill after only fifty minutes, so that they could simply say goodbye and thank you, or if it went very well they would not want to be interrupted at all.' How to manage the end of the meal, he quickly learned, is as important as the welcome, the seating and the taking of the order. It is a question of constant vigilance, observation and looking out for the smallest signals. It is a more streamlined process now that credit-card terminals can be taken to the table.

The recession of the early 1990s also taught this mild-mannered Englishman how to hustle for business. The more obvious approaches were to the concierges of the nearby hotels (and it was always useful, Platts-Martin recalled, to have a mutual passion for football whenever they spoke), as well as the managers of the West End theatres, particularly the Theatre Royal, Haymarket, which was close by. Any visiting Americans were always impressed by an appearance at their table from the very English proprietor with the double-barrelled surname ready on the business cards in his jacket pocket. In the pre-internet days this was an important, inexpensive but very effective tactic in spreading his restaurants' names around the world.

Although he has neither cooked nor served in his own restaurants, his stint at The Square's reception desk also opened his eyes to the wines his customers were looking for, and, importantly, to what they could afford. In the 1990s there was a growing interest in well-priced, well-made white wines from Australia, and Platts-Martin can still recall the pleasure it gave for him to recommend these wines and then watch as his customers enjoyed them. This initial apprenticeship allowed him to develop a more structured approach to the role wine plays in his restaurants. It is, he stressed, more than just business – although well-off wine lovers do tend to flock to his restaurants, where they know that they and their wine foibles will be well looked after – it is another way of establishing the restaurant's reputation, of extending the number of people who will talk about its excellence and

professionalism. 'The wine list is a vital profit centre, because the costs are less than in the kitchen, even taking into account storage and financing. But to do it justice you have to invest as much time in assembling and monitoring the list as a chef does in sourcing the produce for the menu.' The skill in choosing the wines, listing them at the right time and then selling them with enthusiasm, is, he believes, certainly the equivalent of what any chef does. To do this, Platts-Martin spends a great deal of time at wine tastings, regularly reviewing the wines in the restaurants' cellars and continually looking out for up-and-coming producers and wines that may as yet be under represented. As a result he creates a virtuous wine circle that benefits everyone interested in wine: the producers who see him on the tasting circuit, people who want to make a career as a sommelier and who know that they will be encouraged to learn more, and, most importantly, his customers, who know that their interest in wine will be constantly stimulated. They also know that for celebratory occasions, their special bottle will be treated with respect and the corkage charge will not be excessive.

Platts-Martin had originally acquired a fifteen-year lease on The Square, having spotted the agent's board outside as he was on his way from a wine tasting nearby. Three years later, as a sitting tenant with more than a decade left on his lease, he found himself in an awkward but ultimately beneficial position. The Prudential, the owners, wanted to redevelop the whole building, and all the tenants above them were leaving as their leases had expired. His hadn't, and he argued that, despite all the scaffolding, business was still very good. 'I wasn't going to go quietly,' Platts-Martin added, almost unnecessarily. Three years of difficult negotiations eventually saw The Square move to a corner site in Mayfair and into a building designed and fitted out to their specifications, for which the Prudential footed the entire bill – little short of £2 million ($3 million), Platts-Martin reckons. 'It was a struggle all the way because they had to do everything, from getting the planning permission and change of use on what used to be an airline office, to granting me a new and attractive lease. It was very stressful.' The Square reopened in February 1997 and Philip Howard showed his appreciation of his new kitchen by gaining his second Michelin star in January 1998.

Fourteen years later, Platts-Martin still cannot conceal his delight at the consequences of this move. There is no way he could have afforded a restaurant built to such high specifications at that time. More importantly, perhaps, the kitchens have provided the right atmosphere in which Howard has been able to nurture talent such as Brett Graham, who cooked at The Square before he opened The Ledbury. There is now another young chef cooking there with whom he plans to open somewhere new, when he can find the right location at the right price. Here Platts-Martin is again being typically British, but this time in his modesty. He is the only solo restaurateur profiled in this book who has opened more than one restaurant, but has not had to close any. From forgoing a merchant banker's salary in the mid 1980s for what he described as 'a very uncertain future', driven by a passion for food and wine, he has returned one hundred per cent strike record. How has he achieved this in seemingly unconnected and disparate parts of London? The first part of the far-from-simple answer lies in his professional training. A legal career, however brief (he moved on from Freshfields the day he qualified), has clearly proved a useful basis from which to negotiate the legal complexities of five different leases and all the related regulations as he has converted once-unsuccessful pubs or bistros into very busy restaurants.

The second has been not so much the details of what he learned as a merchant banker, as a general approach to what the business will be and its potential. Opening a restaurant, he has realized, is a very different process from running one, and is made up of a series of different processes that all go towards making up one major one. They are dealt with individually, but are closely interlinked. 'From the outset I think of them as transactions, and that allows me to take in what has to be done to minimize the risk involved in opening any restaurant, and also ensures that everything is in place for when the restaurant becomes successful,' he explained. This final factor has certainly underpinned his partnership with his various chefs. If the approach sounds cold and calculated, it is vital to remember that many restaurants fail because these two crucial aspects of the business are overlooked at the outset. Leases are entered into that should never be; partnership deals are struck that, even when the restaurant is successful, leave a sour taste in one partner's mouth; or the chosen location fails to live up to expectations. No restaurant can survive in such circumstances and Platts-Martin is unashamedly delighted that he is still a partner with Poole and Howard after almost twenty years.

To this analytical approach can be added an obvious passion for food, wine and restaurants, one that over the past twenty-five years has changed as his own experience, as both a restaurateur and a customer, has grown.

Nigel Platts-Martin

Having complained about the number of emails he receives daily (which includes a lunch and dinner report from each of his five restaurants every day) in his role as 'mobile head office', Platts-Martin then described what preoccupies him and gives him the greatest professional pleasure. 'What I strive to do in all our restaurants is to ensure a better experience overall for our customers, even if they don't notice or appreciate it.' Without drawing breath, he elaborated on what was a complex, costly but highly successful example of just what he meant. When he bought Chez Bruce, there was no rear access to the kitchen for the deliveries or the kitchen staff to come in through or the rubbish to go out from. Everything and everybody had to come in through the same front door as the customers, and he felt that wasn't right. There was an alleyway from the kitchen door, but this belonged to the house next door. 'So when it came on the market, I bought it, converted it into three flats, which I then sold, but kept the alleyway, which I improved, so that now Chez Bruce is as it should be. No customer will see this but it makes the restaurant a far better space.'

These restaurants, and in particular their kitchens, are better places too, Platts-Martin believes, for two other interconnected reasons. The first is that each restaurant is run by a chef that Platts-Martin is proud to have mentored, the word he chose to describe his role in their career development. 'I've known Phil since he was twenty-four, Bruce since he was thirty and Brett since he was twenty-six. At that age they were quite raw talents and we've worked hard collaboratively, in all aspects of the business, to achieve the very best.' What he first saw in all of them was a natural talent, dexterity and a willingness to learn, and he is proud that he has been able to promote so many head chefs from within the company. An important factor in the collaboration has been establishing each chef as a shareholder in the company that runs each restaurant, an approach that aims to reward them as the business develops and prospers. It is a policy that has enriched them all, Platts-Martin explained, not so much for its equitable nature as for the fact that it mirrors every chef's natural progression. Restaurants mature, and chefs get better and better on the job. 'And that is what annoys me so much about restaurant reviewers, because they rush through the door as soon as any new restaurant opens, but they never come back. They never seem to want to experience how much any restaurant has improved, how much it has changed for the better.'

Platts-Martin acknowledged that his role has now changed fundamentally. He has delegated the wine-buying side to a much younger team and the menu composition to his chefs. The more detailed administration – the accounts, tax returns, rent reviews and HR issues – still fall on his desk, and he also retains one aspect of the business that still excites him and has been an unusual aspect of his success: finding the next site for the next most talented chef from his stable. On paper, the locations of Platts-Martin's restaurants are not just far apart, but also unlikely. Discounting The Square's Mayfair site, which was a stroke of such good fortune, he has shown an uncanny knack of picking locations where a strong consumer demand for excellent food and wine, usually from fixed-price menus that ensure a good average spend for the restaurateur and a fixed cost for the customer, is not being met. This has certainly proved to be the case at La Trompette in Chiswick, which is located in a wealthy residential area that ensures good business in the evening, but is also close to many of the businesses now located between Chiswick and Heathrow, which fill the tables at lunch. Platts-Martin added that a strong demand from private clients is hugely important, as the spend by companies has significantly declined over the past two years.

Another huge factor in his restaurants' success, Platts-Martin was at pains to point out, has been Arvind Vadgama. They first met in 1979 when Vadgama was starting out on his career as a builder. Since then, he and his team have carried out the renovations of all four restaurants other than The Square, and have maintained them ever since. 'Putting all the modern services a kitchen and restaurant demand today into London's old but characterful buildings is incredibly tricky, but working with Vadgama has given me the in-house ability to do things properly. I probably speak to him more than anyone else during the day and I am very proud of this association.' It is a definite sense of pride that will continue to drive Platts-Martin now that he has spotted another, and very different, area of London where there is unquenched demand for one of his restaurants: Hampstead. 'I do get a thrill when people who live or work close by to Chez Bruce or The Ledbury speak excitedly of having one of our restaurants close by. It is a very nice sensation to have generated that community feeling.' He is equally proud that through hard work and good luck his restaurants have been part of such a growth industry during a period when London has developed hugely as a city, and is one in which we can now eat so well. 'Ours is a small family, a stable of good restaurants with no outside shareholders, no borrowing and no central HQ. Other than me and my briefcase, of course.'

In dreams begin responsibilities

The title of this chapter derives from a short story by the American writer Delmore Schwartz, which he wrote in 1937. It is an accurate metaphor for anyone contemplating the legal aspects of life as a restaurateur.

I was given my first rude awakening into these facts of life the moment after I had signed the twenty-five-year lease on 48 Greek Street in London, which as L'Escargot became my professional home during the 1980s. I was in the company of Geoffrey Lander (no relation, but an old family friend), who had acted for me in the complex legal negotiations. No property negotiations are ever straightforward or inexpensive, sadly. In an avuncular fashion, Geoffrey

looked at me and said, 'Make sure you look after and adhere to this lease. It's the most important document in your restaurant.' He was to be proved quite right, in that when the freeholder came to sell the property several years later I was well protected as a tenant. Several years after that, when I sold the business, I was able to assign the lease to my buyer and to pass on all the benefits that Geoffrey had so successfully negotiated on my behalf.

In one aspect, though, Geoffrey was to be proved wrong: it wasn't necessarily the most important document in my possession. In time for our planned opening on 2 June 1981, I hired a licensing lawyer and followed his expensive advice, but my application was summarily turned down. The building was only granted a renewal of its restaurant licence and I had to reconsider everything I had planned to do with the ground floor. Suddenly, it had to be a brasserie, serving more food and requiring more cooks, than I had originally envisaged.

The lease and the alcohol licence are the two sets of documents that underpin any restaurant. Those talented chefs, Brett Graham, Philip Howard and Bruce Poole, are very fortunate that the responsibility for dealing with these less-than-glamorous aspects of the business falls squarely on Nigel Platts-Martin's shoulders. His advice was that most restaurateurs are in a stronger position than they used to be, as landlords wake up to the benefits a restaurant can bring to their building. Given the lease's crucial importance, the negotiations should be handled as confidently as possible.

The most difficult aspect of aligning them becomes apparent itself even before the restaurant opens. No city licensing authority will grant a licence before a final approval of the finished building that is the result of a site visit from a city department official. The restaurateur is therefore caught between the proposed dates for completion offered by the builder and the dates when the licensing authorities sit. Any application made too early will be automatically turned down; any made too late after the restaurant has been completed means a considerable loss of revenue, since no alcohol can be sold until it is granted.

The consequences can go far beyond financial loss, however painful that may be. Because of building delays, Danny Meyer's North End Grill restaurant in New York opened in early 2012 without its alcohol licence. The consequences were fourfold. Firstly, he was unable to train the new staff in how to make cocktails or how to pair wine with dishes on the menu. Secondly, and far more obviously, the shelves that should have been filled with bottles had to remain empty, making for an uninviting first impression of the restaurant for any customer. The financial loss is obviously considerable, not just from wine sales and bar sales but also from the fact that all the private parties booked for the initial period had to be cancelled. These are useful, for the significant revenue they generate at a time when the restaurateur has been spending furiously, and because such events also introduce prospective guests to the new restaurant, allowing the waiting and kitchen staff to practise production and service

to significant numbers without the pressure of order-taking because, as parties, they will be eating from pre-ordered menus.

In London, according to restaurateur Will Smith, these are some of the bureaucratic aspects that need to be dealt with: the local authority for planning, restaurant signage, any street furniture, the alcohol licence and statutory no-smoking signs; through a property lawyer, the lease, the landlord's licence to assign the lease, and the landlord's licence to alter the interior; plus the Fire Authority, Environmental Health and Building Control, and the Performing Rights Society. Finally, he rattled off a list of the specialists that may need to become a restaurateur's best friend: structural engineers, architects, interior designers, mechanical and engineering specialists for the kitchen and air conditioning, kitchen designers, stove manufacturers, electrical engineers, sound engineers, refrigeration specialists, telephone engineers, electronic point-of-sale systems technicians, IT consultants, and reservation diary consultants to interface telephone and internet bookings. Smith ended this recital by commenting: 'But that is not exhaustive!' It is a long haul to realize your dream of becoming a restaurateur. But it can be worth it.

Nigel Platts-Martin

MARK SAINSBURY

Informal urban dining from Moro to Zetter

16

I last met Mark Sainsbury, the man behind Moro restaurant, Bistrot Bruno Loubet and the Zetter Hotel and Townhouse, for breakfast at Caravan on Exmouth Market in Clerkenwell, for two reasons. The first is that Caravan, a restaurant created by New Zealanders Miles Kirby, Chris Ammermann and Laura Harper-Hinton, is a particular favourite of mine. Their menus are appetizing at any time of the day, as are the aromas from the coffee they roast in the basement. The second is that when Sainsbury, with his partners Jake Hodges and Samuel and Samantha Clark, opened Moro in 1997, they transformed the street on which Caravan has been trading since 2010. Before Moro, Exmouth Market was highly unprepossessing during the day and rather unsafe at night. Today it is a striking example of the amelioration of a local neighbourhood that successful restaurants can achieve. There are now more than twenty bars, cafés and restaurants among the shops along both sides of the pedestrianized walkway that dates back to the 1890s. From 10.00 a.m. each morning, stalls selling food from all over the world are set up to attract the many who work nearby, and on Fridays there is a bustling farmer's market. With Sadler's Wells, the highly acclaimed dance venue, only a five-minute walk away, there is considerable pre- and post-performance business, too.

I was about to ask Sainsbury what Exmouth Market had looked like pre-Moro, but we resorted to laughter instead. Sainsbury, forty-three, is such a bundle of joyful energy, rather like Tigger in Winnie-the-Pooh, that no sooner had he parked his bike than he rushed over to my corner table and, in his enthusiasm for Caravan's menu, picked up my list of questions instead. He apologized and we placed orders for cappuccinos, sourdough with avocado and chilli flakes, and coconut bread with lemon curd cream cheese. Then he finally answered. 'This street in early 1997 was very grim, almost post-nuclear. There was rubbish blowing down the street and the place was full of dodgy stallholders. The site that Moro grew into had been a Spar supermarket with a disused bed and a number of dead animals in it.' He remembered the owner of the off-licence next door popping his head in when he saw them and asking them what they were doing there, as nothing good had happened in that street for years.

No more than 500 metres round the corner in Farringdon Road, though, was The Eagle, the first of London's gastropubs, and The Quality Chop House, an old eating house with communal tables that had been reinvigorated by French chef Charles Fontaine. Both were doing great business, particularly as the offices of the *Guardian* and *Observer* newspapers were then close by. Sainsbury can still recall that The Eagle did not take reservations and The Quality Chop House did not accept credit cards. There had to be room for one more good restaurant in the neighbourhood, he believed. There was certainly a good deal to be done: the site was being offered at a rent of £12,000 ($19,000) per annum, with an eighteen-month rent-free period and a subsequent six months at half rent. Although the partners had no experience of opening a restaurant – Sainsbury described himself as 'completely wet behind the ears' at this stage – they were young, strong, healthy and passionate about opening London's first restaurant celebrating the vibrant cooking of southern Spain and Morocco.

The aesthetic touchstone for the restaurant was provided by Samuel Clark, but is sadly now lost, much to Sainsbury's dismay. It was a postcard-sized black-and-white photograph of a bar in southern Spain that had all the ingredients they were to introduce into Moro: a long zinc bar, mirrors along the walls and overhead fans. It was not much, Sainsbury admitted, but there was something about it that summed up their desired simplicity of design and clarity of purpose. Above all, it gave Moro a sense of identity and ruled out the often fatal possibility of its lacking character. 'These images are very important in creating a restaurant because they allow you to slip into an imaginary world from which the answers will eventually come. Today, I love nothing more than a good mood board.'

They squandered their good fortune with their landlords, the Debenham Property Trust, by making the mistake that virtually every new restaurateurs make of not finalizing the design before starting the build, so that their architects could not secure a fixed price from the builders. The partners kept changing their minds, instructing the builders to do things and not informing the architects, and consequently pushing the cost higher and higher. Then disaster almost struck. The district surveyor demanded further excavations by the kitchen area to make it safe, and the quote for the work was £50,000 ($80,000). Sainsbury recalls going off with Hodges for a pint in a local pub to debate whether they could afford this, or whether instead to abandon the project and cut their losses. Fortunately, the landlords agreed to pay half and Moro opened like a breath of fresh air.

I was one of the first writers to review Moro in May 1997, and it is remarkable to recall how innovative it was then, and quite how stylish it has remained. The large Spanish tortilla is still on the bar, along with the open kitchen with a wood-burning oven in which they make their bread, a char grill, and a string of peppers hanging from the ceiling. Dishes I enjoyed then and still look forward to eating now include a broad bean and potato soup with cucumber; monkfish with Swiss chard and an exemplary romesco sauce; homemade yoghurt with pistachios and honey; and any of the tapas and sherries at the bar.

Moro and its customers were all to be beneficiaries of the fact that Sainsbury had introduced his old friend Samuel Clark to his university friend, Samantha Clark. They had subsequently married and before Moro opened had taken their honeymoon in a camper van around southern Spain and Morocco. To the image provided by the miniscule photograph was added the authenticity of numerous recipes they learned at source – enough, Sainsbury admitted with another laugh, to hide the fact that he knew little about the cooking from either country. But he came to the roles of shareholder and restaurateur having had two important experiences on either side of his time at Bristol University. The first resulted from a three-month stint at La Varenne Cookery School, which was run by the American Anne Willan in Paris's 7th *arrondissement*. A bedsit in the Bastille, being the only man in a class of women, daily routines that started with cookery classes, eating what you had prepared, and ended with afternoon lectures on wine, cheese or wild mushrooms: all of these experiences convinced him that becoming a chef was to be his vocation. 'It was the happiest time of my life,' he recalled.

Six years later, after an unhappy stint working unpaid for three months as a *stagiaire* (intern) in the kitchens of the renowned chef Jean Bardet in Tours, France, where the welfare of the staff seemed to have no importance whatsoever, Sainsbury took on the job of 'assman' (assistant manager) at the Union Café off Marylebone High Street, and learned just how to get the best out of his team. He remembered that Caroline Brett was the owner then and he learned from her that however far a restaurateur is prepared to go for their staff, it will be repaid tenfold, and to make sure that those whose job is hospitality are happy. 'She paid for massages for the chefs, mountain bikes for the kitchen porters on their birthdays and trips to Mallorca,' he explained. On the more mundane side, he learned that the only way to acquire the authority to ensure others do the dirty jobs properly, such as washing the floors or the toilets, is to have done them yourself.

One reason why Sainsbury speaks so enthusiastically about restaurants is that he is continually aware that this was not the most

obvious career path for him. As the son of Lord John Sainsbury, who had built up the family's supermarket business, a future in a different form of retail beckoned. His father had put no pressure on him at all to follow in his footsteps, though, for which Mark remains eternally grateful, and he only recalls one occasion when it was even discussed. 'He took me to lunch at Christopher's in Covent Garden before we had found Moro, but I knew even then that corporate life wasn't for me.' A very different life awaited Sainsbury as restaurant manager. Although Moro opened to excellent reviews, life on the ground was not peaceful. 'Closing up at night was scary and the behaviour of some of the kids on the nearby estates was feral. The stereos were stolen from our cars; staff bikes were stolen; they ran in and stole the float from the tills and threw chairs through the windows, so eventually we had to put shutters on them. Worst of all was Bonfire Night when they all had access to fireworks – it was just anarchy.' Sainsbury believes that this inherent scuzziness, as he described it, actually played into their hands. There was definitely a buzz about the area, an edgy feel, and customers seemed to delight in the sense of discovery, that Moro was a modernist, sleek and shiny restaurant, serving exciting and unusual food, in what was then such an unknown part of London.

This tension lasted for five years until Sainsbury had the idea of bringing all those who traded along the street together to form the Exmouth Market Traders' Association. A highlight of this has been their annual summer festival at which those who live nearby can perform and put their energy to less destructive purposes. Almost overnight, Sainsbury recalled with relief, the nastiness stopped: 'Moro was OK.' The wider role of what restaurateurs can do for their neighbours, the local community and beyond had begun to take on increasing importance in Sainsbury's mind. He mentioned with admiration all that American restaurateur Danny Meyer had written on this subject in his book Setting The Table, and how it was to be one of his prerogatives when they opened the Zetter Hotel, and, on a much wider scale, when he came to found the Sustainable Restaurant Association.

Recalling his seven years at the coal face brought back happy memories and many hard-earned lessons. The first was the sheer excitement of being involved in the setting up of a new company, and of quite how much can be achieved out of so little. He ran Moro with Michael Benyan, who has been his business partner since, out of a tiny office, which was really no more than an unventilated cupboard. 'It was beautifully simple, and that sensation can never be repeated, sadly. Our offices in the Zetter are bigger

and far more comfortable.' Other lessons have been learned, such as not repeating their initial skimping on the robustness of the fridges they installed at Moro, which as a result had to be replaced after only six months. Sainsbury has stuck firmly to his policy of not putting his name above the front door because he believes that to do so would limit his flexibility, and has also stuck to the practice of sharing as much financial information as possible with his staff. Equally important at the outset was not to open on Saturdays until they were ready to do so, a policy that allowed them time to recover and stoked consumer demand. For similar reasons, Danny Meyer opens each new restaurant for lunch only for the first two or three weeks, in order to give his team a chance to settle in before opening for dinner. This caution did not, however, stop him investing in Maquis, a French restaurant that Samuel Clark decided to open in 2001 across town in west London. Although the timing proved far from propitious, what really sank the restaurant in Sainsbury's view was poor management and the fact that it was simply too far from Moro to be controlled effectively. His next venture, he promised himself, would have to be no more than a ten-minute bike ride away from Moro.

The inspiration for the fifty-nine-bedroom Zetter Hotel was to come from yet another photo, this time of The Ace Hotel in Seattle, which Michael Benyan had seen on his travels. It was a Moro customer who led them to the building. An imposing corner site, very close to Moro, it had once been the headquarters of the Zetter pools company, a business that could not survive the competition from the recently established National Lottery. Sainsbury described the move from successful restaurateur to wannabe hotelier, as the next logical step – the next test – but I believe the impetus goes deeper than this. Restaurateurs and hoteliers are jealous of one another. The formers' jealousy derives from the fact that they believe hoteliers generate very easy profits while their customers are asleep, at a time, when restaurants are closed for business. Hoteliers, on the other hand, desire the glamour that restaurants exude and want to see their dining room and staff open for the essential breakfast, tea and early evening services, as well as being busy at lunch and dinner.

Enthusiasm and naivety, the combination that had underpinned Moro, was ultimately to ensure the hotel's success – but only just. It was almost a disaster and Sainsbury nearly had a breakdown. 'The most we had ever spent until then was £220,000 ($350,000) on fitting out Moro, and here we were undertaking to spend £15 million ($24 million) on a building that only had one staircase, so from the perspective of the fire regulations the design was incredibly complex.' He was confident that the location between the City and the West End was wonderful, however, and although he never did any market research he never doubted its success.

Doubt may not have been an issue, but neglect of the one element – the hotel's restaurant – which Benyan and Sainsbury had just proved themselves so successful at with Moro, was to haunt them for the next six years. Sainsbury candidly confessed that they focused far too heavily on the hotel and just assumed the restaurant would succeed; that they simply failed to appreciate the far more complex demands that would be placed on a kitchen within a hotel; that the management structure was not right; that they didn't support the chef adequately; and that as a result, neither the consistency nor the margins nor the levels of customer satisfaction were anything Sainsbury could feel proud of. Most poignantly, they seemed to have failed to find the same exciting niche in the market as they had done with Moro. Since this neighbourhood had been where so many Italians had settled in London in the nineteenth century, Sainsbury thought it would be the logical venue for a modern Italian restaurant. It wasn't, and, gallingly, the hotel subsidized the restaurant for five years. 'The restaurant business was harder than I thought.' In essence, the restaurant had failed because it was not good enough, and because it had not established an identity for itself independent of the hotel.

The hotel had opened in 2004, and by 2008 Sainsbury realized that a drastic change in the restaurant was called for. He had no idea that it would lead to one of the best meals of his life, one that would emerge one lunchtime from two cold boxes in his kitchen at home, although he still regrets to this day that his wife had gone out and didn't enjoy it with him. By this stage he had already had discussions with Mark Hix, the ebullient exponent of modern British cooking, and Yotam Ottolenghi, the Israeli cook-restaurateur, about their potential management of the Zetter's restaurant. This type of negotiation can fail for various reasons, but not surprisingly, it is usually either over money or control, or a combination of the two. Then Guillaume Rochette, a Frenchman based in London who has successfully placed top chefs and hotel general managers around the world, called him to say that Bruno Loubet was back in London and that Sainsbury ought to meet him. He was reluctant to do so. 'I never, ever thought French food would work in Clerkenwell,' he smiled ruefully. Rochette persisted. Loubet had been one of the most exciting chefs in London in the 1990s, initially at the Four Seasons, then Inn on the Park, then Bistrot Bruno and L'Odeon. These successful stints had been followed by an ill-judged foray into a large Italian restaurant, after which, disillusioned with London, he had taken his family to Australia. The charms of old Europe had brought them back, although his final destination, whether behind the stoves in a London restaurant or those of a pub in the English countryside, remained unclear.

Sainsbury relented and Loubet came to cook. Two years on, he rattled off the dishes as though he had just eaten them the night before: three first courses, which were a skate terrine and Loubet's versions of the classics *salade Lyonnaise* and potted shrimps; and seven main courses, including slow-cooked spiced beef, mackerel with piccallili and a fish cassoulet. 'On top of all this, Loubet explained how his interest lay in executing good-value dishes using inexpensive cuts of meat and fish, and on putting his own interpretation on classic French dishes. It was as though he were looking inside my head.' Happily, Catherine Loubet, Bruno's wife, was equally excited about the prospect of the family name appearing next to that of the Zetter Hotel, and in February 2010 the first Bistrot Bruno Loubet opened its doors.

It did so to universally good reviews – a combination of the food and friendly service, the return of a long-lost prodigal son, and the fact that Loubet had been put in charge of a kitchen whose management shared the same approach to the care of its customers as he did to the ingredients he cooked with. Bistrot Bruno Loubet became a place not just for lunch and dinner, but also for breakfast, and thereby achieved the holy grail for any hotelier of being equally attractive to the hotel guests as it is to those who live and work nearby.

It is achieving and maintaining this successful interface that means the most to Sainsbury. He repeatedly used the word 'cleavage' to explain the professional divisions he continually tries to bridge: between the kitchen and the waiting staff in the restaurant, and between the hotel staff and the restaurant team in the hotel. 'It's great teaming up with intelligent chefs and my job is to make life as enjoyable and stress-free as possible. To ensure, for example, that if we don't achieve the requisite margin on one dish that we make it up on another. If the brigade are happy and friendly, then everything else follows. It's about happy staff and not about marketing.' I believe he manages this through strength of character and his own personal charm.

Sainsbury concluded by adding that he hoped he had never been too hard-nosed in any deal, and that he believes his strength has always been to create spaces for far more talented people to do their thing. At Moro this has led to the Clarks expanding into the shop next door to establish Morito, a stylish tapas bar, while at the Zetter, Sainsbury brought in the cocktail-shaking talents of Tony Conigliaro and Camille Hobby-Limon when he converted a Georgian townhouse almost next door to add another thirteen bedrooms. He still gets a thrill every time he walks into Moro, the Zetter, Bistro Bruno Loubet or the Townhouse. And he knows that at every Christmas party he can make the same speech: 'I can truthfully tell the staff how proud I am that I regularly see the words helpfulness and kindness used so frequently on the customer comment cards we use. What a lucky guy I am,' he added with a smile, before walking out on to the busy, safe street that he and his restaurant have been instrumental in transforming.

The sustainable restaurant

In 2010 Mark Sainsbury decided to confront and find workable solutions to a major issue, of which he has amassed a good deal of first-hand experience. It is an issue that now confronts every restaurateur: how to make restaurants more sustainable. The first step he undertook was to align the Mark Leonard Trust (which had been established through his family connection to the Sainsbury's grocery business, and which takes a particular interest in the environment), with the Esmée Fairbairn Foundation, the Garfield Weston Foundation and Sustain (an organization that promotes good farming and food practices), to establish the much needed, not-for-profit, Sustainable Restaurant Association: www.thesra.org.

The goals of the SRA are straightforward: to provide restaurateurs and chefs with the information they need to make their businesses more sustainable, and to provide the restaurant-going public with information about those who are following best practice in this field. It is a hugely worthwhile and effective organization that provides a great deal of useful advice, contacts and support. It certainly has a big job on its hands, as any restaurant's environmental footprint is threefold. The first element is what goes into its design and layout; the second, and most obvious, is in everything it consumes to give its customers so much pleasure: and the third, quite obvious early every morning when the deliveries arrive and late at night when the rubbish goes out, is what to do with all the leftovers: the food, cardboard, empty bottles and daily detritus from a busy lunch and dinner, a mound of stuff that the customer does not usually see and doesn't really want to.

In the UK, architects and kitchen designers working on any new building now have to meet the requirements set out in the 427-page consultative document compiled by the Building Research Establishment's Environmental Method (BREEAM). This aims to mitigate the impact of new buildings on the environment and grades any finished project from pass to outstanding. The design and treatment of the kitchen and the restaurant will obviously play an important role in this verdict, but come at some cost. Induction hobs are now increasingly common because they only use energy when a pan is put on top of them, but they are still more expensive to install than the more common gas or electric equivalents. According to kitchen designer James Lee, who has been responsible for over 2,000 kitchen designs, other areas under scrutiny include heat recovery from the kitchen's extraction system to pre-heat the water, thus saving energy; water and energy savings from dishwashers that use far less water than in the past; and dry-waste management that leads to energy saving, more composting and, collectively, to far less waste going to landfill. Not glamorous, but essential.

The most obvious, and most overdue, change in many menus' composition has been in the sourcing of the fish, a constant challenge for restaurateurs ever since Charles Clover first highlighted the impact restaurants have on the world's diminishing fish stocks in his excellent book *The End of the Line*. This is a particular challenge for restaurateurs as supply is decreasing, while demand, and therefore the price of fresh fish, is rapidly increasing. Many restaurateurs have responded sensibly by stipulating on their menus that all their fish are from either sustainable sources, or caught by day boats, which cause the least environmental damage and tend to deliver the freshest fish. There are, however, menus that declare that their fish comes from sustainable sources while continuing to list caviar from wild sturgeon, which is an endangered species.

One of the biggest challenges that every restaurateur and chef has to confront is quite how far they intend to go in sourcing seasonal and local produce. There is no doubt that using local produce minimizes air miles and packaging and generates local employment, but it does come at some cost, albeit one that is not immediately obvious. Many farmers and producers in developing countries depend for their livelihood on exporting the foodstuffs they grow. If we were to turn our back on them completely, the economic and social impact could be devastating. The ensuing menus would also be less varied; the absence of rice, for example, which is an ingredient not grown in the UK, would be a big loss. Restaurants are part of a global economy and those in charge of buying need to be aware of the impact their choices will have well beyond any restaurant's four walls.

JULI SOLER

THE INFLUENTIAL MANAGEMENT OF EL BULLI

17

Juli Soler is the restaurateur who made elBulli famous. It was his partnership with the far better-known chef, Ferran Adrià, that took elBulli to heights that no other restaurant has ever reached and, quite possibly, no other restaurant may ever emulate. The restaurant's website records that over 2,500 articles have been written about it, most of them carrying a photo of Adrià or one of the 1,846 different dishes he created with his brother, Alberto. There are far fewer profiles of Soler, even though he arrived at elBulli in 1981, two years before Adrià. In fact, Soler was running the restaurant when Adrià first arrived as a *stagiaire* in the summer of 1983. Adrià became a permanent member of the kitchen brigade the following year and then chef de cuisine in 1987. During those initial years, elBulli's reputation rested on Soler's extensive and unique skills as a restaurateur.

So too did the seemingly faultless execution of the menu at the new elBulli as it gradually changed its modus operandi during the mid 1990s, going from offering a fairly standard à la carte menu to a new menu of more, smaller dishes that were initially served for lunch and dinner during the six months of the year it was open. It was Soler who oversaw how this menu, which grew from around twenty-four fairly small dishes in 1997 when I first ate there, to between forty to fifty dishes before it closed forever on 30 July 2011, could be served to a room full of fifty very eager and highly expectant customers without any apparent hitch or longeur. Just to put this into perspective, elBulli was serving close to 2,500 dishes on any one evening. This was obviously a challenge for the forty-eight chefs under Adrià, but it was no less a challenge for Soler's team of twenty-five waiting staff, particularly as the latter had no point of comparison. To serve this many dishes during the four hours or so the customers spent at their tables is the equivalent of any other busy restaurateur profiled in this book serving four courses, admittedly larger, to over 600 customers in the same time period. How Soler did this becomes apparent upon looking at his classical French training.

It was particularly difficult because Soler had to impart his professional expertise all over again every spring when elBulli reopened for business after its winter closure. The team would invariably include many new members who only knew of the restaurant's reputation and had certainly never eaten there, nor, probably, had ever even walked inside it before they started work. Soler only had a week to do this, and it included cleaning the whole restaurant inside and out after it had been closed for the winter, before they opened the doors to their first customers.

An added challenge for Soler, but a definite bonus for anyone fortunate enough to have a reservation at elBulli, was its stunning geographical location, which borders on isolation. The nearest town is Roses, a fishing port that has spawned scores of holiday flats over the past couple of decades, since it is only 157 kilometres (98 miles) up the picturesque coast of the Costa Brava from Barcelona. As the road climbs out of Roses towards Cala Montjoi, the promontory to which elBulli clings, the first sign appears that an unusual adventure is about to begin: drawn onto the rocks, at varying distances, are the heads of the bulldog that once belonged to elBulli's original owner, Marketta Schilling. It was she who, with her husband Dr Hans Schilling, first opened what was to become the world's most famous restaurant. In 1961 it was originally a mini-golf course with a small café attached. The precipitous narrow road climbs and turns, and as it does so the views of the Mediterranean become ever more alluring. When elBulli was open for lunch this drive was pure pleasure. In the evening, however, the oncoming drivers of the cars containing couples and families who have spent the day on the beach just below elBulli faced the additional challenge of driving into the still-powerful rays of the setting sun. Many of them were on the wrong side of the road as they turned a bend, which ensured that every arrival at elBulli was a mixture of culinary excitement and relief.

The car park was certainly the most memorable of any restaurant car park I have ever visited anywhere in the world. On the way in, it was fun to perch on the car park's walls and look down at the beach and the bay (in which some friends once moored their yacht, leaving their children on board while they joined us for dinner) with the mountain range of the Cap de Creus National Park beyond. On the way out, it was just as much fun to lie on one of the walls and try to count the stars in the sky while listening to the waves below. It was while walking into elBulli that guests experienced one of the most unusual contradictions of this restaurant, though. On the one hand, it was the most innovative restaurant of its time, but on the other it was home to Juli Soler for the six months it was open (during that period his wife, son and two daughters, the elder of whom, Rita, is now a chef and has worked at elBulli for two years, took an apartment in Roses). Once inside, there was always the enormous contrast between the ultra-modern state-of-the-art kitchen, which was built in 1993, and the sequence of small, whitewashed, almost kitsch dining rooms with pieces of old wooden Spanish furniture that could have been found in any dining room along the coast. Perhaps only Heston Blumenthal's The Fat Duck, which is housed in a seventeenth-century pub in Bray, Berkshire, has the same intimate physical presence, albeit without such a homely feel.

This sense of welcoming his guests into a restaurant that was also his home was extremely important to Soler. When we met judging the Copa Jerez in Jerez (in which six chefs and sommeliers from across Europe had to impress a judging panel led by Soler with their menu and sherry pairings), and later at San Sebastián Gastronomika, a chef's conference, he stressed that from the very first day at elBulli, he had realized that the very best way of running things was to work as a team. 'We were to work in a very coordinated way as a family, with the same respect given to the chefs, waiters, pastry chefs, the driver, the dishwashers, the sommeliers and all the interns.' Soler unquestionably possessed the appropriate physique and charms to present himself as the *pater familias* of elBulli to all his staff, as well his guests. He is tall, has a mop of swept-back hair that has gone greyer over the years, seems to possess a highly mobile, languid frame (a consequence of years in discos perhaps, since Soler is a great Rolling Stones fan), and he has a great memory for people, names and faces. He wanted to make you feel welcome. No customer could fail to respond to his heartfelt warmth and interest in you as he moved to take you into his restaurant home.

This notion of welcoming all those who wanted to experience elBulli soon became impossible, of course, as the restaurant accommodated only fifty guests, and was open for only six months of the year. Faced with the extraordinary demand for tables as Adrià's star ascended, Soler instituted a system whereby those who wanted to book could try to do so on one day each January, with all reservations for the whole season inevitably taken in just a few days. This inability to satisfy demand was one major reason for Soler to close elBulli, as he explained to me one Sunday afternoon in Tokyo. I had travelled to Tokyo Taste, another chefs' conference, in spring 2009 with Heston Blumenthal. On the Sunday we joined up with Adrià and Soler for sushi and a few beers before the serious demonstrations began the following day. Some time before this trip Adrià had explained to me that he would not want to carry on cooking once he felt that there were no new dishes inside him, that he had exhausted his creative talents. Now it was Soler's turn to give me a premonition of why they would eventually close elBulli: he did not go into this business to say no to his customers. For him, the greatest satisfaction at the end of the evening had always been seeing his customers leave the restaurant extremely happy. 'But now I am the

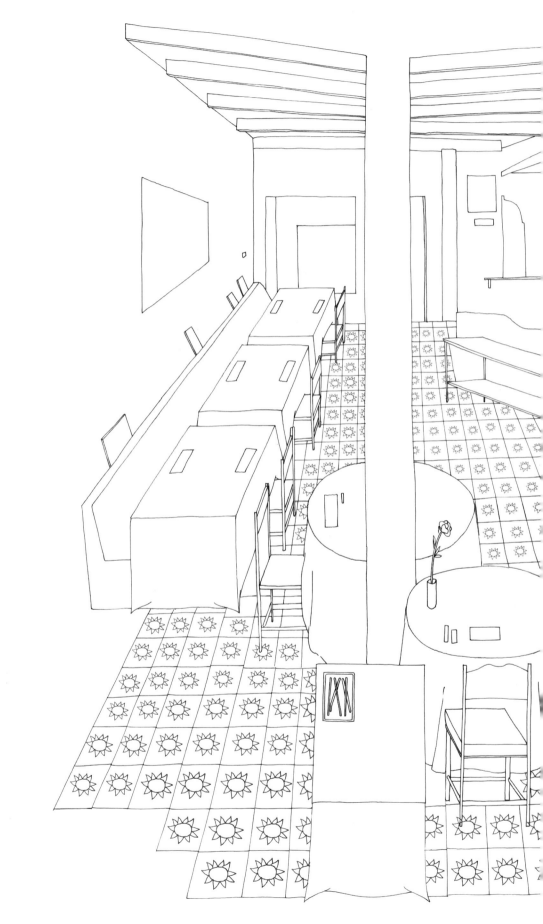

restaurateur who can only say no, from virtually the moment we open our booking lines one year to the same time the following year.' He had worked all those long hours to be in a position to say yes to his customers, not no.

In quite what distinctive and empathetic fashion Adrià and Soler chose to manage their teams was made clear to me during conversations with the chef Jason Atherton at the bar of his restaurant, Pollen Street Social in Mayfair, and with Ferran Centelles, one of elBulli's long-time sommeliers, over a beer in San Sebastián. Atherton was the first British chef to work at elBulli in 1999, but it wasn't the recipes or the techniques that have left the deepest impressions on him, now that he runs his own successful restaurant. The biggest lesson he learned there is that if you want a happy brigade in the kitchen, you must look after your kitchen porters. 'They have to be happy and working well because they are the bedrock of everything the kitchen does,' he recalled.

Ferran Centelles worked for thirteen summers at elBulli. He was initially taken on in 1999, straight out of catering college, following the management principle that excessive enthusiasm for the job will more than compensate for any lack of experience or expertise. He rose during that period to be one of the restaurant's two sommeliers and one of the core team of fewer than a dozen who stayed on and worked throughout the winter too. 'Juli was the soul of the restaurant,' he explained, his admiration for his former boss all too obvious. 'It was he who introduced a sense of calm into the dining room, who made us feel at home so that we could serve from the heart. He was also very funny and irreverent and, by giving the impression that nothing was too serious, he managed to take the pressure off us all.' Centelles also explained that elBulli's organizational structure was very different from the hierarchical norm. They all felt very close to Juli and Ferran, as though there were no bosses. There were no head waiters and no head sommeliers. 'Those are lonely positions, I once heard Juli explain, so we are going to share the work-load between us. From a personal perspective, this way we had far more opportunities to develop.' Centelles then recalled an example of how Soler had taught him how to be a better waiter. It was his first year as a sommelier and he had just taken a wine order. He had shown the bottle to the host, poured some into two glasses, and then just before he was to put them down in front of them, he swirled the glass around to release some more of its aroma. 'No sooner had I stepped away than there was a tap on my shoulder. It was Juli. He'd seen what I had done and he wasn't happy. He quietly pointed out that what I had done was something the customer could do himself, and it could easily have caused an accident by allowing the wine to spill.' Centelles never did it again.

This minor incident reveals one aspect of the restaurateur's art that Juli demonstrated better than anyone else, except perhaps the late Anders Ousback, the restaurateur who first alerted me to this essential aspect of the profession. Ousback, whose Swedish parents moved with him to Australia where he grew up, lived and worked, was responsible during the 1980s and early 1990s for many of Sydney's most successful restaurants: The Summit, The Wharf at Walsh Bay, Bennelong at the Sydney Opera House and the Hyde Park Barracks. Yet Ousback never considered himself a restaurateur. 'I'm a loiterer,' he would say, 'I believe that is the role of the restaurateur.' Once, before his suicide in 2004, Ousback elaborated that the most successful restaurateurs are those who loiter with intent. The intent is to ensure that the service goes as smoothly as possible and that everyone leaves happy and overwhelmed – not an easy proposition when your restaurant is considered to be the best in the world.

Soler managed this via a combination of his personality – Centelles kept referring to the fact that Soler had a very special way of talking to his customers and his staff – and the particular layout of elBulli that he turned so effectively to his, and every customer's, advantage. A long narrow passage led from the front door to what was a bustling reception point. The patio looking out onto the beach was on the left, the kitchen that everyone wanted to visit was on the right. Soler invariably took up a position just to the left of this important intersection, which gave him a clear line of sight right across to see who was coming and when. If the patio was already full, then the guests were diverted instead straight into the kitchen and from there to their table. This was absolutely crucial as, with forty to fifty dishes going to every single diner, the worst thing for Adrià and his team was to find that too many tables were sitting down simultaneously. Soler ensured that this did not happen. After the meal, when Soler had appeared in the dining room less frequently than a normal restaurateur because of his faith in his young team, had his photograph taken numerous times with Adrià, and shaken innumerable hands, he was back on the patio in full control of its several tables which, as they frequently comprised other chefs and restaurateurs, would be occupied until the early hours of the morning.

While this aspect of Soler the supreme restaurateur was visible to any customer, the principles that underpinned Soler's confidence in this role were much less so. They came from a perhaps unexpected source: France. During the decade from 2001 to 2011, when elBulli ruled the restaurant world, its success was hailed as the coming of Spain, the era when Spanish cooking finally dislodged French and Italian cuisine as the world's most exciting. This, however, is a rather simplistic interpretation of what was going on in the restaurant. elBulli was unquestionably a huge influence in Spain's overdue culinary renaissance but, as its reputation surged, so too did its interaction with the rest of the world. Ingredients from China, Japan and South America appeared on its menu. At my last meal there we were expertly served by a waiter from Mexico City. And its clientèle, too, was from all over the world.

The service principles, however, were French, and were laid down when Soler first arrived in 1981 when the Michelin guide was the unquestionable arbiter of taste, particularly for a small restaurant that opened only for the summer season. In 1981 he had started taking his chefs and waiters to visit the very best restaurants in France, to instil in them the fact that every day they had to make the restaurant better in the kitchen, service, food on offer and the décor, Soler explained. 'I continued this practice with much respect and friendship for the great chefs of France and their restaurants. And after Ferran arrived we carried on doing this for many years.' What Soler was referring to was not just the daily obsession in the best restaurants with making today's service even better than yesterday's – a phenomenon that Enrico Bernardo referred to when he went to work at the George V in Paris – but also that this was the foundation upon which Adrià's culinary experimentation depended. The more-than-tenfold increase in the number of dishes, the creativity of so many talented chefs, the sheer pleasure of eating in such an unusual setting: all of this novelty depended on the fact that Soler was steeped in the most rigorous principles of French service that evolved 150 years ago and were all about the sequence of courses – first course, main course, dessert - here multiplied thirteen-fold, of course. And behind that exceptionally warm and welcoming smile, he ensured that all his waiting staff were too. Just as most avant-garde artists have been steeped in classic art techniques, at elBulli Adrià's culinary artistry was served by a waiting team trained with the longstanding rigour of a Spaniard imbued with classic French techniques. However outrageous the food, the hugely intricate service would only be possible if the waiters followed the same rhythm of service as a more formal restaurant in Paris or Lyons.

278

In Soler's case, these principles were being added to a career that, by the time he joined elBulli in 1981, had already involved stages in numerous restaurants. He had started aged twelve working in his friend Miguel Ristol's restaurant in the great casino in Terrassa, Catalunya, where he was born. Then, at thirteen, he went to work for a season in the golf chalet at Puigcerda, and the next year in the great restaurant Reno in Barcelona. The following year he was planning to go and work on a cruise ship and see the world, but his father proposed that they worked together with Juli's mother to manage a restaurant-cafeteria inside a large electrical factory in Barcelona. Around this time, in the afternoons, nights and weekends, he started to get into music and travelled to France every weekend, and two or three times to England, to import records that hadn't yet come to Spain. At the end of the 1960s he became a DJ, opened two nightclubs and a shop selling his mixes. At the end of the 1970s he closed the shop. 'In December 1980 I met Marketta and Dr Schilling, who asked me to take over elBulli, since the chef then, Jean-Louis Neichel, was leaving to open his own restaurant in Barcelona. I accepted. I opened elBulli in March 1981 and since then I have been living in marvellous Cala Montjoi.'

This period, as well as the ensuing thirty years, have left Soler with some very strong personal likes and dislikes about life in general, and restaurants in particular. The former include rock'n'roll, the dish of *calamares a la romana* (fried squid), langoustines in any guise, smoking, sherry, coffee with friends, wines from the classic regions of Bordeaux, Burgundy and Champagne, and, above all, his family. A far shorter list of dislikes includes water (he describes himself as 'aquaphobic'), formality, making people wait in restaurants, and, that perennial occurrence in far too many restaurants, disturbing customers when they are eating. When I asked Soler to describe his ideal style of service, what he sought to achieve and emulate every day when elBulli was open, he thought for a moment and then answered: 'Dynamic, where there is a sense of speed, of inter-action between the waiter and the customer, but no conversation is ever too long to divert the waiter's attention from what he has to do, nor interrupt the customers from why they have come to the restaurant: to eat well and to talk to one another.'

By the mid 1990s, once Adrià and Soler had decided to move elBulli towards such a creative style of cooking that it was rendered unprofitable as a commercial entity, they also began to explore new business associations. These were not all that different in style from the model that many three-Michelin-starred chefs and restaurateurs have followed, whereby the restaurant represents the tip of the iceberg, the visible symbol of the business, while the whole is supported by many far less glamorous commercial arrangements including books, endorsements of culinary products, personal appearances and associations with wealthier companies. Such was the set-up at elBulli: fifty customers, forty-eight chefs, twenty-five waiters and a trading period of a maximum of 180 days, and a not-excessive menu price of €290 (£240 or $385). An unsubstantiated (but likely to be accurate) rumour was that the restaurant lost over €500,000 (£420,000 or $660,000) every summer. When I put this to Soler, his response was, as ever, far more complex than I had envisaged: was much more complicated than it may seem. 'We had decided that if we wanted to be creative, then we couldn't be a business. We could have made it profitable by increasing the price of the menu, but we didn't want to do that, to make it a rich person's club – although we had such a demand for tables that people would have paid it.' It wasn't unprofitable because it couldn't generate a profit, it was simply that they never intended it to be a business. What they did instead was to build a series of businesses around elBulli. 'These have been fascinating projects because we have learned from working with all of them, companies such as Nestlé, PepsiCo, Lavazza, NH Hotels, Damm beer and now Telefónica. We built up a team of fifteen to twenty people to handle this business, and the fact that these have gone so well has been down to them.'

Juli Soler was an exceptional restaurateur. Today, although any conversation about elBulli is naturally tinged with sadness because the restaurant is gone forever, he remains committed to passing on his knowledge and experience to the next generation of Spanish restaurateurs on his extensive travels or at the elBulli Foundation that will arise in place of the restaurant in 2014. Soler knows too that he has been extremely fortunate, not just in arriving at Cala Montjoi in 1981 as a young, snappily dressed restaurateur keen to prove himself to the world, but also in meeting, working with and, most importantly, getting on with Ferran Adrià. That this partnership has developed while Spain was going through a period of economic growth they refer to as *el boom* – and now can only barely recall, so changed are Spain's, and the world's, economies – has also been hugely important. While Adrià and his team provided the culinary magic, Soler and his team provided elBulli's soul. Neither individual could have done what they did without the other. But neither, both stressed to me, could have done what they did without their respective teams.

In praise of kitchen porters

It seems only appropriate to juxtapose the skills of restaurateur Juli Soler, half of the duo that established elBulli as the world's most exciting restaurant, with the mundane task of looking after the kitchen porters. As his partner, Ferran Adrià, stressed from the beginning to *stagiaire* Jason Atherton, looking after your kitchen porters is an essential element of being a successful restaurateur. On one visit to elBulli I joined in the staff meal early one sunny evening, when the queue of fifty members of staff snaked its way through the restaurant. I was struck by how both Adrià and Soler talked to everyone, encouraged them to eat as much as possible, and when it was their turn to eat, made a point of sitting next to people with whom they would not normally come into contact. The memory of chef and restaurateur peeling tangerines and joking with their kitchen porters will be a lasting one.

Kitchen porters do all the dirty jobs. They carry in all the raw ingredients and usually end up peeling most of them. They wash up all the kitchen equipment, crockery, cutlery and glassware. They have to keep the kitchen floors clean so that no one slips, and they have to be quick on their feet when one of the cooks shouts 'bin change' and a full, and often messy, bin needs changing immediately. They are also responsible for taking all the bags of food out at night in time to meet the final rubbish collection, and the front of the restaurant is often their responsibility too, which means washing it down at least twice a day. Their reward is a salary not much above the minimum wage, as well as the staff meals which, not surprisingly after so much physical activity, they attack with gusto.

Kitchen porters merit a good deal of attention from any restaurateur, not only because of all they do, but also because their career path is far more limited than that of a talented chef or waiter. Their work is far from glamorous; it is essential to the well running of the kitchen in particular, and therefore the restaurant in general; and it is not a role many aspire to, so a policy of continuous encouragement mixed with praise and a shared joke, will often generate considerable loyalty and persuade them to recommend working in your restaurant to their friends when they move on. Since kitchen porters handle everything that comes into and out of the kitchen, a dishonest one, working in collusion with a delivery man or even a fellow kitchen porter, can pose a real threat to the restaurant's profitability. Over the years there have been numerous such instances, where KPs, as they are commonly known, have mishandled goods on the way in or taken out with the rubbish expensive and pristine ingredients that can readily be sold for cash. Regular stock-takes and technology can mitigate the number of such misdemeanours, but they still happen.

Secondly, as part of their daily routine kitchen porters handle toxic chemicals that can lead to unexpected problems. One such experience involving my most trustworthy KP is still firmly lodged in my memory, almost thirty years after it happened.

This KP was called Martin, a blunt and very loyal Yorkshireman, who supervised all the others while he remained firmly in charge of the enormous industrial dishwasher. The kitchen was in the basement and linked to the three floors of the restaurant above by shafts holding two electric lifts, one for the food and one for dirty crockery. The dishwasher required chemicals that we bought regularly from the same supplier. That evening something went horribly wrong: either the wrong chemicals were delivered or the incorrect proportions were mixed together. Smoke ensued. Not thin wispy clouds of it, but thick billows of the stuff that promptly engulfed the kitchen and, most alarmingly, started moving up the building through the lift shafts and into the restaurant. We promptly got on the phone to the fire brigade, who fortunately were just around the corner.

The restaurant was already busy. There were forty customers sitting down in the very top room. The second dining room was booked for another party who were to arrive somewhat later, and the main dining room was fully booked, too. The ground floor brasserie was humming and I was nervously waiting to meet a demanding client who had arranged to meet me to discuss her son's forthcoming wedding reception, which she planned to hold in my restaurant. Fortunately, she and her husband were already in the restaurant when the fire brigade told me to close the front door and not to allow anyone else in. If, as at the time seemed most likely, we had to close, there would be a lot of explaining to do and a considerable amount of lost revenue.

The firemen made their way down to the kitchen, past a line of chefs and kitchen porters who were only too pleased to see them, and soon found the cause of the problem. The washing machine was disconnected, the pavement skylights and the windows at the front of the restaurant were flung open and quite soon – far sooner than I had initially imagined – normality was restored. Martin was naturally embarrassed, and that night had to do all the washing-up by hand, but the evening ended happily. I just lost a few more hairs: I had realized once again quite how much any restaurant depends on everyone doing their jobs properly. KPs tend to come from some of the most vulnerable and least well-off sections of society, and fulfil all manner of roles that affect every plate and every customer. When well looked after – and I do recall how much they enjoyed our staff outings – they play a vital but often overlooked role in the success of every restaurant.

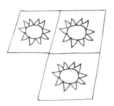

ADAM TIHANY

THE RESTAURATEURS' DESIGNER

Adam D. Tihany has designed many of the world's top restaurants for the world's best chefs. Tihany Design, the company he established in 1978 and which now operates from offices in New York and Rome, was responsible for Daniel Boulud's Bar Boulud, which can serve 700 customers a day, and Heston Blumenthal's Dinner, which can feed a further 300, both in the Mandarin Oriental, London. In New York, Tihany designed Le Cirque 2000 for restaurateur Sirio Maccioni, and Aureole, Per Se and Jean Georges for chefs Charlie Palmer, Thomas Keller and Jean-Georges Vongerichten respectively. His empathy for restaurants and hotels – I once saw a drawer in his office labelled 'the hotel bedroom of the future' – has also seen his designs emerge in restaurants for chefs Wolfgang Puck in Las Vegas, Vineet Bhatia in Geneva, Nobu Matsuhisa in Cape Town and Paul Bocuse in Geneva. Anyone travelling to eat, drink or stay at the King David Hotel, Jerusalem, the Beverly Hills Hotel on Sunset Boulevard, Los Angeles, or The Breakers, Palm Beach, Florida, will also experience the Tihany design ethos.

Four hours with Tihany, which began at his favourite table at the Gotham Bar & Grill on East 12th Street in New York and ended with a tour of his office, revealed several professional achievements of which he is proud. To begin with, he was the first designer to hang a sign outside his office that specifically read 'Restaurant Designer'. This initially went up outside his New York office in 1981. The second is that, as a result of his design for the wall of wine that has been such a striking feature of Charlie Palmer's Aureole restaurant in the Mandalay Bay Hotel, Las Vegas, he has created a new profession: the 'wine angels', who use ropes to climb the thirteen-metre (forty-three foot) wall to collect whichever of the 10,000 bottles stored there the customers have chosen for their meal. The third is that he was for several years a highly successful restaurateur himself.

I could see immediately why Table 29 at Gotham Bar & Grill has become Tihany's regular table, a fact the receptionist let slip as she seated me. It is in the corner of the raised area in the far corner of the dining room, which has lost none of its lustre since it was first opened in 1984 by executive chef and co-owner, Alfred Portale, and is a great place for surveying New Yorkers at work and play. No sooner had Tihany arrived than he added one other reason for this choice for our rendezvous, 'I believe this is a style of restaurant New York does better than any other city in the world. It's dependable, civilized, smart yet casual just like Gramercy Tavern', which is another of his favourites.

The route that has taken Tihany to his exalted position in the restaurant world has been far from straightforward. He was born in 1948 in Transylvania, south-eastern Europe, to parents who had survived the Holocaust. They moved to Israel when he was two years old and he grew up there in time to fight in the Six Day War in 1967. After three years of compulsory military service, Tihany was ready to leave Israel and he discovered that certain Italian universities were then offering subsidized places for Israeli students. He had a choice – veterinary studies at Bologna or architecture at Milan – and he knew that he didn't want to spend the rest of his life looking at animals. He set off to Milan with a bank of memories locked away: the strong sense of light that suffuses Jerusalem, the city he grew up in, and the glow of sunshine on its buildings. Doing his utmost to replicate this would remain a constant goal in his designs, for the benefit of chefs and restaurateurs as well as their customers. Perhaps the most striking example of this is the glass box that surrounds the kitchen at Dinner in the Mandarin Oriental.

The communist upheavals sweeping Italy in the late 1960s and early 1970s did not frighten Tihany after his stint in the army, but they did have one particularly beneficial effect on his career. The economic uncertainty that prevailed as a result meant that there was absolutely no work for architects, who were turning their professional hands to all forms of other design work to survive, whether in packaging, furniture or the elegant Italian cars of that era. This was crucial for him when he came to design Remi, his own restaurant, in the 1980s and then many others: 'I learnt immediately that it is not about the big picture, it is all about the detail.' An exhibition devoted to Italian design at MoMA, New York's Museum of Modern Art, in 1973 led to Tihany crossing the Atlantic. An American company wanted to form a joint venture with the Italian company he was then working for and, as he was the only English speaker in the company, he was promptly dispatched. 'I was thrilled,' he added. 'At that time every young Israeli wanted to come to the US.'

The American approach at that time did not favour the jack-of-all-trades Tihany had become until three high-profile jobs came his way. The first was to design the vast apartment in the new Olympic Tower on Fifth Avenue for the Saudi arms dealer Adnan Khashoggi. The second was designing the layout of the DDL Food stores in New York and LA for film producer Dino De Laurentis. These eventually failed, but from the pictures I saw of them they were in scope and scale spectacularly glamorous

Adam Tihany

precursors of Whole Foods and Eataly on Madison Square. It was here at DDL Food that Tihany was to meet chef Francesco Antonucci, with whom he was to open four branches of Remi and to develop a friendship that has lasted to this day. Then came the biggest break of all: the opportunity to design New York's first grand French café, to be called La Coupole and modelled on the Parisian restaurant of the same name, which finally opened in heavy snow in 1981. Recalling as if it were yesterday, he enthused, 'This was the hottest ticket in town with queues round the block. And when Andy Warhol couldn't get in, the place was made.'

Restaurants, Tihany was beginning to realize, are businesses that allow the designer the opportunity to control every discipline: the menus, the furniture, the graphics, the lighting, the finishes and the uniforms. They were a microcosm of everything he had wanted to do. Like every designer since, he has appreciated that as restaurants are public spaces they double up as the designer's showrooms in which to show off their talents just as much as the restaurateur's.

Our first courses, a butternut squash soup and a salad of beetroot, creamy goats' cheese and fennel, had just been served and Tihany displayed his Jewish origins: 'If you eat, I will tell you more,' he quipped. I started eating and he continued. He had been working on the design for a new restaurant, which needed backers to the tune of $300,000 (£190,000), when a conversation with Antonucci led to the somewhat reckless decision that they should do it themselves. Savings were scraped together, Antonucci took charge of the kitchen and Tihany the dining room, and the first Remi (the Italian word for the oars of a Venetian gondola) was born on the Upper East Side. The New York Remi, which was very stylish and certainly conveyed a sense of being in Venice, provided that magical combination of good food, wine, friendly service and fun – certainly far more so than many of the city's French restaurants of that era – and was to last for over twenty years, moving once to Midtown on 53rd Street and spawning siblings in Santa Monica, Mexico City and Tel Aviv. The other branches were eventually sold or closed, but Remi New York prospered under Tihany and Antonucci's management for more than twenty years, generating at its peak an impressive annual turnover of over $8 million (£5 million) before they sold it.

For the first three years Tihany worked as a designer during the day and then, at 6.00 p.m., switched career and took on the mantle of a restaurateur. 'I had no clue but I loved the transformation. I loved the fun, my

customers and, above all, I loved the control being a restaurateur gave me. I was like a fish in water.' He stressed the importance of the friendship he had established with Antonucci, his only partner and with whom he has remained on the friendliest terms since the initial Remi opened. (Antonucci still has his own restaurant, Antonucci's, on the Upper East Side.) The friendship almost foundered, though, after the first week, when both learned a significant lesson in what restaurants must do to survive. Gael Greene, then the city's most powerful restaurant critic as a result of her column in New York magazine, had eaten at Remi in its first week and subsequently called Tihany. Antonucci was from Mestre, near Venice, and they had opened serving the simple, unadorned Venetian food that his mother had cooked, which was low in salt and garlic. Greene thought the food was wonderful, but she was equally convinced that if Antonucci carried on cooking in that simple, Italian style, Remi would close very quickly. His style was too pure: by the standards of New York of that era it was simply not 'Italian' enough and too refined for the American palate, which then wanted more tomato-based sauces and, above all, demanded quantity. It seemed New York wasn't ready to appreciate authentic Venetian fare, so that night Tihany sat down with Antonucci for a confrontation that he did not relish, but is all too common between the restaurateur and the chef. Chefs tend to believe that they know best what their customers want to eat, even though they spend most of their time in their kitchens. Restaurateurs spend their days listening to their customers and therefore know what they really want.

Happily, Antonucci was willing to adapt and upped the flavours to include more seasoning and garlic, and included more drama in the presentation to create New-York style Venetian dishes such as ravioli Marco Polo (which was stuffed with tuna and served with fried ginger), pumpkin gnocchi, monkfish with radicchio and polenta, and some quite fancy desserts. As Tihany put it, 'Franco displayed no ego. If this is what the food critic says, she knows best, he told me. And the huge lesson we both took away with us is: in order to prosper, cook for your customers, not what you like to eat.' These three years also taught Tihany that the design of any restaurant has to incorporate the absolute need for synergy between back of house – the areas that support the kitchen brigade and the waiting staff – and the more attractive and exciting areas that the customers' eyes will focus on. Design, food and service are all equally important, but to build loyal staff the designer must give them the tools and the space in which to work comfortably and efficiently. If not, the staff will keep on changing and, whenever they do, the quality of the cooking and the standards of service will decline. It is not just about the finishes the customer will see: a successful restaurant design has as much to do with the ergonomic flow from the kitchen to the dining room; how well appointed and easy to use the waiter stations are, enabling staff to clear and re-set the tables as efficiently as possible; and choosing finishes that ensure the surfaces and corners can be cleaned as easily as possible. Restaurant design is more to do with service than the customer, Tihany learned.

He recalled the words of Joe Baum, the pioneering American restaurateur who was responsible not only for the success of the Rainbow Room in the Rockefeller Center, but also for Windows on the World at the top of the World Trade Center, the world's largest-grossing restaurant until 9/11. 'The first thing I do when I walk into my restaurant,' Baum used to say, 'is look up at the ceiling and make sure everything is working as it should. Are all the lights working properly or do they need adjusting? Are they focused on the appropriate tables? Then I look down at the floor, at the spaces between the tables, in the corners, around the service stations. Is everything as clean as it ought to be? Then, if I am happy with everything I have just seen I never take my eyes off my guests.' What Tihany learned, and has incorporated into his designs since his own time as a restaurateur, is that he must empower the restaurateur to control everything by making the design as effective as possible.

This approach was appreciated by chef Heston Blumenthal when he and Tihany began to design Dinner, a process that took more than two years. The brief from David Nicholls, the former chef who now sets the vision for Mandarin Oriental's restaurants worldwide, was a 'contemporary British brasserie', a phrase Nicholls kept repeating at every meeting, according to Tihany, although no one could name anywhere comparable. Blumenthal's plans for the food concept, which is inspired by historic British gastronomy, took Tihany to meet Ivan Day, one of the UK's leading food historians, who knows more about historic British recipes than anyone, and who cooked roast beef and all the trimmings for them both over his spit in his kitchen at his home in the Lake District. It also took them to the librarians at Hampton Court Palace, who provided another source of historic British recipes Blumenthal has successfully tapped. Tihany also appreciated that he had to mirror Blumenthal's modern reinterpretations of these classic dishes in the dining room, hence the absence of tablecloths and place mats, which are the norm in hotel dining rooms, and an overall sense of modernity and lightness. Wall-mounted light fittings in the shape of large transparent jelly moulds, amongst other things, create a link with the past. 'You walk through the hotel's heavy and somewhat gloomy lobby, and suddenly there is all that light, and you think "now I can relax".' What impressed Blumenthal so much about Tihany's approach was that, as a former restaurateur, Tihany was able to tell him about certain crucial areas, particularly the connection between the kitchen and the restaurant, where things would and would not work. 'I was genuinely surprised,' Blumenthal told me, 'by the breadth of his technical knowledge. It was incredibly helpful. Tihany intuitively knew about how the flow would work best, how we could ensure that the plates would stay as hot as possible and, on their return to the kitchen, in which direction they would cause the least disruption.'

Tihany's years as a restaurateur were not only fun and beneficial to his future customers but also, he believes, crucial in one other important respect. 'Remi was a portrait of Franco and me, and those first few years were enough to satisfy my ego. Obviously, ego still plays a part but I believe it is less significant now and certainly less so than that of my clients.' That, he believes, is what they appreciate because what they are looking for, as internationally recognized chefs and restaurateurs, are monuments to themselves, and not to him. What Tihany is doing as a designer is painting a portrait of his client – he often refers to his designs as similar to the contours of a custom-made suit – and that it is these differences between people that he is always trying to evoke. His fun, quirky designs for Le Cirque 2000 on East 58th Street are the way they are because he sees its restaurateur, Sirio Maccioni, as a traditional Italian ringmaster, pulling the strings on all those around him. Even though it is only a few blocks away across Central Park and he was working on the two projects simultaneously, his design for Jean-Georges is very different, and more plush, because Vongerichten is very different: 'an extremely precise, cerebral, Prada-wearing, Alsatian' was how Tihany described him. It is his customers' different personalities that keep Tihany fresh.

It was this approach that led to the wall of wine and the creation of the wine angels. Tihany was taken on a hard-hat tour of the Mandalay Bay Hotel in Las Vegas while it was under construction and shortly after the management had reached an agreement with New York chef, Charlie Palmer, to open a restaurant there. Palmer, physically, is a big, broad chef and Tihany realized that his designs would have to reflect this, as well as the powerful presence of New York. It could be no shrinking violet. During the tour Tihany saw three massive fifteen-metre (forty-five foot) cube-shaped holes in the ground-floor slab; these were intended for staircases, although one, somewhat surprisingly, was superfluous. Tihany was told that if he could come up with a better use for the third hole it could be incorporated into the restaurant, but the building programme was advanced and he had only until 9.00 a.m. the following morning to come up with an alternative. Over dinner that night, Tihany pondered the question of wine storage in the restaurant, but inspiration deserted him. Unable to sleep, he switched on the television at 2.00 a.m. in the morning and was confronted by Tom Cruise dressed in pure white in the first *Mission: Impossible* movie. He was struck by the size and simplicity of the images he saw and he began to sketch an outline of what would appear: wine angels using ropes to climb a tower of wine. It would be a sight that was at once both very Las Vegas and very New York. The following morning he persuaded the hotel management of his vision, the third staircase was cancelled, and a new profession was invented.

While opportunities such as this one, and that of working with chefs like Blumenthal and Vongerichten, are highlights of his long career, Tihany was quick to stress that the importance of the lighting in the restaurant and the kitchen has been a long-term bedrock of his approach. He was the first designer to install on top of the pass (the junction where the food finally leaves the kitchen) the same type of lighting as there is in the restaurant, thus allowing the chefs to see the food as the customer does. If that is not physically possible, a light box under which the food can be placed temporarily is the next best option. As all designers know, if the lighting in the restaurant makes people look and feel good, there is every probability that they will spend more money - peach-tinted lights around the mirrors in the lavatories are not an expensive addition, he disclosed as an example of how to make your customers look good.

Tihany also observed that restaurants have become the meeting places of choice for much of the developed world, the places where people want to socialize. Although he pointed out that it will be fascinating to follow what happens in India and China, in this respect he too is of the opinion that we may be witnessing the swansong of the more formal, fine-dining establishments. However, as more and more people become interested in what he refers to as 'fine eating', creating a successful and

Adam Tihany

fully integrated design becomes even more important. He is aware of how much the designer's role is changing. In a world of rising commodity prices it is much harder to justify the inclusion of so many natural resources, such as hardwood and the finest linen, that were once the staples of any restaurant design. In a warning to future restaurateurs, he repeated the beginning of his address to the students at the Culinary Institute of America in Hyde Park, New York, of which he is now Art Director and which he visits twice a month. 'I always begin by saying that for any prospective restaurateur out there, it may seem that I am your worst enemy. As a designer I am going to cost you more than any student loan and far more than any lawyer. But the most appropriate design is crucial to a restaurant's success, and it is never cheap.'

Tihany's current projects include what he describes as 'the dream commission' of designing a new *enoteca* (wine bar) and restaurant for the Cipriani Hotel in Venice looking out to the sea. As we parted by the lift in his office, he repeated something that he had touched on over lunch. The most fun he'd had was working at Remi. 'I could control how my customers felt, I had the ability to change their mood – a definite sense of power. If things weren't going well, then equally I had the opportunity to fix things. This becomes a drug and I now know that once I had done this, I was cured.' For Tihany, being a restaurateur was an unforgettable experience.

Taming the designer

As the peripatetic career of Adam Tihany reveals, the professional worlds of the restaurateur and the designer exist side by side and often overlap, usually to everyone's benefit. Tihany is not the only designer to have crossed into the restaurateur's camp. In the UK, the eminent designer Sir Terence Conran turned restaurateur with the opening of Bibendum restaurant in 1987, in which he still retains a significant shareholding, before going on to establish a large group of restaurants around the world that now trade under the name of D&D. Conran was also responsible for initiating the career of furniture maker Sean Sutcliffe, whose company Benchmark Furniture has been designing and making bespoke furniture and fittings for restaurants over the past twenty years.

There are many reasons why designers are lured towards restaurant work, and why several others as well as Tihany and Conran, most notably David Collins and Martin Brudnizki in London, David Rockwell in New York, Grant Cheyne in Sydney, Hecker Guthrie in Melbourne and Pierre-Yves Rochon in Paris, have made such a name for themselves in the design of so many stunning restaurants. Alan Yau even managed to lure such hugely talented designers as Christian Liaigre to help him reinterpret what was once a car park, and today is the seductive home of the original Hakkasan.

The first is that restaurants are so adaptable, thereby presenting the designer with a wide range of artistic challenges. It is usually the most modern interpretations that seem to attract the most attention, such as the various branches of Nobu around the world, M on the Bund in Shanghai, the reworked Le Bernardin in New York or Rockpool in Sydney, but that would be to ignore how today's restaurants manage to make the best use of buildings built many years ago. No other purpose than a restaurant could have put the old, tall, narrow buildings of Soho, London, to such effective and popular use as L'Escargot and Quo Vadis, or the challenging spaces now generating such pleasure in New York, such as Union Square Café or Gramercy Tavern. And Ballymaloe in Ireland certainly resounds to more laughter in its dining room today now that it is a restaurant open to the public than it would ever have done had it still remained a private house.

The second is that the restaurateurs who introduce designers to these buildings are exciting clients to work with.

They have a strong vision, a burgeoning reputation, exude enthusiasm, and although the restaurant business may involve inherent financial risks, it is at least blessed with a strong cash flow. Payment may not reach the designer precisely when it should, but it will arrive. Finally, restaurateurs will be bringing in happy and appreciative customers keen to absorb the designer's aesthetic taste.

To these three factors must be added the ultimate professional challenge for any designer working in a restaurant: having an assortment of talents across many disciplines. It is not just the practical challenge of linking the kitchen to the dining room, but also doing this in such a way as to encompass basic human needs, good sight lines, good acoustics, warmth and comfort, alongside all the more tactile elements that will enable the customer to enjoy this to the full: the crockery, cutlery and glassware.

Above all, restaurants allow their designers to show off their work to the public. Unlike their other main sources of commission, such as private clients or big corporations, restaurants are open to diners most of the time, with no entry fee other than the menu prices. Every good-looking restaurant is a calling card for its designer and I have long wondered how many designers have earned commissions from those clients who have left their restaurants initially as well-fed customers.

Many restaurant designers are, at heart, wannabe restaurateurs. Their experience alongside the professional restaurateur tends to bring out in many the notion that they can cross the divide (my designer tried twice). And that leads to the title of this chapter. Inspired design, however apparently simple, can be very effective. It is a great pleasure just to walk in to Maialino and enjoy the sense of being in Italy that David Rockwell has cleverly replicated in the Gramercy Park Hotel, New York. One of the reasons, in my opinion, that Isola and then Mocoto failed in the same location in London's Knightsbridge, first as an Italian restaurant and then as a Brazilian, were that both were over-designed. Hotel restaurants often suffer this fate because there is often no restaurateur to stand up to the designer or the hotel's general manager.

Ultimately, the harmonious working relationship between the restaurateur and designer comes down to the individuals' personalities and the restaurant's success. If the initial restaurant prospers, opportunities will present themselves to expand. If this does not happen (and over-design can lead very quickly to failure), then their personal harmony will never be tested. The professional union does provide a very strong bond, though. Restaurateurs want to have their vision interpreted spatially to everyone's benefit. What they do not want, and this must be made clear from the outset, is too much interference beyond this – although they do want their imaginations to be extended and excited so that they can do the same for their customers. What Christian Liaigre has designed for Alan Yau, and the five partners at Bentel + Bentel have created for Danny Meyer, and Grant Cheyne has done for the interiors of Neil Perry's restaurants, demonstrates just how successful this relationship can be at its very best. Even if, along the way, there may be a few disagreements.

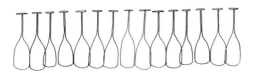

MARIE-PIERRE TROISGROS

CLASSIC FRENCH LUXURY

When Marie-Pierre Troisgros and I first sat down to talk about her career as a *restauratrice* (which is how her profession is listed in her passport), she rather shyly confessed that this was the first time she had formally discussed her work, despite having been the force for change in the three restaurants with which she has been so intimately involved since marrying chef Michel Troisgros in 1983. Today, the name Troisgros, with its large T logo, is synonymous with the very finest French cuisine, and Maison Troisgros (illustrated page 305), their main restaurant with rooms, has held the ultimate accolade of three Michelin stars since 1968. Its importance to the town of Roanne in eastern France, which over the past thirty years has seen the demise of its two main industries – textiles and engineering – and its population fall from a peak of 80,000 to around 30,000 today, is reflected by the signposts that point the way to Maison Troisgros as soon as you drive into town. The Troisgros restaurants spread the name of Roanne, and the culinary reputation of France itself, around the world. It was also to have a strong impact on the future of Californian cuisine, as it was chez Troisgros that a young, hungry Judy Rodgers, the chef-partner of restaurateur Gilbert Pilgram in Zuni Café, San Francisco, spent a year as an exchange student in 1973–4 and fell in love with the family's French cooking.

Our initial discussion took place in Troisgros' tiny office behind the reception desk of La Colline du Colombier, a restaurant with rooms eighteen kilometres (eleven miles) north of the French city of Roanne, which has been her home since marrying into France's longest established culinary family. It was 6.00 p.m. on a Saturday evening and Troisgros was just gearing up for what is always the busiest night of the week. 'I will stay here until about 9.00 p.m. because we are very full,' she explained. 'Then I'll drive into Roanne and spend some time at Le Central [their café-épicerie], before finishing up at our restaurant next door. I will be there until the last customer has gone to bed.'

Appreciating quite what, and how, this talented, determined and resilient woman has achieved over the past thirty years involves both delving into the history of the top restaurants in France, and considering what the atmosphere must have been like a generation ago inside a conservative, family-owned business where the men were used to taking all the major commercial decisions and the women were accustomed to playing a decidedly subservient role. A series of chance occurrences, however, has allowed all this to change significantly. Had Marie-Pierre and Michel had their way in the early 1980s, their planned restaurant in Sydney, Australia, would have been so successful that they might never have returned to France to work.

Maison Troisgros had been opened as a humble café in 1930 by Michel's grandfather Jean-Baptiste, who recognized the importance of its location opposite the town's train station. In the 1950s he retired and handed it over to his two sons, Jean and Pierre, who were part of the new wave of French chefs who challenged, and then changed, the much richer style of cooking bequeathed to them by the godfather of classic French cuisine, Auguste Escoffier. The unique Troisgros contribution to this movement was their famous dish *escalope de saumon à l'oseille* (escalope of salmon with sorrel), which has unquestionably stood the test of time. By the late 1970s the Troisgros restaurant was built on solid foundations, with Pierre's two sons, Claude and Michel, being groomed to take over. And then the first chance occurrence happened. Michel, sixteen, had been sent to hotel school at Grenoble in 1973, where he enrolled in the same class as Marie-Pierre Lambert. Born in Valence into a house where her father loved to cook, Marie-Pierre had wanted to carry on her studies at university, but her parents insisted on a vocational training. On her visits to an aunt who lived in Grenoble, she had seen the hotel school and, simply on the basis of this brief encounter, decided to enrol, thereby joining the ranks of the world's many accidental restaurateurs. It was, she consoled herself at the time, at least a profession that would allow her to earn, to be independent and to travel the world.

Marie-Pierre and Michel finally became a couple in their last year as students (she is one year older than him), and in 1976 she came to Roanne for the first time with a group of twelve friends, where she met the family. What made the strongest impression on her was a meal cooked by Michel's Italian grandmother, although she recalled that this brief visit did not prepare her at all for life chez Troisgros in a few years' time. The following few years certainly tested their love and the strength of her character. She accompanied Michel while he cooked at Frédy Girardet's restaurant in Switzerland, The Connaught in London, and at hotels in New York and Brussels, but in that era the top hotels were extremely reluctant to take on couples, particularly unmarried ones. In early 1983 they returned to Roanne, ostensibly to work there for six months before setting off for Australia. But Jean, Michel's uncle, died suddenly in August, and by the end of the year she and Michel were married. She was now Madame Troisgros and part of a restaurant dynasty. Thirty years later, it is still clear what first attracted Michel to Marie-Pierre in what both separately described to me as a *coup de foudre*, or love at first sight. Although neither is tall, both exude a physical energy that seems to galvanize each other as well as all those around them. Within her restaurants, Marie-Pierre has a constant smile that vanishes the moment she sees something she dislikes or disapproves of. But it is her eyes that are her most professionally valuable asset. In fact, Michel listed her eyes, her intelligence and her confidence as the characteristics that first seduced him. An old friend who lives close to Roanne recalls watching Marie-Pierre walk into Le Central one very busy Saturday night and as she stood by the reception desk she immediately spotted something that was not right. A napkin had been laid out, nicely ironed and correctly folded, but still with a couple of small stains on it. Before her maître d' had even noticed, she swept it up and replaced it with another one that met with her approval.

Returning to the events of the early 1980s, she recalled that 'the problem we both had to face up to at that time is that there had always been only two Troisgros, Jean and Pierre, as far as the world was concerned.' In those days the menu cover was simply a portrait of the brothers' two faces in front of an outline of the railway station. Claude had already left, so Michel had to stay to cook alongside his father: he had no choice, and nor did she. The fact that Claude, the elder brother, had flown the family nest to make his restaurant career several thousand miles away in Brazil spoke volumes about the household Marie-Pierre was moving into. It was nothing personal, she stressed, and she adored her mother-in-law, Olympe Troisgros; it was just that there was a well-established way of life with little room for change. Most depressingly, the ten members of the family, spread over three generations, all lived on one floor directly above the restaurant, and such was their dedication to the business that there was very little separation between work and home. 'Nobody would survive in an atmosphere like that today,' she continued with a laugh. 'They would probably all kill one another.'

She lasted only two months in that constrained atmosphere before finding herself and Michel a separate apartment to live in, while establishing her own sphere of influence in the restaurant. This began slowly at the reception desk, and then, having won her mother-in-law's confidence, she was able to introduce their first computer and began to modernize their style of service. The changes were not initially welcomed by the inhabitants of Roanne, who had come to use the bar at the restaurant as a local meeting point. This became incompatible with the growing number of visitors from all over the world who now wanted to stay at the

restaurant as Michel's culinary reputation blossomed. This was particularly true of visitors from Japan, where he had taken over an association with a restaurant in Tokyo initially planned by his uncle, a working relationship that continues today through Michel's association with a French restaurant in the Century Hyatt Hotel, Tokyo.

On my return to Roanne, Troisgros kept repeating what for her has been an absolutely essential factor in allowing her to breathe vital change into an already established and highly revered restaurant. 'I'm not materialistic and I'm not possessive. This isn't my house, it's really Michel's, but that does not mean that I cannot see what needs to be done to make it even better.' These thoughts began to crystallize in her mind after a decade of running the restaurant and the birth of their three children, two of whom have chosen to follow in their parents' footsteps, much to their surprise. César is already a talented chef who has worked at The French Laundry in Napa, California, among other top restaurants, as well as alongside his father, while his younger brother Léo has recently embarked on a career in hotel management. I am sure they were helped on their way by the decisions that lay behind the opening of Le Central in 1996 and then La Colline du Colombier in 2008.

Le Central was to be, as its name suggests, a place for the locals, the Roannais who were beginning to find the main restaurant too expensive and whose custom, support and loyalty both Marie-Pierre and Michel were determined not to lose. 'It's your clients who make a restaurant, who fill it and who in turn give us our living. We have to respect them.' My only complaint about Le Central is that it is too far from London for me to eat there once a week, because it manages to combine so many fascinating and attractive aspects of what a restaurant should be. It occupies the ground floor of what used to be a hotel, right next door to the Troisgros' main restaurant, so it is a mixture of the old – a splendid early twentieth-century wash basin, high ceilings and a tiled floor – with modern features such as cheerful floor-length curtains, polished wooden tables that make tablecloths unnecessary and, in the smaller back dining room, a full-length glass swing door into the kitchen. The front-of-house team has been led almost since the beginning by Patrice Laurent, who combines charm with the authority of a sergeant major. The kitchen is visible from the main dining room, along with the chefs in their tall white hats behind a counter that is home to a set of antique red weighing scales, and on some days a large tarte tatin that gets smaller as the evening progresses.

Several other factors also have contributed to the success of Le Central, which has been full since it opened, serving ninety to a hundred customers every day. The first has been the Troisgros' obvious willingness to share any approval for what they are doing with the suppliers who make it possible by hanging black-and-white photographs of everyone they buy produce from around the walls close to the kitchen. The second has been to make Le Central more than just a café, of which the centre of Roanne has plenty, but a café-épicerie, or grocery store, with several walls of shelves full of the kind of ingredients that can make a good meal even better, such as vinegars, sauces, chocolate, wines and – the latest addition – sardines she had discovered from a small artisanal producer in Lisbon during a recent Relais & Châteaux conference. It is a clever way of bringing the world to the centre of a relatively small provincial French town whose citizens have been obsessed with food and wine for many years.

Another aspect of Le Central that always brings a smile to my face is the paper place mats. Underneath the white napkin, which is wrapped in a paper coil with the name of the restaurant on it, is a circular white plate, again with the name Le Central around the rim. Below that, printed on the pale purple place mat, are the outlines of precisely where the cutlery, plate, water and wine glass should be placed. It is incredibly simple, efficient and professional. My reference to the efficiency of this place mat prompted Troisgros to give an example of why restaurants continue to fascinate her and Michel. She had been in a meeting all morning with Isabelle Allegrette, their interior designer, because she is planning to change a lot of the main restaurant's interior: the chairs, what is on the walls, the general look of the place. One of the things they were discussing is whether, given their status, they can do away with tablecloths. 'I am very conscious that cloths are synonymous with the best French restaurants, but I am also increasingly concerned about the environmental damage that doing so much laundry is causing. We've already replaced the bathrobes in the bathrooms with even larger bath towels for the same reason.' She asked for my opinion, but having left home at 5.00 a.m. that morning, I was instead eyeing the attractive menu with some interest. Right on cue, Laurent was at our side, pen in hand, to take our order for bowls of pumpkin soup with almonds and a lamb tagine for me, and a steak for Troisgros, which she insisted had to be without any sauce. I observed that Heston Blumenthal's Michelin-starred restaurant Dinner, designed by Adam Tihany, had opened without tablecloths, and she responded that a trip to London was long overdue.

This then led her to slip, unprompted, into explaining the unique pitfalls and attractions of life as a restaurateur.

'It's a wonderful life, but it's a façade,' she explained. In order for everything to seem so effortless, there must be a series of teams, all doing their jobs well. Teams in the dining room, teams in the kitchen, teams of washers-up, all of whom have to be extremely well managed – and the client must never see anything. 'That's the misunderstanding so many people have when they decide to open up their house and take in a few paying customers, to run a bed and breakfast, on even a limited scale. I know what is involved and I would never do that in my own house.' What she and Michel still find so fascinating, though, is the absence of routine, an opinion with which most restaurateurs would concur. Of course, there is a rhythm to the day in the life of any restaurant, and particularly one associated with a hotel, but it is the unexpected, which also seems to occur regularly, that can be such an attraction professionally. 'Michel and I hate routine, and in this job there certainly is never anything routine.' As our conversation took place in French, Troisgros on three separate occasions used a memorable phrase to describe her professional life: 'c'est riche'.

Life for the Troisgros family and their customers was to become considerably richer when she started dreaming of opening something in the rolling countryside that surrounds Roanne. 'I think it was more me than Michel at the outset, because this is the Troisgros house – their safety net, if you like. Because it isn't really my house, I had the capacity to think of something beyond these walls.' She knew exactly what she wanted: an extremely good restaurant in the countryside where they could go as a family on their day off. Somewhere that was definitely not another Michelin-starred restaurant and, equally importantly, one at which the food had not come from a cash-and-carry or the deep freeze, as is so often the case in rural French restaurants today. The search for what they eventually opened as La Colline du Colombier (it takes its name from a former dovecote) took eight years, but has brought with it immense professional satisfaction because Troisgros set her own goals so high. 'All the estate agents showed me initially were crumbling châteaux and maisons bourgeoises (country houses). But what we wanted was something that expressed the Troisgros style, somewhere far more relaxed and in keeping with the twenty-first century.' They finally settled on an abandoned series of farm buildings with uninterrupted views of the countryside in all directions, and began to plan a renovation that eventually concluded with the large stables being converted into a striking restaurant with an open kitchen. The rest of the farm buildings have now become bedrooms with en-suite bathrooms, and, more unusually, there are also three *cadoles*, or sleeping quarters in the shape of long half-igloos, built in front of the building on tall steel struts to allow 180° uninterrupted views from the terraces in front of them. The inspiration for these buildings came from the huts in which the local winemakers used to store their tools in the vineyards, but they now incorporate all the accoutrements of a modern hotel room, as well as a log-burning stove. They have proved so popular that they are even booked over the weekends in the winter, when the rest of La Colline is closed, with the Troisgros delivering a breakfast service.

The impact that the transformation has had on Marie-Pierre is obvious from the sheer enthusiasm with which she recollects the whole project. From the outset they decided to take their time and to plan everything not only from the perspective of what the customer would want, but also from how they could learn the most from everyone they came into contact with, which they hoped would make La Colline even more sympathetic. They were particularly invigorated by the architect Patrick Bouchain and Troisgros learned a lot from him, as well as the masons and the botanists she met. 'The whole process was incredibly stimulating and at the end, when it was all over, I remember crying because that was a part of my life that I really, really enjoyed.'

For a *restauratrice* as professional as Marie-Pierre Troisgros, the opening of any restaurant, let alone something as architecturally complex as La Colline, means a new shift in her responsibilities. She considers what she does as no more than 'dispensing humanity,' though, and I subsequently learned one small aspect of how she does it. Every May, when the main restaurant closes for a short period, she turns one of its main rooms into a *brocante*, or a posh car-boot sale, and puts up for sale all the items she believes have outdone their usefulness: glasses, cutlery, salt and pepper sets, crockery, anything and everything that no longer meets with her approval. The proceeds from this sale go to support a village in Mali in sub-Saharan Africa.

As she sipped the hot *citron pressé* she had ordered in the hope of warding off an incipient cold, I put to her the one question that she chose not to answer directly: would she and Michel have been happier in their own restaurant in Sydney? 'I dream all the time, and that includes doing many other things. I think I've opened more than fifty different restaurants in my head. But now that we have three, I know that that is enough. I couldn't do a fourth.' Here, I believe, she was referring not only to her role, but also that of Michel, her husband and business partner. She has had the good fortune of marrying a great chef whose restaurant has long had close working relationships with many top winemakers because of its proximity to the vineyards of Beaujolais, the Rhône and Burgundy. She has, therefore, not needed to preoccupy herself too much with the challenges of the menu or the wine list. However, to this business, which comprises three restaurants and two hotels, all very different in character, she has brought two unique and enormously valuable traits. The first is a grasp of detail combined with a determination to achieve the highest standards. *'J'organise'* was how she summed up her working day, and there is no question as to where the power in the organization lies outside the kitchen. The second is her feminine presence in a business that had, until her arrival, been singularly masculine. The consequences of this are now enjoyed by any customer who appreciates the sense of modernity, freshness and lightness, as well as extreme comfort in the bedrooms, that she has brought to all three establishments.

It came as no surprise, then, when she described the thing that has given her the greatest satisfaction over the past thirty years. Although it involved her staff, it did not take place in any of the restaurants. She had organized a staff outing for everyone, about seventy-five of them all from all three restaurants. They went go-carting in the morning, then for a picnic at her daughter's riding school. 'It was incredible to see all of them having such a good time, to appreciate quite how many jobs we have been able to create, and to know that all these people are in a position to help me pass on so much happiness to our customers.' Of all the restaurateurs in this book, Marie-Pierre Troisgros has probably faced the biggest challenges to realizing her dreams. She fell in love with a member of a culinary dynasty, which prevented her pursuing her professional dreams in the emerging restaurant scene in Sydney, Australia. As a result, she has spent her working life in France, the country that gave restaurants to the world, but on the whole has been slow to welcome innovation in a profession that many considered their own prerogative. And she has accomplished all her innovations away from the stimulating competition of a capital city. In the same way that Australians are very fortunate that Neil Perry never left Sydney, French people, and any visitor to Roanne, are very fortunate that Marie-Pierre Troisgros never left their shores.

Continuous innovation

Of the many qualities that unite the restaurateurs in this book – a love of food, wine and the magnanimity they show to their staff and customers – nothing has contributed to their success more than their willingness to innovate continually. This is a characteristic, I believe, that distinguishes the best from the rest, and it is a principle that begins even in the very first restaurant. What is important is simply never to stand still – to ensure that your customers want to return because there is something on the menu, on the wine list, or even on the walls, that they have never tasted or seen before.

Innovation is equally crucial whether it relates to just one or a small number of restaurants, as in the case of the Troisgros, or to a series of new openings, as in the case of restaurateurs like Danny Meyer. And it is often at its most effective when it is most subtle: a rehanging of the pictures on the walls, a change of the font that is used on the menu, or the incorporation of the wine list on to the menu. All of these, often subconsciously but most effectively, provide an extra reason to return.

It can be easier to achieve than it sounds, because from the beginning there is often a partnership that allows ideas to flow between the restaurateur and the chef or between the restaurateur and his or her business partner. In the case of Danny Meyer it was his early association with his chef Michael Romano that laid the foundation for his varied restaurants. For Russell Norman it was the enthusiasm and *joie de vivre* of his partner and oldest friend, Richard Beatty, that provided the basis for their development into Venetian wine bars, American diners and Mishkin's, a Jewish deli with cocktails. It is not expansion for expansion's sake – that is what leads to the plethora of restaurant chains – but instead an expansion driven by excitement, the feeling that no one else could pull off this new idea quite as well, and that the new departure, as well as being financially rewarding, will be fun, too. Since restaurants tend to be quite hierarchical organizations, with only limited positions at the very top, it is also vital to follow a path of continuous innovation in order to make room for the new, young and enthusiastic staff coming through the ranks. If they cannot be promoted within your restaurant, there is sure to be somebody else who will poach them.

One reason why innovation is possible is that each of these restaurateurs has a deep interest in food and wine, and both of these are subjects for which the more you know about them, the more you realize how much there is to learn. Of all the restaurateurs who have effectively put this theory into practice, none, I believe, has done so quite as thoroughly as Marie-Pierre Troisgros. Others may have travelled further (although the Troisgros do have a restaurant in Tokyo and an association with the restaurant in the Hotel Lancaster, Paris), but none will have started with quite the obstacles that she faced when she first arrived chez Troisgros in 1983. She was a woman in a man's world, with relatively little experience of the professional world she was entering. The world of haute cuisine in France at that time was dominated by men, and, many would maintain, still is to this day. Today, though, the Troisgros business is unrecognizable compared with what it was twenty years ago. By stages, Marie-Pierre has transformed the dining room of the three-Michelin-starred restaurant and given the whole hotel a modern design that was distinguished from the outset by her purchases of modern art for the walls, particularly the works of Japanese artists; she has opened a café-épicerie next door, an unusual combination for a small provincial city; and finally she has opened a restaurant with three unique bedrooms in the countryside. It is an impressive record.

It is obviously a great advantage that she is Madame Troisgros and partnered with her husband Michel, who is as talented in the kitchen as she is in the various restaurants, and has an exemplary set of professional standards and values.

But this could just as easily have been a reason not to implement so many changes, and not to open anything new. Instead, she has chosen to innovate. The shelves on her walls display foodstuffs she has seen on her travels; the restaurant in Japan brings in young *stagiaires* keen to spend several months in a Troisgros kitchen; and their varied restaurants, from the more relaxed to the far more structured, provide an excellent training ground for their waiting staff, whose skills can then be developed in different ways.

Continuous innovation is a factor common to the success of many businesses worldwide, such as Apple and Dyson, most obviously. And what is so unusual about the world of restaurants is that its essential building blocks – food and wine – provide the basis for this principle to be put to such exciting ends. Embrace this principle of continuous innovation, as so many excellent restaurateurs have done, and the rewards are enormous and fairly immediate. Your customers will be delighted and, crucially, return and recommend your restaurant. But the most satisfying aspect is that you lay down a fascinating path of future knowledge, pleasure and enjoyment for you and your colleagues to follow – a path that has no end and no limit.

ALAN YAU
SLICK, FAST-PACED AND EXCITING FOOD

Alan Yau is the restaurateur who created wagamama (illustrated page 318–319), Hakkasan, Yauatcha, Cha Cha Moon and Sake No Hana, none of which he has an interest in any longer, as well as Busaba Eathai and Princi in London, which he still controls, along with Betty's Kitschen in Hong Kong. When he slipped into the banquette of Racine in Knightsbridge for lunch with me one Saturday, he was looking better than I had seen him in years. Once we had shaken hands and exchanged pleasantries – we have known one another for more than fifteen years – Yau ordered a pot of hot water and asked me to explain what I wanted to talk to him about. Of all the restaurateurs I had wanted to include, Yau had been the most difficult to track down. He now explained apologetically that this was not because he did not want to participate, but because he was under a vow of silence not to answer any press or media requests at the suggestion of Patrick Wong, his feng shui master in Hong Kong. He had broken this vow for me because he appreciated the opportunity (in between his trip from Hong Kong to London, and then back to Asia for his first visit to Tibet) to talk about his extraordinary career as a restaurateur. And when I explained what I was doing, he applauded.

The first ten minutes of our conversation, however, included many painful memories. The first related to Yau's six-week stay in autumn 2010 in Wat Phra Dhammakaya, a Buddhist temple in Thailand, after which he had been enrolled as a Buddhist monk. It had been spartan in the extreme and Yau had had to be both mentally and physically tough, and equally bloody-minded, to survive. He'd first had to call on these traits at an early age, however. Born in Hong Kong, the eldest of four, at age twelve he had moved to the UK in 1975 to join his parents who had already settled in King's Lynn, a market town in Norfolk, 110 miles north east of London. Life was not easy. He spoke no English and the family was housed on a very poor and tough housing estate, which meant an equally uninspiring school. 'For the first time I encountered racial prejudice and social antagonism, phenomena which simply had not existed in our small village in Hong Kong.' His father, who had been a tailor in Hong Kong, had turned to cooking as that was the only profession easily accessible to immigrants at the time, and had become the chef and partner in an eighty-five-seater restaurant, which further alienated Yau. 'I disliked it intensely,' he explained, 'and at that stage of my life I really wanted to run a mile from a career in restaurants.'

Although I knew that Yau's story was to have a happy ending, I was now feeling pretty downbeat and I suggested we ordered. A crab salad with herb omelette followed by duck confit with lentils were Yau's choice, and Racine's signature dish of a saffron mousse with mussels followed by cod, brown shrimps and cucumber were mine. Then Yau's unlikely life story really got under way – a story that has taken him from King's Lynn to London, seen the restaurants he has created open all around the world as a result of collaborations with several of the world's leading architects and designers; and taken Yau, as a restaurant consultant, to projects in Moscow, Dubai, New York, Doha and Bangkok.

Underpinning it all was Yau's position as the eldest son and the expectations that rested on his shoulders in a traditional Chinese family, even one a long way from home. 'I needed to accumulate wealth for my family, and to do so quickly,' he explained matter-of-factly. His initial career working for a steel stockholding company in Watford made it apparent that corporate life was not for him and that his future lay as an entrepreneur. His eye was caught by an advertisement from the Peterborough Development Corporation that was seeking bids for a series of buildings they were planning to let on favourable terms to individuals starting new businesses. With the help of an accountant colleague, Yau filled in the forms and secured a building. His restaurant career was under way, albeit in a very low-key fashion. In 1990, with £25,000 ($40,000), the family's entire capital, Yau took a punt on opening a Chinese takeaway called Capitel. It served the standard Chinese fare then popular throughout England, and prospered immediately. 'I made my investment back in six months. Now I felt ready to conquer the world.'

Growing up in his father's restaurant had shown Yau the hardships of the business – the very long hours combined with minimal rewards – and reinforced his determination to go for broke. He was fascinated by McDonald's, which has been a huge if unlikely influence on so many restaurateurs of the past generation. (McDonald's had also interested Drew Nieporent, who worked in a New York branch during his school holidays.) This fascination related to the then unusual levels of hygiene, speed of service and value for money it represented, all underpinned by an unprecedented array of systems. Yau invested £65,000 ($100,000), using the cashflow and profits from Capitel, to try to create a model for an equivalent to McDonald's that could serve Chinese food just as swiftly and efficiently.

Despite his ingenuity, and the support of the late David Acheson at the accountants BDO Stoy Hayward, Yau's dreams came to nothing.

Alan Yau

'It was not possible,' he recalled, 'because the de-skilling process involved in producing even the least complicated Chinese menu was was far too difficult. It needed too many chefs and too many processes.' He continued to work at the coal face, though, encountering what he described as 'racial bombardment' while working at a branch of KFC in west London. He then worked at a McDonald's in Hong Kong because he realized that the colony then was home to six of the company's top ten performing sites worldwide. He was even offered a McDonald's franchise in what was then the New Territories, which would have certainly made him a very wealthy man, but he turned it down. He wanted his own restaurant, but he still had no idea what it would be.

Yau was introduced to ramen noodles by Ayumi Maeda, a young Japanese student who was on the same hairdressing course as his sister Linda (who now owns Cocorino, a café and ice-cream bar on Marylebone High Street and a good example of an easy-to-remember brand name). He had found the ability to put all that he had been dreaming of into practice, albeit with Japanese rather than Chinese food. He recalled that they were talking one night and Ayumi had mentioned that the food she really missed now that she was living in London was ramen noodles. 'I had no idea at the time what these were, but as soon as she explained them to me, a light went on in my brain.' Here was a style of very popular food that only required three components in its cooking: the soup; the noodles and the topping. Ayumi, with whom Yau has since lost touch, also mentioned her nickname *wagamama*, which is Japanese slang for a spoilt rich kid.

Yau was focused, his father sold a second restaurant to support him, and in 1990 the search for the first London site began. The risk of failure was a spectre too, and Yau recalled visiting prospective sites with letting agents almost hoping that they would not be suitable. Then, under the influence of personal development trainer Anthony Robbins, Yau's approach changed. Firstly, he got his balls back, as he described it, and realized that there is no such thing as failure, which is just part of life's learning curve. Six months as a vegetarian restored his energy levels and provided the template for the raw juice and healthy eating components that would be key and novel ingredients in the success of the first wagamama. Yau rattled off the details of the first site in a basement just off Gower Street as though he had opened it yesterday, rather than in April 1992: 278 square metres (3,000 square feet); six long communal tables that sat 104 in total; an average main-course price of £3.80 ($6.00);

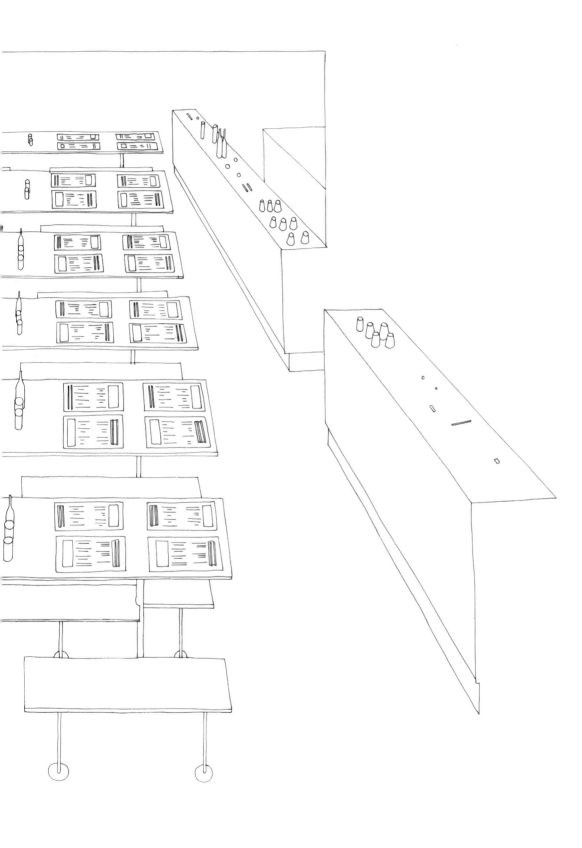

an investment of £388,000 ($610,000) – over budget, as Yau's restaurants have frequently and often fatally been. All the wagamama innovations were there from the beginning: no booking, the paper table mat as menu, the bench-style seating, and, long before it became compulsory, a no-smoking policy. Yau recalled standing in the restaurant on its opening day, proud and nervous, alongside his father, who hardly knew London at all. Their attention soon had to turn to how to keep the people who were waiting for a table happy, often as many as a hundred, with the queue on many days stretching all the way up the stairs and out onto the street. Yau recalled doing a deal with a Japanese brewer so that he could hand out small cans of beer as a way of thanking them for their patience.

Wagamama's instant success was due to some very favourable reviews, a great location close to offices, the British Museum and a large student community, and the novel and extremely good-value food it served, which many people had not come across before. Yau also recalled that it managed to exude an almost political (what would now be called lifestyle) appeal for his customers and, in retrospect, a romantic one for him. John Pawson, the architect, and he were also keen to incorporate the Japanese principles of *wabi-sabi*, the beauty of transience, and *kaizen*, the philosophy of continuous improvement. 'These, combined with the motto that positive eating equals positive living, led to what we were doing reading rather like a party manifesto. Our customers became our community,' Yau explained. The spareness of the elements of Japanese design they incorporated into the bowls that the noodles were served in, and the set-up of the kitchen, intrigued their customers, who were young, and, in those days before the advent of inexpensive travel and Muji, had not been exposed to such influences. The success also related to the simple principles of ramen cooking that Yau was first exposed to by his sister's flatmate: the hugely important stock, then always prepared on site, the noodles and the different toppings. What he ensured, based on his own experience and his lessons at McDonald's, was that the short distance between the kitchen and the customer precluded too many mistakes or delays, and kept menu prices as low as possible.

As it prospered, the restaurant engendered emotions in Yau that he has never been able to repeat. 'Your first restaurant is very like your first meaningful relationship. There is definitely a sense of running it with a great deal of love. I wish all my restaurants could have been like that one.' The note of regret is partly to do with the fact that the success of the first wagamama was quickly followed by the appearance of one of the restaurant industry's few maxims: that the second restaurant is invariably the most difficult opening. There are a variety of reasons for this. The company doubles in size, the restaurateur has to give up many of the pleasurable aspects of the business and learn to delegate, and the second site is bigger, more expensive and more complex. It was a combination of all these factors, but principally the final one, which brought Yau's involvement in wagamama to an end during the construction of a much larger, and at the time seemingly more impersonal, basement site in Lexington Street, Soho. Since 1998, Yau has had no connection with his first love, wagamama, of which there are now more than 115 branches in seventeen countries. But his ignominious exit following a boardroom coup (it is now jointly owned by its management and venture capitalists) doubled his already resolute determination to succeed elsewhere.

As we enjoyed our first courses, which Yau studied and tasted critically before eating, I asked him about the development of his palate. 'It was not something I was aware of until the 1990s, but then it developed, first from everything I ate and then from the increasing number of sites and restaurants I spent time in. I began to develop a sense of visual aesthetics, how a room should look, an ability to engineer space, and, through meditation, a sense of energy. Space planning and ergonomics are crucial to the success of any restaurant.' Yau was continually in demand, although he is the first to admit that during the 1990s several chefs around the world were making Asian food more accessible and therefore his role somewhat easier. Nobu Matsuhisa was changing the face of Japanese food at Nobu in New York and London; Australian chef David Thompson, with whom Yau was later to collaborate on the menus for Busaba Eathai, was doing the same with Thai food at Darley Street Thai in Sydney; and Hong Kong chef Susur Lee was modernizing Cantonese food at his first restaurant, Lotus, in Toronto, Canada. Asian food is visually exciting, healthy and fresh, and Yau was soon to make it glamorous and profitable in two very different guises.

His creation of Busaba Eathai, a Thai equivalent of wagamama, and then Hakkasan, a far more expensive Chinese restaurant in a cul-de-sac off Tottenham Court Road, London, again came about indirectly. The initial Busaba site on Wardour Street in Soho (there are now six), was bought by a fellow restaurateur who wanted Yau's input to make it succeed. While thinking it over they took a trip to Chiva Som,

Alan Yau

the renowned spa in Thailand, from which Yau returned convinced of the attractions of fresh and inexpensive Thai food in stylish surroundings. Busaba adopts some of the Yau principles, but in a warmer Thai-style setting. The pricing is keen and no reservations are taken, a combination that can lead to long waits. It has proved more challenging to find sites for Busaba because its menu requires a series of high-powered woks that in turn require high-powered air extraction, which is not easy to install in old buildings in crowded city centres.

The genesis of Hakkasan lay much closer to home. The management of the Mandarin Oriental hotel in Knightsbridge called Yau in because they wanted him to create a Chinese Nobu in their hotel, as Yau recalled it, to compete with the original Nobu in the nearby Metropolitan Hotel. Ultimately, these plans came to naught (the space is now home to Dinner by Heston Blumenthal), but Yau was smitten by the challenge. 'I really didn't have any experience at that stage of restaurateuring in the true sense of the word and I was excited by the challenge of transcending from fast casual into fine dining, especially with top-quality Chinese food, which was not being served in London at that time.' There were the usual contradictions: a basement site (a former garage), which was available at a very low rent, the hiring of the hugely talented and expensive French designer Christian Liaigre, and very detailed planning. Hakkasan was conceived in 1998 and finally opened in 2001. With it came immense professional satisfaction, not only from the commercial successes of Busaba Eathai and Hakkasan, as well as Yauatcha, his dim-sum tearoom that opened on Berwick Street, Soho, in 2004, but also from a sense of the personal progress he was making as a restaurateur.

What he found so exciting, Yau explained, was dealing with what he described as the 'soft architecture' as he began to organize the space within these restaurants: the width between the corridors created by the tables, and the height and width of the tables themselves. Here he paid particular tribute to the design of the tables and chairs in the Cipriani restaurants worldwide, which are much lower and narrower than normal, making the setting much more intimate. 'It is these aspects of being a restaurateur that really fascinate me.' The initial Hakkasan had satisfied all his sensibilities as a restaurateur. 'I inherited a rectangular box and we succeeded in energizing all four sides of it. The north became the kitchen; the east the lounge; the south was the bar and the west was the tea station. I was very pleased with that.' If Yau was happy with the design of Hakkasan, so too were the people who ate there and enjoyed its atmospheric black interior, which accentuated the exotic food and stylishly clad waiting staff.

As our main courses were served Yau rattled off a series of professional reminiscences, explaining that the real pleasure in any restaurant lies in the development stage, and the real work lies in any restaurant's first twelve months. This is when it can be hard and stressful each and every day. 'But once it is established, it is magical. Everything you touch turns into pleasure and turnover, and you look forward to implementing changes and improvements. It is like surfing in the middle of a wave.' Not even the most successful are impervious to the odd rogue wave, however. Yau suffered a conspicuous failure with the closure of Anda, a rustic Italian restaurant on Baker Street, the site where Galvin Bistrot de Luxe now flourishes. The success of Hakkasan had disproved the long-held theory that any restaurant's success is all about 'location, location, location,' and Anda had a highly talented chef in Francesco Mazzei, who has since been responsible for the success of L'Anima near Liverpool Street, but the restaurant failed, I believe, principally because of its timing. It was just too early in a rapidly changing area.

From a chance encounter at Anda with a retired Italian banker, who had sought Yau out because he was so surprised that a Chinese restaurateur was serving such authentic Italian food that he wanted to meet him, came an introduction to Rocco Princi, the master-baker of Milan, and Yau's opportunity to reverse the failure of Anda with the remarkable success of Princi in Soho. Princi was a friend of this banker, who was astounded by the baker's talents but frustrated by his inability to convert them into commercial success. Princi and Yau finally met in Milan, where they got on very well despite the absence of a mutual language, and Yau was 'blown away', as he put it, by the quality of the bread he had enjoyed. Another three years were invested in planning before a site opposite the original Busaba Eathai on Wardour Street, which had failed first as an Indian and then as a Korean restaurant, became available. In late 2008 two large windows finally revealed a wood-burning oven that produces some of the capital's finest bread, and a retail and café site that seem to throb with energy from the staff in their white bakers' outfits serving their far more colourful customers. Princi resonates with the aroma of bread, coffee, pastries and pizza. In ergonomic detail, it is very close to the blueprint for wagamama that Yau had introduced sixteen years earlier, and which, over our lunch in Racine, he proceeded to draw for me.

Alan Yau

The left-hand side is the long, linear, kitchen, the engine of the room; the far side is the bar and drinks-dispensing area; and across the body of the room is a series of horizontal communal benches and tables packed with happy customers. Yau smiled as he recalled a conversation with his building contractor in early 1992 at the original wagamama, who, in an avuncular fashion, had tried to dissuade him from this style of seating on the grounds that the British don't like sharing. It is fair to say that wagamama singlehandedly disproved that principle.

The proximity of the original Busaba and Princi introduced Yau to another aspect of his career as a restaurateur that he has embraced over the past decade. In 1999 a series of inexplicable mishaps and comments from the managers that they thought the restaurant was haunted as they closed up at night, were beginning to bother Yau. A chance encounter with his friend and lighting expert, Arnold Chan of Isometrix, over dim sum at Royal China, Baker Street, led Chan to introduce Yau to Patrick Wong, the feng shui expert, at another table. Although Yau was initially sceptical, Wong read his palm with accuracy and was asked to visit Busaba to see whether he could exorcise the spirits. This, apparently, he managed to do successfully, Yau knows not how, but most memorably, as they were standing outside Busaba, Wong looked across the street at what would be Princi nine years later and said to Yau that that particular site, in which he then had not the slightest interest, would one day be his. Since then for any new sites Yau now uses an English psychic to clear the land of any pollution or negativity, and then calls in Wong.

Princi also brought new personal challenges, including learning how to be a retailer and adapting a business that in Milan does sixty per cent of its turnover before 6.00 p.m. into one in London where the evenings are much busier. Yau recalled the moment of greatest satisfaction: 'I was stopped by someone and asked whether I was Alan Yau. When I said yes, he continued that he wanted to thank me so much. He was a third-generation Italian living in London and his grandfather who lived in Golders Green never used to leave his flat. But now that Princi is here, he sets off down the Northern Line to buy his bread and have a cappuccino. He is so happy.'

Having learned from his experience of his early exit from wagamama, Yau chose to sell Hakkasan, Yauatcha and Sake No Hana (his multi-million pound transformation of the former *Economist* building by the renowned Japanese architect Kengo Kuma) at a considerable profit to a company that intends to exploit the international appeal of these restaurants. A second branch of Hakkasan has opened in Mayfair, London, and the first in the US, in New York's theatre district. Yau's original plans were to settle back in Hong Kong, where his parents now live, and he has quickly established professional roots with the opening of Betty's Kitschen in the International Finance Centre, a fun French bistro that tips its hat at the Mad Men era. Here too Yau, despite his vast experience, is having to learn to accommodate unexpected cultural norms. 'I was obviously prepared to accept a corkage fee, when the customer brings his own wine, but I had never before heard of cakeage, where a customer brings their own cake and then pays the restaurant for plates and cutlery,' Yau smiled.

I asked him whether he is tired of restaurants. 'Yes and no. I was thinking of a complete career change in 2012 when I'm fifty, but the prospect of creating something that could produce fast and good-quality Chinese food in China is still very alluring and there are some interested partners.' He concluded with a set of vivid recollections: of how life as a restaurateur has definitely satisfied his soul, of how proud he was to have been able to take his father to Buckingham Palace to see his son awarded an OBE for his services to the British restaurant industry, and of how eternally grateful he will always be to David Acheson (head of franchising at BDO Stoy Hayward) who, as Yau put it, 'for some reason took this young, and then very naive, Chinaman seriously.'

Alan Yau

Maximizing your space

Neither Drew Nieporent nor Alan Yau could have been more specific: the success of their diverse restaurants over the past twenty-five years has rested firmly on the intense management of their internal space, and this element has become almost the most fascinating part of their plans for any proposed new site. In many respects, however, space planning is one aspect of the restaurant that few customers will notice. Certain issues may bother them during their stay – such as why there is such a long walk to the lavatory, – but even with a less-than-successful layout most restaurants can be made to work.

The issue is that those whose space has not been correctly planned, discussed and then laid out will always be far less profitable than they should have been. And once the layout is fixed it is usually extremely expensive to modify it. In financial terms, of course, the rent that is agreed usually applies to the total area, although it may be less for any mezzanine or basement space than for the ground floor level, as customers often find these less attractive.

The most immediate challenge for any restaurateur taking over a new space is that a significant proportion becomes non-revenue generating. The reception area, the entrance to as well as the lavatories themselves, the manager's office, storage facilities for the food, wine and laundry, the whole kitchen plus changing facilities for all the staff, a small office for the chef complete with a safe, and perhaps a small staff room: all these have to be taken out of the total area before the balance is left for the space for your customers to sit down, relax and spend money in.

The final percentage that proves non-revenue generating depends on the style of the restaurant. If it is to be an informal bar, café, bistro it can be as little as thirty per cent. In a more formal restaurant it can be as high as fifty per cent, as more space has to be given to more comfortable lavatories, changing facilities for the staff, a private dining room that may only be busy in the evenings and better storage for the wines and spirits. While this part of the equation firmly puts the emphasis on maximizing revenue-generating space for the restaurateur, there is the opposite side too, which has to be minimized. The areas where the customers walk in, or the path along which the waiters walk to collect the food from the kitchen are referred to as 'dead spaces' and these need to be kept to a minimum.

Nigel Platts-Martin, standing in the lobby of The Square, which he had been able to design from scratch, pointed out that, as a result of this unusual blank canvas, he had been able to place the entrance to the lavatories adjacent to the front door and alongside the bar area so that they created one joint 'dead space', rather than three separate ones. This has not only maximized his space for tables at The Square, but also provided a blueprint for what he was to do at three subsequent restaurants, in all of which he went to the considerable expense of moving the front door. At the Ledbury, for example, the new entrance for the customer also encompasses the entrance to the disabled lavatory, and the area at the top of the stairs where the waiters arrive with the food from the basement kitchen leaving far more room for tables.

Tables cannot go everywhere, of course. Nobody wants to sit at the table next to the entrance to the kitchens or right by the door to the lavatories, so these areas have to be dealt with sensitively. Nor does anyone want to be next to a waiter station where the waiting staff are noisily entering orders or swapping gossip about their customers. The trick is to get the very best out of the space that is available, and generate the very best overall experience for your customers. It is not easy. Platts-Martin, quite an accomplished player at this game, described it as 'the restaurateur's equivalent of three-dimensional chess'. This is a game that becomes somewhat easier over time.

However, help for the restaurateur can come not just from the professionals who have considerable expertise in this field, but also courtesy of the most unlikely quarters. For example, throughout central London many of the buildings were originally constructed with coal-holes, arched and bricked, into which the coal was delivered directly from the street outside.

They are a huge boon to any restaurateur because they provide extremely inexpensive, dry, safe and secure storage facilities that are also a vital aspect of planning your restaurant and kitchen. L'Escargot was blessed with two such coal-holes, one we referred to as 'wet' because it could hold up to fifty cases of mineral water (these were the days when there was still constant demand for this drink – although the current trend for tap water has removed an easy source of profit, it has also released valuable storage space and reduced the strain on many a waiter's back). The other held all the dry goods a busy kitchen needs. Since these areas were not considered of any commercial value, we did not pay rent on them, but cracking one's head on their low ceilings could be very painful indeed.

Despite the immense popularity of Princi, his self-service Italian café in Soho, from the day it opened, Alan Yau soon came to realize that its layout could be improved. Displaying the crucial traits of continuous innovation and space maximization, he totally redesigned the seating area in autumn 2011. The communal tables that had formerly been arranged down the length of the room were replaced by five tables that ran crossways, each seating twelve rather than the previous ten. This new arrangement not only generated more seats for the customers, but also meant that there was more space around the counters where the customers stand to choose their food. This, in turn, induced them to wait longer, instead of walking out and eating elsewhere, as the queues now appeared shorter. Thanks to the new layout, Princi can now serve 2,000 customers every day, which is a significant increase on even its busiest days.

Alan Yau

THE LIFE OF A
RESTAURATEUR

The stories of the world's most successful restaurateurs have, I hope, yielded many insights from their very different routes into this extraordinary profession. They display as many intriguing characteristics as the different flavours on their menus and wine lists, but let us now focus on what we can learn from them about what it takes to be a successful restaurateur.

The life of a restaurateur is not an immediate or obvious path to riches, and this is not just because of the long hours involved, or because it is increasingly a seven-days-a-week occupation. The basic economic principle behind restaurants is that the gross profit is inversely proportional to the quality of the food served: in other words, the better the food, the wine and the service, the lower the margins, and the lower the financial reward to the restaurateur. None of the people in this book chose to become a restaurateur to get rich quick. In fact, in most cases they will have had to subsidize their own income for as long as a couple of years, or live off their savings, until the restaurant can afford to pay them a salary, and it will usually be a relatively small one to begin with. This is certainly how my life as restaurateur began. In this aspect, they have all adhered to those fundamental three principles that the late Parisian restaurateur, Jean-Claude Vrinat of Taillevent, described as the profession's imperatives: a love of food, a love of wine and a love of one's fellow human beings.

At the outset, the excitement of being so intimately involved with these three factors makes up for a lack of cash, and there is usually neither the time nor energy left to spend it in any case. After that, while the growing interest in food and wine go some way towards making up for what a restaurateur would earn in another profession, the love of one's fellow human beings always ensures that whatever money the business does begin to generate is promptly spent on others. Altruism is in the DNA of every successful restaurateur. But although the practice of altruism is increasingly essential in our world, it is not a significant contributor to profitability. Nor is one other quality which is just as common in all these restaurateurs, and many others: they are romantics. By this I mean that they possess from the outset a strong vision in their minds of how they see their customers enjoying their meals as soon as they start dreaming of their restaurants. In this context it does not matter what the menu is, however simple, or the location, however humble, or the amount of money that has been invested, however small.

None of this has any real bearing on how the restaurateurs imagine and construct the setting for their future customers to relish. Two lines by the English satirical poet Alexander Pope encapsulate what distinguishes the best: 'True wit is nature to advantage dressed, / What oft was thought, but ne'er so well expressed.' Pope was writing long before the first restaurants opened in Paris, but he does, I believe, get to the heart of why these exceptional restaurateurs have achieved so much, quite frequently from what were initially nondescript surroundings and in limited circumstances.

With hindsight, it may seem obvious that modern Japanese sushi bars, restaurants celebrating the freshest American or British ingredients, the wine bars of Venice, or noodle bars where a Duchess could sit next to a student at long, communal tables, would become so incredibly popular. But it is a tribute to these restaurateurs that they not only conceived of them, but that they then replicated them in more popular locations, and finally made them hugely successful. The combination of having a business that is not profitable, along with a large helping of altruism and a romantic rather than hard-headed vision, partly accounts for the reputation of restaurants being highly risky ventures. Before addressing the personal characteristics that these restaurateurs have demonstrated to become so successful, there are, I believe, three other preliminary qualities that unite them.

The first two, a sense of humour and a sense of proportion, are very closely related. Restaurateurs are great fun to be with. They realize that however taxing their jobs may be, however awkward and demanding certain customers can be, theirs is a fascinating profession that brings them into contact with an extraordinary range of people every day. These might be customers, suppliers, winemakers, chefs and cooks (temperamental or otherwise), kitchen porters, knife sharpeners, or even the man I always remember as the key to my staff's good humour each morning: Mr Necchi, who arrived on his motorbike every Tuesday morning to ensure that the espresso machines were working properly. On top of all this there are the media in their increasingly diverse aspects. The sense of proportion comes from the growing recognition, usually absent at the beginning, that with enough good will and humility, most mistakes can be put right quite quickly and most customers can be placated with a smile, a sincere apology and a gesture of generosity. Correctly handled, situations like these can convert a seemingly unhappy customer into a loyal regular in the future. All good restaurateurs know

how to deal with situations like this because they have come to realize
that one of the most demanding aspects of this profession – that it involves
two performances a day in quick succession – gives them an immediate
opportunity to ensure that whatever went wrong at 1.30 p.m. will not be
repeated at 7.30 p.m. The ability to take advantage of this vital opportunity
is very important. So too is a thick skin and the composure to conceal it.

There is not a restaurateur in this book, or anywhere in the world
for that matter, who has not been on the receiving end of a critical review.
They hurt; they tend to linger in the memory, regardless of how many
good reviews there are; and they are a fact of restaurant life that no one
can escape. In fact, the more successful the restaurateur, the more keenly
awaited each new opening will be and the keener every reviewer will
be to spot faults. A restaurateur has to respond swiftly and efficiently
to such criticism, and how well they do this is a tribute to their sense
of humour and to this thick skin.

Customers benefit from these qualities, but they rarely see them.
What is far more obvious, and of far greater joy to them, are the corner-
stones of any exceptional restaurant experience: great taste and vision,
allied with an outstanding appetite. Let's start with the latter, as I cannot
stress its importance enough. Even as a restaurant reviewer I have always
been struck by how the best restaurateurs want to take maximum
advantage, usually in other people's restaurants, of what they can taste,
eat, experience, and what they can learn. By this I don't mean that they
are gluttons; far from it. Since restaurateurs are lucky enough not to have
to worry where their next meal comes from, most of them eat and drink
sensibly, but they do at every stage want to see what their counterparts
and competitors are up to. And, when the opportunity presents, to taste,
taste and taste again.

The other meaning of the word 'taste', of course, affects not only
what goes onto the plate and into the wine glass, but also everything
that surrounds them. Restaurateurs need a plethora of professionals to
help them convert their dreams into reality, but in the cases of the most
successful, they usually provide no more than a guiding light. In terms
of the overall design, restaurateurs are far more likely to choose to work
with those who can best interpret their own vision, rather than imposing what they may think the most suitable. Sticking to these principles,
particularly as restaurants multiply and more people become necessary
for their ongoing success, has to be a guiding rule for restaurateurs.

How well a restaurateur manages to achieve this is a direct result of two other inherent qualities, the first of which is simply how determined the restaurateur is to achieve their dream. Opening a restaurant is a remarkably complex journey. It requires dealing with the finance, the planning, the law on several different fronts, securing and getting on with your partners (unless you have very broad shoulders and choose to do it on your own), managing architects, surveyors, builders, insurers and designers, and possibly all of these before you have even found your chef and enjoyed what will, you hope, be an exciting first tasting. All of these come after what is for any restaurateur the most challenging aspect: finding that first elusive site. In this, the odds are stacked heavily against the newcomer. Any potentially good site will always be circulated first to those already trading. Without a financial track record the new restaurateur will always be regarded with suspicion by any potential landlord who, in turn, will always demand more financial security than if he or she were dealing with a restaurateur already trading. Since this location is to be the first restaurant, the prospective restaurateur will always be looking for that perfect dream site which, as they will later learn, simply does not exist.

This determination has to be underpinned by high energy levels. I hope I have managed to convey quite how much effort the restaurateurs in this book had to put in at the outset to ensure that their restaurants opened as close to the proposed opening date and budget as possible. I don't believe that, even as a father of young children, I was ever quite as exhausted as I was during the spring and summer of 1981 as L'Escargot came to life. And I never, unlike so many in this book, faced the challenge of being responsible for more than one restaurant. This involves not just the additional management challenges and the need to delegate, but the realization that the anticipated pleasures that drove you to open the first restaurant will now have to be shared with colleagues. These include welcoming your guests, setting the lighting and the music, and being at the door to say goodnight. Finding other people to do the elements of running a restaurant as well as you think that only you can is, as many of these restaurateurs have proved, another of their many talents.

Above all there is the confident, but never cocky, ability to communicate their passion to an audience that ranges from the kitchen porter, who may well have never eaten in an expensive restaurant, to the customers, who may eat out even more frequently than the restaurateur.

The best manage to do this not only from a management perspective, transmitting succinctly their vision for the restaurant, but also from the perspective of the customer: what they have learned from experience, travels, their own taste and sensibility about how people should be looked after. As a result, whenever a thoughtful member of the restaurant team encounters a loyal customer, the experience can be enjoyable, exciting and memorable for all concerned.

There is no doubt that we will all benefit from the next generation of restaurateurs. Although restaurants are an essential part of any city's retail landscape, they are perhaps the only ones that have benefited from the arrival of the internet. While so many of us have switched from buying goods in bricks-and-mortar shops to shopping online, this is not, and never will be, an option available to the restaurant-goer. In order to enjoy, to experience, to eat and to drink at any restaurant, we will still have to go out and enjoy it in person. Cookery books, television shows and even the occasional book on restaurateurs may well whet the appetite, but they cannot deliver the ultimate pleasure of enjoying a great meal, good wine and charming service in good company. That is, and will always remain, the restaurateur's prerogative.

The Life of a Restaurateur

CAST OF CHARACTERS

Ferran Adrià

The chef responsible not only for the extraordinary success of elBulli restaurant, now sadly closed, but also the high regard in which Spanish cooking is now held around the world.

John Alexander

A publisher and editor whose love of good food led to the inauguration of what has become the *Sydney Morning Herald's* highly influential *Good Food Guide,* Alexander is now deputy chairman to James Packer.

Stephanie Alexander

She ran the highly successful Stephanie's restaurant in Melbourne, Australia, for over twenty years, and is the author of numerous cookbooks, most notably *The Cook's Companion.*

Francesco Antonucci

Born in Mestre, just across the bridge from Venice, Antonucci opened the original Remi restaurant with designer Adam Tihany, where he cooked dishes inherited from his mother. Similar dishes still fill the menu of his Antonucci Café on New York's Upper East Side.

Jason Atherton

The first British chef to work a summer at elBulli, Atherton now practises all he has learned over the years in his own restaurant, Pollen Street Social, Mayfair, London.

Jean Bardet

A chef who ran a two-star Michelin restaurant in Tours, in France's Loire valley, which is now closed.

Joe Baum

The seminal New York restaurateur who, via Restaurant Associates, made such memorable successes of The Rainbow Room in the Rockefeller Center and Windows on the World in the former World Trade Center.

Rainer Becker

The German-born chef who spent several formative years cooking for the Hyatt in Asia. He then returned to London and applied his culinary and management talents to the successful openings of Zuma, Roka and other restaurants.

Vineet Bhatia

A chef who trained at the Oberoi, Mumbai, before moving to England, where he became the first Indian chef to win a Michelin star. He runs his restaurants in Chelsea and the Mandarin Oriental, Geneva, with his wife, Rashima.

Heston Blumenthal

A chef who has had a similar impact as Adrià but for British cooking, initially at The Fat Duck and The Hind's Head in Bray, Berkshire, and more recently with Dinner in the Mandarin Oriental, London.

Chris Bradley

Head chef at Danny Meyer's restaurant Untitled at the Whitney Museum.

Richard Caring

A successful businessman who was the first to appreciate, and exploit, the value of the brand names of the restaurants he started acquiring from his purchase of The Ivy and Le Caprice in London onwards.

Samuel and Samantha Clark
The two chefs behind Moro, who were introduced to one another by their mutual friend Mark Sainsbury, with whom they opened Moro.

Tom Colicchio
Danny Meyer's original chef and partner in Gramercy Tavern. Their split was ultimately public and acrimonious. Colicchio has gone on to an outstanding career in his own restaurants and in front of the cameras.

Sir Terence Conran
A man whose appetite for good food and wine merged with his design talents with the opening of Bibendum, London, and then led to a score of other restaurants in London, Paris and New York.

Chris Corbin
The restaurateur who, shoulder-to-shoulder with his partner Jeremy King, has opened several of London's most successful restaurants since the early 1980s, most notably The Wolseley.

David Doyle
An American businessman who made a large fortune out of selling his dotcom business, the proceeds of which he has now converted into a significant share in Neil Perry's restaurants and one of the largest private wine collections in the world.

Alain Ducasse
A hugely talented French chef who has successfully opened a collection of restaurants around the world, including the Louis XV in Monaco and the Plaza Athénée in Paris, which boast an extraordinary number of Michelin stars.

Auguste Escoffier
The great French chef and codifier of classic French cuisine, whose cookbooks are still on the bookshelves of so many chefs today. His partnership with hotelier César Ritz in the early twentieth century redefined the style of restaurant service in the leading hotels of Paris and London.

Oscar Farinetti
Even more passionate than most Italians about food and wine, Farinetti has been the driving force behind Eataly alongside restaurateur Joe Bastianich and chef Mario Batali, which has been such a success in Madison Square, New York.

Charles Fontaine
A French émigré chef who reopened The Quality Chop House by Exmouth Market, London, in the early 1990s, at a time when the area was very down at heel. Its success was an inspiration to Mark Sainsbury.

Pierre Franey
Born in Burgundy, Franey went to the US in 1939 as chef in the French pavilion at the New York World's Fair. He stayed to become head chef at Le Pavilion, for many years America's finest French restaurant.

Chris and Jeff Galvin
Brothers and talented chefs, both
cooked at L'Escargot before opening
their own restaurants in London,
Galvin at Windows, Galvin Bistrot
de Luxe and Galvin La Chapelle.

Justin Gellatly
The pony-tailed baker at the St. John
restaurants in London, who has been
responsible for its stunning range of
breads, doughnuts and desserts as well
as its Eccles cakes.

Frédy Girardet
The great Swiss chef, now retired, who ran
an inspirational three-Michelin-starred
restaurant at Crissier from 1971–1996
before selling it to Philippe Rochat, who
had worked alongside him for many years.

Michel Guérard
From his first restaurant in Paris in the
early 1970s, Guérard set a new direction
for French cooking as the leader of the
movement that came to be known as
nouvelle cuisine. For the last thirty years his
base has been his hotels and restaurants
in Eugénie-les-Bains, south-west France.

Gabrielle Hamilton
The chef-patron of Prune in downtown New York, and the author of an
extremely funny autobiography
Blood, Bones & Butter.

Henry Harris
Trained by chef Simon Hopkinson
at Bibendum, Chelsea, Harris moved
less than a mile to open Racine in
Knightsbridge, which has been a bastion
of great French flavours for over a decade.

Fergus Henderson
The architect-turned-chef who created
the food that made St. John restaurant
in Smithfield, London, world famous.
In the process, he has inspired a new
generation of young British chefs.

Mark Hix
A chef who began his career behind
the stoves before rising to chef-director
of Caprice Restaurants, then heading
off on his own to open Hix restaurants
across London and in Lyme Regis. He is
also a talented food writer.

Jake Hodges
One of the original team behind the
stoves of Moro, Hodges then went off
on his own to open Cigala on Lamb's
Conduit Street in Bloomsbury, London.

Simon Hopkinson
The original chef at Bibendum restaurant in Chelsea, London, when it opened
in 1987, and still a partner today. An
equally respected author of cookbooks.

Philip Howard
The British chef whose culinary talents
have been responsible for the consistently high reputation of The Square
for over twenty years. He is also involved
in The Ledbury and Kitchen w8.

Rowley Leigh
The chef-patron of Le Café Anglais
in Bayswater, London, Leigh is also
a highly talented writer whose cookery
column graces the food section of the
Financial Times every Saturday.

Yad Joussef and Aga Ilska
The perhaps unlikely combination of a Lebanese chef and Polish restaurant manager who met, fell in love, married and have made a success of their Yalla-Yalla restaurants in London's Soho.

Thomas Keller
Having washed dishes in his teenage years, Keller has become one of the most successful American chefs, initially with The French Laundry in Yountville, California, and then Per Se in New York.

Miles Kirby
Born in New Zealand, Kirby is as talented a chef as he is a coffee roaster. With Chris Ammerman, his great friend, partner and fellow Kiwi, he has made their Caravan restaurant in London an outstanding success.

Dan Kluger
A chef who trained with Michael Romano and Danny Meyer at the Union Square Hospitality Group before moving round the corner to open ABC Kitchen for Phil Suarez and Jean-Georges Vongerichten.

Pierre Koffmann
Having begun his career at the Waterside Inn, Koffmann established La Tante Claire as one of London's finest French restaurants during the 1980s. He is now behind the stoves of the hugely popular Koffmann's in Knightsbridge.

Bruno Loubet
Loubet shot to fame in London in the early 1990s before spending a decade cooking in Brisbane, Australia. Since his return he has been in partnership with Mark Sainsbury at Bistrot Bruno Loubet.

Martin Lam
Martin took over as head chef at L'Escargot and stayed on with Elena Salvoni after I sold it. He then opened Ransome's Dock in Battersea with his wife Vanessa, an equally talented pastry chef.

Susur Lee
Lee trained as a chef at The Peninsula Hotel, Hong Kong, before making his career in Toronto, Canada, initially with Lotus restaurant in 1987. Today, his Lee restaurant is the embodiment of his refined and innovative Chinese cooking.

Alastair Little
The original chef at L'Escargot before he left to open the much smaller Alastair Little restaurant on Frith Street. He now runs Tavola in Notting Hill Gate.

Rebecca Macarenhas
The ever-smiling restaurateur who began her professional career with Sonny's in Barnes, south-west London, in 1986, a restaurant-deli that is still extremely popular. She also runs Kitchen W8 with Philip Howard, and Cantinetta.

Sirio Maccioni
The Italian-born restaurateur and author whose Le Cirque restaurants in New York and Las Vegas set new standards in the US, not just for their food, but also for their service and their sense of style and occasion.

Tony Mackintosh
Tony was responsible for several of London's most successful bars and clubs in the 1970s, before becoming managing director of The Groucho Club.

Stefano Manfredi

The chef who has taught Australians to enjoy the finest Italian cooking at a string of eminent restaurants: Restaurant Manfredi, Bel Mondo, Manfredi at Bells, Pretty Beach House and, most recently, Balla at the Star Casino.

Nobu Matsuhisa

Perhaps the most peripatetic of all chefs, Nobu was born in Japan, and cooked in Peru and Alaska before opening two restaurants in Hollywood. From there a restaurant partnership was formed with actor Robert de Niro that has seen twenty-two Nobu restaurants open around the world.

Francesco Mazzei

An Italian chef whose London career began at Alan Yau's failed Anda. Mazzei is now the head chef of the very popular L'Anima at Liverpool Street.

Barry McDonald

A New Zealander, McDonald worked as a waiter for me at L'Escargot before establishing a food wholesale business. Today, he runs the ever-expanding group of Fratelli Fresh, which combines a bar, an Italian *trattoria* and a delicatessen all under one roof.

Jean-Louis Neichel

A chef from Alsace, Neichel was the first to achieve critical recognition at elBulli before moving on to open his still-successful restaurant, Neichel, in Barcelona.

David Nicholls

Once executive head chef at The Ritz, London, Nicholls is now head of food and beverage worldwide for Mandarin Hotels. His singular achievements have been the highly successful openings of restaurants by Vineet Bhatia, Heston Blumenthal and Daniel Boulud within this hotel group.

Yotam Ottolenghi

Born in Israel, Ottolenghi first worked in the kitchens of Kensington Place for Rowley Leigh before opening the highly successful deli-cafés around London that carry his name.

Anders Ousback

An inspiration to many young Australian chefs, restaurateurs and wine enthusiasts, Ousback laid down the uncluttered principles for many successful Sydney restaurants in the 1980s.

James Packer

The son of the late media mogul Kerry Packer, James has built up an extensive gambling business, Crown Casino, in both Melbourne and Perth, into which he has introduced numerous successful restaurants, most notably Rockpool Bar & Grill.

Jean-Louis Palladin

A larger-than-life chef from Armagnac country in France, who opened his first restaurant, Jean-Louis, in the Watergate Hotel, Washington, DC in 1979. His passion for ingredients was to inspire many young American chefs and restaurateurs.

Charlie Palmer

When Palmer opened Aureole restaurant in New York in 1988 he was among the first chefs to emphasize the importance of American ingredients on his menu. Other restaurants have followed in Las Vegas and California.

Tony Papas

A New Zealander who came to Sydney, Australia, and had great success as a chef with the Bayswater Brasserie. His most recent ventures have been the highly successful Brasserie Bread Company and Allpress Espresso.

Rajat Parr

The wine director behind chef Michael Mina's numerous restaurants in the US. When Parr is not in the US, he is usually to be found tasting in the cellars of his beloved Burgundy.

Jean-Philippe Patruno

The French chef whom Sam and Eddie Hart initially hired and was instrumental in the initial success of their Fino and Quo Vadis restaurants. They have since parted company.

Alberico Penati

The chef for many years at Harry's Bar, Mayfair, and regarded by many of the capital's other Italian chefs as il maestro. He is now the head chef at Birley's, Mayfair.

Damien Pignolet

With his late wife, Josephine (after whom Neil Perry's elder daughter is named), he ran Claude's in the 1980s to great acclaim. Today he is the executive chef at Bistro Moncur.

Bruce Poole

A British chef who has been singularly responsible for Chez Bruce, and overseen the successes of La Trompette and The Glasshouse.

Alfred Portale

The chef and restaurateur behind the continuing success of New York's Gotham Bar & Grill, which has become a byword for consistency.

Rocco Princi

The inspiration behind four outstanding bakeries in Milan, whose introduction to restaurateur Alan Yau led to the opening of the first Princi in Soho, a bustling bakery and café.

Wolfgang Puck

The Austrian-born chef whose numerous restaurants came to define a new direction for the cooking of southern California. The various branches of Spago and Chinois in Santa Monica have been particularly influential.

Trish Richards

A stockbroker who joined forces with her cousin Neil Perry in 1988 to establish Rockpool, and then, with her financial expertise, oversaw the expansion of the restaurant group, Perry's deals with Qantas and his numerous cookbooks.

Eric Ripert

The quiet-spoken French chef who stood next to Gilbert Le Coze at the stoves of Le Bernardin, New York, and then took charge after Le Coze's untimely death.

Jancis Robinson

My wonderful wife, whom I met only after I had signed the lease on L'Escargot. The best wine teacher and dining companion in the world.

Joël Robuchon

The French chef considered by many to have been the one of the most influential of the twentieth century. Branches of his L'Atelier du Joël Robuchon restaurants can now be found around the world.

Judy Rodgers

Having cooked at Chez Panisse in California, Rodgers crossed the Oakland Bridge into San Francisco, took over the stoves at the already established Zuni Café in 1987, established the highest standards for its cooking and has maintained them ever since.

Ruth Rogers

The American cook, who with her late partner, Rose Gray, opened the River Café in Hammersmith and set new standards for Italian cooking in the UK.

Michael Romano

He became Danny Meyer's chef at Union Square Café shortly after its opening, and since then their friendship has provided the culinary bedrock for Meyer's restaurant expansion.

Michel Roux Snr

The charming embodiment of a Frenchman in England, his Waterside Inn at Bray has held three Michelin stars, the highest culinary achievement, for over twenty-five years.

Michel Roux Jnr

Chef-patron of two-starred Le Gavroche, Mayfair, and, today best known as the presenter of the BBC's *Masterchef: The Professionals*.

Ken Sanker

A successful businessman who has backed the Galvins, Chapter One restaurant in Kent, and has generously offered avuncular advice to many in the British restaurant industry.

Alain Senderens

A colleague of French chef Michel Guérard, who after many years as the chef-proprietor of Lucas Carton, a three-Michelin-starred restaurant in Paris, handed back his stars in 2005 and changed the name of the restaurant to Senderens to reflect a simpler style of cooking.

Nick Smallwood

He joined L'Escargot shortly after it opened and was responsible for making it profitable. He left to open the very successful Kensington Place with Rowley Leigh.

Will Smith

A successful London restaurateur whose partnership with chef Antony Demetre has led to the opening of Arbutus, Wild Honey and Les Deux Salons, and many happy customers.

André Soltner

Born in Alsace, Soltner came to New York where his Lutèce restaurant was a beacon of French gastronomy for over thirty years. He has been an inspirational teacher to many young chefs.

Cast of Characters

Jeffrey Steingarten
A hugely perceptive American writer
on food and restaurants and the author
of several books, including the semimal
The Man Who Ate Everything in 1997.

Phil Suarez
The businessman whose financial
acumen has reinforced the culinary
skills of Jean-Georges Vongerichten,
a combination that has led to numerous successful restaurants.

David Thompson
The Australian-born chef, who after
an early exposure to the charms of Thai
cooking in Thailand, transformed how
it is appreciated outside its homeland
with the opening of his own Thai
restaurants in Sydney and London.

Claude and Michel Troisgros
Sons of Pierre Troisgros. Claude flew
the family nest and now runs his own
restaurants in Brazil, while Michel
maintains the three-star Michelin reputation of Maison Troisgros in Roanne.

Jean and Pierre Troisgros
The two brothers who inherited the
family restaurant, Maison Troisgros,
in Roanne, France, and subsequently
took it to its three-Michelin-starred
status in 1968.

Charlie Trotter
A self-taught chef from Chicago who
was responsible for establishing his
home town as a centre of gastrnomic
excellence after opening Charlie
Trotter's restaurant in 1987, which
he closed in the summer of 2012.

Jean-Georges Vongerichten
A chef from Alsace, France, who headed
to the US like many other young French
chefs, where he stayed and achieved
extraordinary success with restaurants as
diverse as Jean-Georges, Mercer Kitchen
and Perry Street.

Jean-Claude Vrinat
Vrinat inherited Taillevent restaurant
from his father and then proceeded to
raise it to the highest professional levels. He was the last French restaurateur
to hold three Michelin stars and was
widely regarded as the consummate
restaurateur.

Alice Waters
The quietly spoken, determined and
principled chef who opened Chez
Panisse in Berkeley, California, in 1971
and has subsequently set a professional
and ethical lodestar for other American
chefs to follow.

Mark Yates
Trevor Gulliver's partner at the now-
defunct Fire Station, London, Yates has
subsequently been a partner in numerous other restaurants, most notably at
Livebait and The Real Greek with chef
Theodore Kyriakou.

INDEX

Numbers in superscript
refer to illustrations

Acknowledgements

This book would simply not have been possible without the achievements of the twenty restaurateurs I have profiled. I am extremely grateful to them all for giving up so much time to me and for selflessly passing on their knowledge, warmth, passion and wisdom. I would also like to thank all their PAs for somehow finding time in their busy schedules for my interviews to take place. Marcus Ford, Kerry Held, Michael Hill-Smith, Barry McDonald, Guillaume Rochette and Michael Steinberger have also been most helpful in Shanghai, Adelaide, Sydney, London and New York.

I am most grateful for all those, whether mentioned in this book or not, who over the years have shared their experience and knowledge with me so that eventually I became a successful restaurateur. I was certainly very naive when I opened L'Escargot and I owe my career in restaurants over the past thirty years to the advice and kindness of many.

I thank my literary agent Caradoc King of AP Watt for so much timely advice, encouragement, commercial nous and the odd lunch. To my friend Julian Barnes, thanks are due for passing on the words of his late wife, the literary agent Pat Kavanagh, that 'if you feel the book is in you, go ahead and write it,' however unresolved the contract negotiations may appear at the time.

I owe enormous thanks to all at Phaidon: Amanda Ridout, Jenny Lea, Emma Robertson, Emilia Terragni who wrote out of the blue to see whether there was a book in me, Sophie Hodgkin, and Laura Gladwin, a model editor. To Nigel Peake, thank you for the remarkable illustrations that have brought this book to life.

My writing would not have been anywhere near as confident without my weekly column at the *Financial Times*. I am extremely grateful to all those who have put up with me at the FT since 1989.

I owe my love of food, cooking and hospitality to growing up in a Jewish home in Manchester where my mother was a wonderful cook. Somehow she always managed to have more than enough to feed the friends who called in, however many and however hungry. My interest in restaurants was, however, sparked by my late father. Having flown as a navigator during the Second World War, he believed passionately that life is for living and that restaurants are an essential part of life. I initially shared this passion with my sister and brother, then with my own family and, whenever and wherever possible, with our friends. Our children, Julia, William and Rose have, not surprisingly, inherited this interest, an interest matched by our son-in-law, Charlie. Our grandson Jake seems, happily, to be following in the family tradition.

Finally, my biggest debt is naturally to Jancis in her many varied roles as wife, mother, grandmother, and as the most extraordinary wine teacher, restaurant-going accomplice and in-house editor anyone could ever have hoped for.

Thank you all. I hope that in the future we will all share many excellent restaurant meals together.

351

for Jancis

Phaidon Press Limited
Regent's Wharf
All Saints Street
London N1 9AP

Phaidon Press Inc.
180 Varick Street
New York, NY 10014

www.phaidon.com

First published in 2012
© 2012 Phaidon Press Limited

ISBN 978 0 7148 6469 3

A CIP catalogue record for this book
is available from the British Library.

Commissioning Editor: Emilia Terragni
Development Editor: Laura Gladwin
Project Editor: Sophie Hodgkin
Production Controller: Vanessa Todd-Holmes

Designed by John Morgan Studio
Illustrations by Nigel Peake

Printed in China

The publisher would also like to thank
Tom Brent, Julia Hasting, Martin Lam
and Teresa Lima for their contributions
to the book.